The History of British Steel

The History of British Steel

John Vaizey

Weidenfeld & Nicolson London

© George Weidenfeld and Nicolson Ltd 1974

Designed by David Gentleman for George Weidenfeld and
Nicolson Ltd, 11 St John's Hill, London SW11

Printed in Great Britain by
Willmer Brothers Limited, Birkenhead

ISBN 0 297 76704 6

Marina
with love

Contents

List of Illustrations   ix

List of Diagrams and Maps   xiii

Preface   xv

1   Introduction   1

2   The Difficult Twenties   20

3   The Watershed   48

4   Revival   69

5   The War   88

6   War and Peace   103

7   The Early Days of Peace   118

8   The Reconstruction of Steel   129

9   New Problems and Solutions   150

10   A New World   180

Sources and Guide to Further Reading   190

Some People Mentioned in the Text   196

Index   200

Illustrations

COLOUR PLATES   *facing page*

Iron ore field in Mauretania (BSC)   14
Unloading ore at Port Talbot (BSC)   15
Coke ovens at Ravenscraig (BSC)   30
Blast furnace at the Abbey works (BSC)   31
The Bessemer process at Ebbw Vale (BSC)   78
Open-hearth furnaces at Ebbw Vale (BSC)   79
Electric arc furnace at Hallside (BSC)   94
Basic oxygen process at the new Anchor plant (BSC)   95
Teeming at Port Talbot (BSC)   126
Soaking pits at Anchor (BSC)   127
Temper mill at Gartcosh (BSC)   142
Making tubes at Hartlepool South (BSC)   143
Hand-forging a steel ring (Brown Bayley Steels Ltd)   174
The Severn Bridge (BSC)   175
Aerial view of Port Talbot (BSC)   190
Lord Melchett (BSC)   191

BLACK-AND-WHITE ILLUSTRATIONS

Between pages 38 and 39
C. W. Siemens (Ronan Picture Library)
Henry Bessemer (Ronan Picture Library)
The Bessemer process (Ronan Picture Library)
Open-hearth furnace, 1889 (Ronan Picture Library)
Puddling iron, 1872 (Ronan Picture Library)
Frodingham Ironworks, 1907 (BSC)
Ironstone mining, c. 1900 (BSC)
Staffordshire ironworks, c. 1918 (J. Patchett)
Slagging a blast furnace, c. 1920 (Collection of W.K.V. Gale)
Dorman Long's Britannia Ironworks, 1920 (BSC)
Delivering miners' strike pay, 1921 (Radio Times Hulton Picture Library)
Filling ladle with hot metal (Park Gate Iron & Steel Co. Album)
Re-lining a ladle (Park Gate Iron & Steel Co. Album)

Illustrations

Between pages 54 and 55
Steel tyres, Sheffield (BSC)
Blast furnaces at Workington, *c.* 1930 (Collection of W.K.V. Gale)
Newspaper report on Clarence Hatry (*The Daily Mirror*)
Montagu Norman (Radio Times Hulton Picture Library)
Jarrow march, 1931 (*Evening Chronicle*, Newcastle-upon-Tyne)
Strike duty at Appleby Ironworks, 1926 (BSC)
Dismantling Trent Ironworks (Collection of W.K.V. Gale)
Sir John Craig (*The Glasgow Herald* and *Evening News*)
Reginald McKenna (Popperfoto)
Steelworks in Middlesbrough (Collection of W.K.V. Gale)
Consett Ironworks (*The Northern Echo*)
Cartoon on Corby development (*The Birmingham Evening Mail*)
Corby blast furnaces, 1933, from *The Development of Corby Works* by Frederick
    Scopes (© Stewarts & Lloyds, 1968)

Between pages 70 and 71
Ebbw Vale works under construction (BSC)
'Batho' type open-hearth furnace (Brown Bayley Steels Ltd)
Axle-rolling machine (Brown Bayley Steels Ltd)
Casting giant steel ingot for heavy forgings at English Steel, Sheffield (*The Northern
    Echo*)
Re-rolling mill at Colvilles (*The Glasgow Herald* and *Evening News*)
Hand-rolling steel sheet, Shotton (BSC)
Shipbuilding at John Brown's yards, Clydeside (Radio Times Hulton Picture Library)
Chassis assembly lines at Cowley (British Leyland Motor Corporation Ltd)
Furnaces at Dudley, *c.* 1935 (Collection of W.K.V. Gale)
Cargo Fleet, Middlesbrough, 1936 (BSC)
Bessemer converter at Corby, *c.* 1934 (BSC)
H.A. Brassert from *The Development of Corby Works* by Frederick Scopes
    (© Stewarts & Lloyds)
Allan Macdiarmid (*The Glasgow Herald* and *Evening News*)
Sir William Firth (Radio Times Hulton Picture Library)
Sir Andrew Duncan (Radio Times Hulton Picture Library)

Between pages 102 and 103
Corby's blast furnaces by night (Stewarts & Lloyds)
Shell production during the First World War (Imperial War Museum)
German aerial photograph of Ebbw Vale (BSC)
Emergency blast furnace in Staffordshire (Collection of W.K.V. Gale)
Bomb damage to mill building (Brown Bayley Steels Ltd)

Illustrations

Removing railings for scrap (*Evening Chronicle*, Newcastle-upon-Tyne)
King George VI visiting Shotton, 1942 (BSC)
Laying the Pluto pipeline (Stewarts & Lloyds)
The Pluto pipeline under construction (Stewarts & Lloyds)
Sir Ellis Hunter (© Dorman Long) from *A Man and his Times, A Memoir of Sir Ellis Hunter* by Charles Wilson
Sir James Lithgow (*The Glasgow Herald* and *Evening News*)
Sir Walter Benton Jones from *The United Steel Co. Ltd 1918–68, A History*
R.S. Hilton from *The United Steel Co. Ltd 1918–68*

Between pages 118 *and* 119
Mining of Lincolnshire iron ore (BSC)
Scrap drive advertisement from *Steel News*, 1949
Stewarts & Lloyds' Clydesdale works (Stewarts & Lloyds)
Welding machine at Corby (Stewarts & Lloyds)
Consett in 1949 (*Evening Chronicle*, Newcastle-upon-Tyne)
Consett in 1949 (*Evening Chronicle*, Newcastle-upon-Tyne)
Open-hearth furnace at Shotton (BSC)
Anti-nationalization cartoon from *Steel News*, 1949 (© *Evening News*)
Steel is Power: The Case for Nationalization, published by Victor Gollancz, 1948
'The Arming of the Knight', Illingworth cartoon from *Punch*, 1948
'The Greedy Fingers of the Steel Moguls', Illingworth cartoon from *The Hawskmoor Scandals* by Bernard Hollowood, Harrap, 1949
Hugh Dalton (Keystone Press)
John Wilmot (Radio Times Hulton Picture Library)
Steven Hardie (Keystone Press)
Herbert Morrison (Keystone Press)
Oliver Franks (Popperfoto)

Between pages 150 *and* 151
Dismantling open-hearth shop at Templeborough (Collection of W.V.K. Gale)
The Four Queens at Appleby-Frodingham (BSC)
Sir Robert Shone (Popperfoto)
Sir Archibald Forbes (Keystone Press)
Sir Andrew McCance and Sir John Craig (*The Glasgow Herald* and *Evening News*)
Lackenby Works (BSC)
Port Talbot (BSC)
Steelworkers' homes in Port Talbot (BSC)
Building blast furnace at Llanwern (BSC)
Control pulpit of hot mill at Llanwern (BSC)
Rolling the first billet at Anchor (BSC)

Illustrations

Between pages 158 *and* 159
Walking dragline near Corby (BSC)
Transport trucks at Ravenscraig (BSC)
Coke ovens, Ravenscraig (BSC)
Pig iron stockyards at Workington (BSC)
Scrap being fed into oxygen converter at Consett (*The Northern Echo*)
Oxygen converters at Abbey works (BSC)
Lackenby works (BSC)
Teeming into ingot moulds at Llanwern (BSC)
Stripping an ingot from the mould for transfer to the soaking pits for re-heating
   (*Iron and Steel Editorial*)
Continuous casting, Panteg works (BSC)

Between pages 166 *and* 167
Forging a boiler drum (*Iron and Steel Editorial*)
Cold mill, Llanwern (BSC)
Galvanizing line, Ebbw Vale (BSC)
Electrolytic tinning line (BSC)
Stelvetite line, Shotton (BSC)
Spiral welded pipes, Llanwern (BSC)
Pipe mill (BSC)
Seemless pipe at Clydesdale (*Iron and Steel Editorial*, © Stewarts & Lloyds)
Galvanized wire at Dorman Long (*The Northern Echo*)
Hand-rolling steel sheet, *c.* 1967 (BSC)
Plate mill (BSC)
Making stainless steel, Panteg works (BSC)
Finishing mill, stainless steel, Panteg works (BSC)
A selection of finished rings and tyres (Brown Bayley Steels Ltd)

BSC *refers to photographs supplied by the British Steel Corporation*

Diagrams and Maps

1 Making iron: Blast furnace   16

2 Making steel: Open-hearth furnace   17

3 Making steel: Electric arc furnace   18

4 Making steel: Basic oxygen furnace   19

5 Location of steelworks mentioned in the text   24–5

6 Steel production 1920–72   46–7

7 Steel consumption by industry groups   154–5

8 Present location of British Steel Corporation works by Division 186–9

Preface

This book has been based on the surviving archives as listed at the end of the book. In form it is a long essay, as well as a detailed narrative. One of the consequences of nationalization is that most of the surviving archives of much of the industry are now available to the student. So far as I know this is the first time that the records of recent date of a substantial number of major companies in a leading industry, together with the records of their trade associations, including the price conferences, have been made available. As a result, a synoptic view has been possible. I have been the first person to whom these records have been opened and a list of archival material is available for the use of other scholars. Printed secondary sources have also been used and my grateful acknowledgments appear in the guide to further reading. In particular, I have relied mainly upon them for the period up to 1920, with which the Introduction is concerned.

Three people must be especially mentioned. Mrs Huldine Ridgway was secretary and assistant to the project and without her skill and tact it could not have been begun, let alone carried through and completed. John Owen, of Brunel University and Trinity College, Cambridge, read through some of the archival material and his extensive notes helped in the preparation of some parts especially of chapters 6 and 7. Brunel University gave me a sabbatical, for which I was grateful, and Mrs Annemarie Maggs, secretary of the Economics Department was a great help.

Sir George Weidenfeld and my editor, Christopher Falkus, have been as helpful as always. At British Steel, my relations have been equally fortunate. This history was written at the suggestion originally of Lord Melchett, and he had continued to take a personal interest in the project until his death, which occurred just after the book was sent to the publisher.

Mr Ronald Peddie and Mr Robert Roseveare were a great support and Mr James Siddons was helpfully the director in charge of the arrangements for the book. Mr Derek Charman, the Corporation's archivist, has been as helpful as it is possible to be, as has Miss Jane Francis, the Corporation's librarian.

Many other members present and past of the British Steel Corporation, who are too numerous to mention, have been most helpful; wherever I have gone I have found a deep interest in the past as well as the future of the industry and they have spared no efforts to be as helpful as possible. Other people inside the industry and outside it have also been most kind especially my colleagues Professor Charles Carter of Lancaster and Professor Patrick Lynch of Dublin who have commented on drafts.

My thanks are due, too, to the staff of the British Library of Economics and Political Science, Cambridge University Library, the London Library, the Public Record Office and, above all, to the library services of the London Borough of Hounslow. I often think we take the public libraries for granted just because their work is so astonishingly good.

The original structure of the book was determined after a thorough reading of the printed sources and many discussions with people in the industry, or who were knowledgeable about it. The flesh of the work, however, was built out of the archives, and in that sense - but not only I hope in that sense - the book is an original contribution to knowledge. One of the fortunate consequences of the reorganization of the industry, following nationalization, is that arrangements have been made for the proper safeguarding of the archives. Much has perished, inevitably; but an astonishing amount survives. In particular, where there has been widespread destruction, in one quarter, records survive occasionally elsewhere. A really thorough search will be possible when the archives have been organized. A note at the end of the book indicates, in a preliminary way, the scope of the collection. It is to be hoped that it will form the basis of a growing series of detailed monographs on the working of a major industry. The present study is not so much a detailed monograph as a synoptic view of the industry's development. In earlier works the present author has made very detailed studies of narrow topics but the time for this in the steel industry is not just yet. First there is a need for extended work based upon the archival material setting the framework of the questions which need to be asked - the answers to which, to be sure, will modify the framework itself. This book, then, is an extended essay based firmly upon sources that for the most part have never been accessible before. Even in the case of United Steel, on which much work has been done, some hitherto unknown material has been brought to light.

The theme of the book is the development of a major industry over half a century. It raises certain important problems, and it suggests tentative answers to them. It would be presumptuous indeed to call it definitive - what work in economics or history could be called that? - but it does challenge a number of prevailing opinions about the recent history of the industry. In particular it illustrates the extensive nature of the reorganization from 1928 to 1933 and its profound subsequent consequences.

Preface

The illustrations are not gilt on the gingerbread. From the beginning they have been thought of as integral to the text. Since modern techniques of illustration became lavishly available and book designers learned how to use them, it has not been necessary to add illustrations as extra material because they can become fully part of the book. Paragraphs of laboured technical description and elaborate explanation can be avoided since the photographer and the artist can do the job better. It has been a matter for pride that David Gentleman designed the book so beautifully and efficiently. We have been fortunate to have the assistance of Martha Caute and Jasmine Spencer, who have done so much work with the illustrations and diagrams, in collaboration with the British Steel Corporation's design staff, especially Phil Nunan.

Lastly, after a decade and a half of industrial histories it is hardly necessary to add that the book has been produced under conditions of complete intellectual freedom. So far as I am aware nothing has been kept from me, and I do know that great efforts have been made to open a great many doors. I have not sought to pull any legitimate punches or to avoid friendly commendation. I can only hope that the result is thought to be reasonably fair and balanced. There are understandably errors, which I regret, but I hereby acknowledge full responsibility for them and hope that my successors will put the record straight still further.

I

Introduction

Steel has seemed for so long the basis of our national life, the synonym for the endurance, resilience and subtle strength that are thought of as our characteristic natural virtues, especially if we are Scots, that it comes as some surprise to realize how recent its dominance is. And it is a surprise, too, to realize how profound are the changes that are now occurring, so that the industry's story from 1918 to the 1960s is virtually a self-contained story, a chapter of great importance lodged between an introduction and the future, a story well worth telling in its own right and also because of its significance for so much else. In the story of steel there is to be found the place that innovation, science and technology played in a great basic industry. Steel's output reflected and exaggerated the economic ups and downs of Great Britain. Its place in world trade was a reflection of the balance of payments of Britain and the world. War, peace and politics played their important parts.

In this book, after a brief look at the history of the steel industry in the United Kingdom until the end of the First World War, we shall look at three main periods. The first is from the end of the war till about 1932. Before 1914 Britain's steel industry had been rapidly falling behind that of the United States and Germany. During the war it grew in response to the urgent national need for shells and armour plating, and for ships. At the end of the war there was a brief boom, followed by a collapse. For the next fifteen years the industry was in the doldrums. Its chief response was to try to get foreign imports of steel reduced, preferably by a tariff, which it achieved finally in 1932. The industry also tried to reorganize itself, partly by strengthening its central organization, partly by increasing prices, partly by the regrouping of firms, and partly by opening new works on new sites, to meet changing demands.

It is during this period that some questions that had been put before the First World War became dominant; they asked themselves so clearly and with such persistence that they had to be answered. In the course of the narration of the events between 1919 and 1932, the questions will emerge and an attempt will be made to judge whether or not the answers were satisfactory. They are, briefly, these. Was the persistently depressed state of the steel trade merely an inevitable and necessary reflection of the depressed state of the economy (as it obviously was) or was there in addition a special situation in Britain which made British steel react worse and less constructively than its counterparts elsewhere? Was the structure of the industry appropriate to the conditions in which it had to operate, or would a different structure have been more flexible, more responsive to opportunity, and less defensive? Was management unduly timid and was technology unnecessarily backward?

Financial policy certainly laid up major troubles for the industry. In the 1920s expensive borrowing was undertaken on onerous terms, and the resultant cash shortages led to a neglect of plant maintenance and new development. It was at the end of this period that the old steelmasters came to be replaced in many instances by accountants, a change of great significance. In short, it seems that the industry continued to fall behind, and added to its special legacy of old equipment and conservative management as it came through the years of depression. A leading authority on the period has argued somewhat along these lines and, importantly, the trades unionists then in the industry thought it to be like that at the time. Their pamphlet, published in May 1931, *What is Wrong with the British Iron and Steel Industry?* was the first authoritative and documented case for nationalization, precisely on the grounds that the industry had in some sense 'failed the nation'. At the same time, as subsequently, contrary opinions about the industry were held by those in power, especially by the Bank of England, and were usually dominant. But from 1931 onwards, the debate in the industry and about the industry tended to be about such matters as how to reorganize the industry under central control. By 1944 the radical views were civil service orthodoxy.

After the slump touched bottom, in 1931-2 in Great Britain and in 1932-3 in America, the steel industry began to revive. By about 1936 a powerful upswing was apparent throughout the world. True, it was interrupted in 1937-8 by a sudden renewed onset of the American depression, but that was a mere hiccough, and the strong upswing continued. It was recovery and rearmament, the one succeeding the other but powerfully accelerating it, that revived the steel industry. The war itself led to a great growth in the demand for steel products of all kinds. Britain had its own special problems. Not only were imports from Europe cut off so that arrangements had to be made with America, but ore sources had to be switched. Bombing, labour shortages, and all the problems of the war affected the industry. In the Second World War, however, not much extra crude steel-making capacity was created, because steel ingots were imported from the United States, and the new plant was specialized rolling mills, forges and other capacity for making armaments. Steel did not end the Second World War, therefore, as it had the First, with a legacy of ill-designed and ill-located surplus steel-making capacity. Once more, however, the question has to be put: what was the nature of the industry's response to the crisis and the opportunity? Since the war was won, and its progress was not unduly affected by shortages of steel, it might be supposed that the industry made its due contribution to the war effort and answered in the most direct way the questions that had been put to it. But whether, given the support that it got, there was an adequate preparation for its postwar circumstances has been much debated. The coalition government's civil servants, notably Oliver Franks, argued that the industry needed drastic changes. At the end of the war a Labour government was elected, seemingly determined to nationalize steel largely because of its alleged prewar failures, and the industry itself, partly at government request, put forward plans for the future. These plans, like the government, assumed at first that a slump would recur. It was only after a couple of years that it was realized that the postwar boom was not as ephemeral as that of 1919; and it was not until after the Korean War of 1950-3 that it was apparent that the twenty years after the Second World War were to be the greatest boom the world had ever seen. Soon, then, the industry's plans were to be criticized - as by the Treasury in 1954 - not for their extravagance in the face of a slump, but for their inadequacy in the face of a great boom. Steel allocation by the government, indeed, lasted until 1957 and was then abandoned, unwisely it was thought by many even then.

The first nationalization of steel and the rearmament boom associated with the Korean War coincided with and also threw into relief three major questions. What ought the size of the industry to be? How ought it to be organized? And, lastly, how was it to be kept technologically ahead? All three questions were, of course, interdependent. If the industry were organized in one way its size would be bigger and its rate of technological advance would be faster than if it were organized in another way - or so the protagonists and opponents of nationalization argued. In changing demand conditions, it was argued, its flexibility of response and so its rate of technological change would be faster if it were organized on the one basis rather than the other. Separate from the question of nationalization, but related to it, were the questions of the supply of finance, the location of new plant, the relations with the European Coal and Steel Community, and the appropriate organization of the firms, whether by final product basis, by technique, or as conglomerates. Above all, the relation between government itself and the steel industry remained a matter of central concern as did the matter of the financing of successive development programmes.

From the end of the First World War these questions had recurred – questions that had been raised half a century before that. What sort of steel industry was desirable? How should it be organized and run? What plants should it have and where should they be? What relationship should its policies have to those of the government? To look at these questions, we begin by briefly surveying the origins of the industry.

Iron ore is one of the earth's commonest minerals. It was used in the earliest years of civilization though in very small quantities. By extrapolation it may be suggested that perhaps a few hundred tons of iron were produced annually in the world by the time of the early iron age; production at the time of the Roman Empire was several thousand tons a year, and Britain was a major exporter of iron; in recent years world production has been running at over half a billion tons a year. Surges of iron production took place under Rome, in the early Middle Ages, and in the seventeenth century. But the great curve began its sharpest ascent in the industrial revolution. It is at that time that the modern history of steel-making began, and two critically important inventions took place in the 1850s that made steel a mass production industry.

Iron is extracted from iron ore by being heated in a furnace. The quality of the ore varies considerably – rich or poor in iron from magnetite to haematite, as found in Cumberland, and low-quality ores like limonite and siderite which are found in Lincolnshire and Northamptonshire. The ores have chemical contents which present different problems for smelting and it is the varying qualities of ore than determine many of the characteristics of different iron and steel processes. Iron can be extracted by being heated with charcoal, or with coke, and limestone over a fire, in a furnace. Originally, the furnace was lined with silica. In the resulting brew, which depended on the heat being kept up, the slag floated to the top, like fat on stew, while the pure iron was left at the bottom. The trick of all iron furnaces was to tap the furnace at the bottom, like the bung at the bottom of a barrel, and drain out the iron; and this was a process that could be kept up, by repeated further additions of fuel and ore. Abraham Darby was the man who invented the process by which coke could be used instead of charcoal; this invention, in 1760, allowed the industry to produce iron more cheaply, and led it to locate itself on coal fields; it also enabled it to expand, since there was far more coal available than there was timber to make charcoal.

What was made was iron, and it was this iron that was the basis of the first industrial revolution. From it the early industrialists made iron machines and iron rails for the early railways. The iron was tough enough and cheap enough to enable steam to be used on a widespread basis. Steel was still a specialized product, the sort of thing from which swords and razors were made. Steel and iron are the same metal - iron - but in steel the impurities, especially carbon, which cannot be entirely excluded in the manufacturing process, are controlled carefully, whereas in pig iron and cast iron impurities remain and the carbon tolerances are outside those required in steel. By adding other metals, such as nickel, different kinds of steel can be made for different purposes. Cast iron is malleable when it is hot, but gets hard and brittle, because of its high carbon content. Wrought iron, from which gates and railings were made, is cast iron reheated with iron oxide to remove practically all the carbon. The 'puddling' process enabled small furnaces to operate, producing 500 to 1,000 tons of iron a week. The blast furnaces were located near the sources of iron ore and coal, especially high quality coal; and that is one of the major reasons for the early location of the iron industry, a location pattern that in some respects has persisted to the present day.

By the mid-nineteenth century, then, Britain produced considerable quantities of iron (about 3·2 million tons of pig iron and 1·25 million tons of wrought iron in 1855) and a little steel. The steel was produced chiefly in Sheffield by Huntsman's crucible process, where pig iron and scrap were heated in a crucible furnace to produce fine steels. In 1853, there were 1,500 crucible furnaces in Sheffield and 40,000 tons of steel were produced. Its chief uses were for steam engines and associated products. In 1856 Bessemer invented a process of blowing cold air through molten pig iron. This got rid of the excessive carbon, silicon and manganese and raised the temperature to the critical level - 1600°C - where iron melts and releases its impurities, so that molten steel could be tapped. The Bessemer process initially ran into snags but it was widely adopted on the Continent and in America.

The process invented by Siemens was equally simple. Coal was turned into coal gas, which was then burnt, raising the temperature of the air which was blown into the steel-making furnace, through a series of hot chambers. This raised the temperature of the molten iron even higher (because he started out with *hot* and not *cold* air) to about 1750°C. Siemens produced not only better steel, but reduced costs by using the coal more effectively. His open-hearth process became the most widely adopted in the United Kingdom and elsewhere. In 1866, then, with the Siemens invention, steel entered into its modern phase. It is convenient to bring the story into focus, then, in that year.

In 1866 the steel industry was on its way up to unprecedented heights. In 1865 Britain produced 4·8 million tons of pig iron; 3 million tons of wrought iron were produced in 1870; steel was still not separately enumerated in those accounts, but in 1875, J. S. Jeane estimates that Bessemer steel output was 0·62 million tons. But what was significant about this figure, achieved nearly twenty years after Bessemer's invention, was that it was overshadowed by a world output consisting of an American output of 0·38 million tons, a German figure of 0·32 million tons and a French figure of 0·24 million tons. International competition in steel was virtually simultaneous with the great inventions by Bessemer and Siemens; whereas, in the iron trade, Britain's supremacy had been virtually unchallenged for a century until the late 1850s, when the American and German iron industries really got under way, as part of their industrial revolutions. Those industrial revolutions, be it noted, were based on steel.

The first thing to note about British steel, then, is that it began in an atmosphere of international competition. The next thing is that it seemed early on to tend to lose in that competition. Outside observers and steelmen themselves were from the beginning critical of the industry, on several counts - mainly that it was technically unadventurous and that its prices were too high. Both these points were connected with another major feature of the steel industry, its intensely cyclical nature. In 1873, when there was a general depression of trade, steel was especially badly hit. At these points in time, steel prices collapsed and there was a flood of low price imports, leading to allegations of dumping - allegations that were often correct, since at times of great overcapacity, marginal output that could bring in any income at all was important in keeping up the cash flow of foreign steel firms, and so they exported whatever they could at rock bottom prices. Foreign steel firms were for the most part protected by tariffs.

In 1869 the Iron and Steel Institute was set up to further research and development possibly largely to counter adverse criticism encountered at the Paris Universal Exposition of 1867 about the quality of British iron and steel. From the first meeting the Institute was a success. Technical discussions helped to spread knowledge of new processes, and the speed of change and development helped to bring the industry together to consider common problems. Essentially, however, the industry was composed of strong-minded individualist steel-makers. They were to be found in Sheffield, in South Wales, in the Black Country, in Scotland and Durham – in most of the places where the industry is located today. In the industrial depression of the early 1870s, the iron industry which had expanded to meet a rapidly rising demand at home and abroad, took a nasty knock. Steel replaced a great deal of the iron trade – in railway lines, for example, which were a very large market. Tube making grew, as the firm of Stewart's (to be part of Stewarts & Lloyds) got well established and the Bessemer process, adopted in West Cumberland where low phosphorus ore was available, led to the great growth of the steel industry there, at Barrow and at Workington. Ore

6

was mined locally, and elsewhere in Britain, the Northamptonshire and North Lincolnshire ore fields were being opened up, while Spanish ore also became an important source of raw material.

Thus, by the late 1870s the steel industry was well established. The iron trade was largely a contributory industry to steel. Ore was being imported, and steel exported in large quantities, so that steel was an important part of British international trade. John Brown in Sheffield was supplying rails, parts for railway carriages, iron armour plate for the navy. Thomas Firth was supplying ordnance for the army and the navy; Cammell and Vickers were growing; Samuel Fox was making special steels in Sheffield; Whitworths were in Manchester; there were wireworks in Warrington – many of the firms which were to survive (often in amalgamations) to nationalization seventy years later were already well established. Steel fell in price as techniques improved, and it became an important part of total national output. With Thomas and Gilchrist's discovery of the basic steel-making process by finding the way to eliminate phosphorus in the processing of pig iron into steel at the end of the 1870s, a great leap forward took place. Basic steel was relatively cheap because it allowed the use of the plentiful high phosphoric ores from Lincolnshire and Lorraine, and as the Gilchrist Thomas process was widely adopted steel output rose dramatically, exports almost doubling between 1878 and 1882. Would international competition be controlled? Other steel-making countries, after all, were vastly expanding their steel-making capacity too.

But at this stage an important technical problem can be neatly pinpointed. Before 1875, British and American blast furnaces were similar. But by 1880, the Edgar-Thompson works in Pittsburgh had a bigger furnace than any yet in use in Britain; according to Lowthian Bell, writing in 1875, there was 'nothing either in the construction of these furnaces or in the working superior in efficiency to those used in the Middlesbrough district. . . . The whole secret lies in forcing the air at a high pressure, 8-9 lbs, and immense volume.' According to Gayley, writing in 1890: 'Although the practice of rapid driving has been much decried yet in many ways it has resulted beneficially. It has brought in an equipment . . . sufficient to accomplish a large amount of work without a constant strain on every part - a condition very rare prior to 1880; and it has also developed a construction of the furnace stack, in which larger outputs from a single lining can be obtained with less irregularity in the working.' This and similar developments put the Americans ahead of the British.

How did this situation arise? It was inevitable that the United States, with its abundant raw materials and a big railway system should expand its iron and steel industry. Also, in America skilled labour was scarce, a fact which perhaps explains why American blast furnace techniques were more capital-intensive than those in England. This explains American efforts to increase labour productivity. But do they explain the 'technological gap' between Britain and the United States ? The problem must be put in perspective and it concerns coal prices. What we are effectively looking at are small cumulative modifications of a basic technique used on both sides of the Atlantic. Coal is one major clue to what happened.

For much of the period between 1870 and 1913 British coal prices moved in an opposite direction to that of most other prices. This was the very period during which the Americans established their lead over the British in pig iron manufacture and in coal production. In the British coal industry productivity actually declined between 1880 and 1913, from 318 tons to 260 tons per man year, while American productivity increased substantially. These fuel costs significantly affected the costs of producing pig iron. The explanation of the British attempts to save fuel, and so to avoid many new techniques that used a lot of coal, seems to lie somewhere along these lines. New American techniques saved labour, while British steel-masters tried to save fuel. History was on the side of the Americans.

Tinplate, shipbuilding - a whole series of major trades - were profoundly affected by the changes in steel production at the end of the century and by the late 1880s, steel existed as a powerful, progressive industry in the main centres it was to continue to be located in for the better part of the coming century. It was established as a key industry, basic to engineering, shipbuilding and railways. It had a large export trade. Yet, already, steel imports were formidable and worried British steel-makers. Overseas steel producers, especially those in Germany and the United States, were becoming technically more progressive; they were protected by tariffs and price rings and the scale of their production was already generally getting larger. In 1896, of an estimated world production of steel of 18·36 million tons, Britain produced 4·13 million tons, compared with 5·28 million tons in the United States and 4·63 million tons in Germany. Moreover, Britain's exports of iron and steel represented two-thirds of its output, so that the British steel industry was deeply dependent on foreign markets, chiefly in countries that were themselves industrializing and so developing their own iron and steel industries.

The consequences of these developments were threefold. By the end of the nineteenth century the growth of steel production capacity had been so rapid that conditions of almost permanent 'over-production' were threatened. Secondly, international competition was seemingly ruinous, in the literal sense of the word. Because steel was a decreasing-cost industry with big economies of scale, 'dumping' paid. Thirdly, amalgamations and price-fixing arrangements were becoming common in the international market. In the course of the competition Britain fell rapidly behind the United States, and what marked the industry there was rapid growth, accompanied by vast fortunes and spectacular bankruptcies. The effect of these bankruptcies, of course, was to write off capital values. The industry increasingly consisted of firms that were operating with the latest and most up-to-date plant, organized in firms like Andrew Carnegie's United States Steel Corporation with a relatively large output. Germany shot ahead too, with its big firms organized in cartels.

By 1906, world output of steel was 50·40 million tons with the United Kingdom producing only 6·46 million tons, while the United States produced 23·40 million tons, and Germany 10·53 million tons. The authoritative historians of the industry write that '1896 inaugurated a new era of world expansion. . . . The British steel industry, its leadership of the world already gone, faced fundamental problems of production and trade and found no answers.'

This is, perhaps, a little exaggerated but it is the essence of the matter. In the years around 1900, a series of amalgamations produced many of the firms that were to form the steel companies that were eventually nationalized – Stewarts & Lloyds (1903), Dorman Long (1899), Bolckow Vaughan amalgamated with some other firms around the turn of the century, Furness Withy (1891), Guest, Keen & Nettlefold (1902), Baldwins (1902), Vickers (1897), Armstrong Whitworth (1897), Cammell Laird (1903), Workington Iron & Steel (1909) – were some of them.

Bessemer steel production based on low phosphorus ore fell behind and the basic open-hearth process based on high phosphorus ore advanced. This tended to shift the geographical emphasis of the industry away from Wales and North-West England to the North-East and the Midlands. The industry was regarded by many observers as stagnant, even though its output increased with each major economic upturn and, a most serious indicator of loss of confidence, it regarded itself as an industry with 'problems'. The problems were overseas competition, severe losses of output in frequent slumps, and technical backwardness.

The response of the industry, then, to the problems that faced it was to demand protection, for firms to amalgamate, and to attempt to push ahead technically in the kinds of steel that were likely to be in future demand, which seemed to mean a switch to a more efficient open-hearth process. Chamberlain's unofficial Tariff Report of 1904 which advocated tariffs for iron and steel of between 5 and 10 per cent, became the basis of a strong political campaign. From this time on the industry's problems became partly political. The steel-masters threw in their lot with the tariff reform party and one of them, Baldwin, was to become twenty years later, Conservative prime minister. At the same time the industry became increasingly preoccupied with technical problems, since its costs had to be brought down, and the firms did not have the vast internal market enjoyed by the Americans. The way to do this seemed to be through technical progress. The development of the open-hearth furnace, of the electric furnace, and of alloy steels (using chrome and nickel) were especially important, but above all there was the rolling mill. Yet in almost all these fields Britain seemed to fall further and further behind especially in the development of rolling mills.

It was at this time, just before the First World War, that the general complaint about the industry was that it was dominated by family firms, with a great deal of traditional knowhow but a dislike for up and coming brash scientific technologists; that the firms had (on average) a strikingly low profit rate; and that the equipment was chronically old-fashioned. These complaints were of course all linked; a low profit industry cannot be expected to invest heavily, and a 'stagnant' industry is unlikely to promote brash young men and fire the existing boards of directors, especially if they happen to own large parts of the equity. In 1906, for example, L.D. Whitehead, the works manager of the Tredegar Iron and Steel Works, took the business over at the age of twenty-nine, founded the Whitehead Iron and Steel Company and put down a semi-continuous Morgan mill. He did very well; had he been in another firm, and had he not managed to lay his hands on the Tredegar Company, this important development would have been still further delayed.

In the steel firms the succession of sons to the board was based less on their formal technical qualifications, of which there were few in Britain in any case, than on a family tradition of 'the sound businessman'. These people recruited outsiders from business circles rather than from technology or accountancy. The accountants and company secretaries were looked upon as book and minute keepers, and paid accordingly. As a result the firms were technically and managerially less professional than those in America or Germany. But the businessmen were 'shrewd', in the tight-fisted sense, about buying and selling, and consequently often made money out of technically backward plant. In the 1920s, however, the financial complexities became too great – as we shall see. It was then that the accountants took over and began to emphasize technical qualifications.

The industry's other explanation for the slowness of technical development was that most innovation in America was for large-scale production, the British market for steel was far smaller, and at home and overseas the demand was for a great variety of specifications of product, which splintered production into small lots. This was of course a marketing problem, but, without protection, how was the industry to achieve some degree of standard-ization? Without protection, special requirements could always be cheaply imported.

This was the state in which the industry entered the First World War. From a condition of chronic surplus capacity the industry moved to a chronic deficit. The munitions crisis was a sign of steel shortages among other things and the steel shortage in part was due to a shortage of iron ore – so it went on. Steel output rose by nearly a quarter over the four years of the war. After a bout of inflation, steel prices were controlled. Because of competing demands for steel by the Admiralty, the Ministry of Munitions, and other users, in 1916 steel output was put under the control of the Iron and Steel Department of the Ministry of Munitions, and steel-making capacity was extended on a higgledy-piggledy basis – five extensions of major works were undertaken, and innumerable other minor extensions – all at high cost, and most of them neither technically sound nor well-located.

As a result of this growth in demand for steel for the war and the control of raw materials and production, firms had to collaborate; inevitably amalga-mations took place. At Templeborough, for instance, three firms joined to begin a new steel works, using cold pig iron based on home ores. Harry Steel (whose name makes the whole thing like Happy Families) of Steel, Peech & Tozer, sought amalgamation with Samuel Fox in order to ensure a supply of pig iron, and joined with Samuel Fox to buy the Frodingham Iron & Steel Company at Scunthorpe to safeguard its raw material supplies. At the same time the problem of coal supplies was acute and the Rother Vale collieries were bought to ensure supplies. Steel, Peech & Tozer launched the Templeborough project for a melting shop and billet mill with govern-ment support. Similarly David Colville, the Scottish steel firm, bought other firms at government request in order to extend their total steel-making capacity as rapidly as possible. Dorman Long, Baldwins, Richard Thomas, John Brown – all grew by amalgamation.

All this activity naturally led to speculation as to the future of the industry. Would the wartime boom persist?

In 1919 the British steel industry consisted of hundreds of firms, but the greater part of the output was in the hands of a relatively small number of them. For the most part the activities of these firms were confined to one main centre each, but already several of them were geographically widely dispersed as a result of amalgamations that had brought together sub-sidiaries which were scattered – and, also, a point of importance, with diverse interests. If we take for example a firm like United Steel Companies we find that it was an amalgamation in 1918 of Samuel Fox & Company with Steel, Peech & Tozer. These firms amalgamated with the Workington

Iron & Steel Company, the Frodingham Iron & Steel Company and the Rother Vale collieries. They, in turn, were the product of earlier mergers and takeovers. The new firm now had major plants in Sheffield, Cumberland and Lincolnshire; it had coal mines, ore fields, and all stages of iron and steel production. Other big examples could come from Scotland and from Wales; and other, though smaller, examples could be given from Lancashire and the Black Country.

This structure was based upon a series of individual companies which had merged, but not necessarily on any coherent basis other than personal and financial links. Yet some industrial sense could be made of the pattern. The industry, for instance, had strong tendencies towards vertical integration. Many firms owned coal mines, iron ore mines, quarries, and went in for making iron, steel and steel products. If we take the case of United Steel we see such a pattern. Often the integration had come back from the final user; Harland & Wolff, for instance, who were shipbuilders in Belfast and Glasgow exchanged shares in 1919 with David Colville & Sons of Scotland, so that they could control in part their supplies of steel. Similar moves were seen on the North-East coast.

In thinking about steel companies, therefore, it is important to remember that their interests were diversified, chiefly into coal, shipbuilding and heavy engineering, and that the steel component was not necessarily the major one. It so happened that all these industries tended to be affected by the same economic forces – a slump drove down the demand for coal, steel and new ships disproportionately to demand in general, for instance – but difficulties in one field could adversely affect a firm whose steel interests were all right in themselves. The prolonged coal strikes and lockouts of 1920, 1921 and 1926, for example, badly affected the steel companies most of the larger of which had coal interests. The effects on the cash flow and market position of steel firms seeking new capital was obviously affected by the results of their non-steel operations, especially in coal.

In 1919 the capital position of the industry was affected further by the merger movement, since the mergers were accompanied or followed by financial reconstructions and new issues. These represented in part the capitalization of wartime investment projects, and in part the raising of finance for projects planned by the new companies. United Steel, for example, generated a big issue in 1919 (of $1\frac{1}{4}$ million £1 ordinary shares) as well as £1 million on a debenture issue on its formation in 1918, and a £1$\frac{1}{2}$ million issue of 8 per cent preferred ordinary shares in 1920 to finance a subsidiary, the United Strip and Bar Mills at Templeborough. More serious than ordinary share issues was the issue of debenture fixed interest stocks such as the Ebbw Vale Steel, Iron and Coal Company's £3 million seven-year notes floated at 8 per cent in November 1920. These major issues were grave hostages to fortune because they meant that if the profit level fell in money terms, the payments due for capital were bound to be a heavy burden. In the next decade, in fact, the greater part of the industry was on or over the verge of bankruptcy from this very fact.

By 1919, then, the industry was buoyantly making plans for growth based on the hope of rising money profits. It was quickly seen that these plans were not only unrealistic; they were profoundly unwise. Why was this?

The background to these changes was a complex one. Immediately after the war there was a great industrial boom and steel output switched rapidly from shells, ships and tanks to its normal pattern, to meet a peacetime demand. In 1919–20 output of iron and steel reached a peak of 9·0 million tons a year. Yet in 1921 output was down to 3·7 million tons. As the postwar slump set in steel prices first soared, till mid-1920, and then fell, and fell far more rapidly than prices in general. The effects of this experience were catastrophic, especially in blowing sky high the carefully drawn-up plans for the postwar reconstruction. The industry needed public support and a policy of protection against imports. Yet in 1919 the industry had indignantly resisted proposals for support and protection.

During the war the Balfour Committee on Commercial and Industrial Policy after the War had a committee (under Scoby-Smith) on the iron and steel trades. The war showed that centralization of the industry had enabled capacity to be expanded rapidly and production to be rationalized. Self-sufficiency, both in steel and in ore, was possible, so that tariffs were feasible. During the war the firms were apprehensive about the future demand for their expanded capacity, and they also faced financial problems, especially if the government did not guarantee postwar markets for the expansion it was exhorting the industry to undertake for the war and was helping to organize and finance.

The Balfour Committee supported protection in some circumstances – the government that appointed it was composed partly of tariff reformers – and the Scoby-Smith Committee proposed it especially for iron and steel on the grounds of likely serious postwar competition arising from the greatly enlarged steel capacity and the formation of an export association. What price was the industry to pay for protection? None, it seemed, for the Scoby-Smith Committee recommended no continuation of government control as a quid pro quo for protection. There were dissentient voices, but the general opinion was that tariffs, and no other government regulation, would keep the industry going.

It had been suggested in 1918 that imports from Germany should be banned and other imports restricted in order to let the British industry make the transition to peacetime production in due and careful order. Yet such was the deep sense of security of the steel-masters that by the late summer of 1919 imports were once more allowed. Once this had happened, an easy shift to a policy of protection was out of the question. Similarly with public support and control. The government ended its wartime commitments as fast as it could, and subsidies to the iron and steel industry were ended, together with most price and other controls, in the spring of 1919. It was clearly in the industry's immediate interest that this should be so, since a great boom in prices and expectations was already under way. But it left no government mechanism for supporting the industry when the slump came.

Why did the slump come so quickly? The first explanation was that (as was to be made particularly clear in 1931) the demand for steel fluctuated far more widely than the general level of activity, and when there was a general slump, steel was especially badly hit. But the other explanation was that international competition became especially intense because of the general over-capacity that had arisen from the war. Wartime plans came to fruition at the end of the war and at the beginning of the peace, and it was as a result of this that the capacity of the industry suddenly became much bigger.

The slump, when it came, affected the British industry more than it did those of several other countries. British free trade allowed the dumping of foreign steel and at the same time gave the industry no bargaining counter to protect its vulnerable export trade. This was nothing new. Before the war, too, a situation had developed where in times of international shortage, out-of-date firms missed too many opportunities for new business. In time of world surplus they plunged faster into financial crisis. The allegations were revived, not without justification, that the industry was technically backward and badly managed. How far was this true?

Opposite *The lunar landscape of the big iron ore field in Mauretania.*

Opposite *The shipping of ore by sea (here to Port Talbot in Wales) is a major reason for putting steel-works next to deep water.*

A

Making Iron: Blast Furnace

The blast furnace showing iron ore, coke, limestone and sinter being put into a skip. The mixture is taken up a hoist, and put into a double bell at the top of the furnace. The furnace is extremely hot, blown by blasts of hot air. Gas is drawn off at the top and molten iron is drawn off from the bottom, while the slag (or waste) is run off.

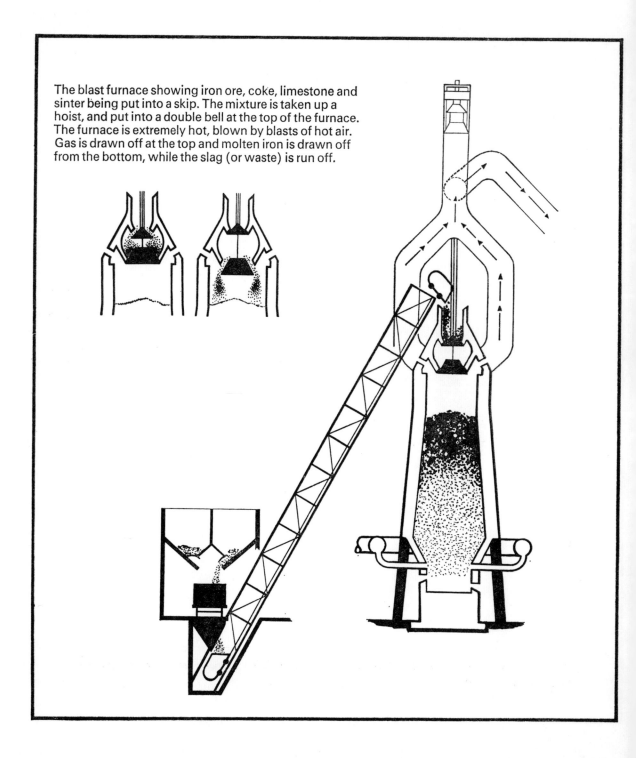

Making Steel: (1) Open-Hearth Furnace

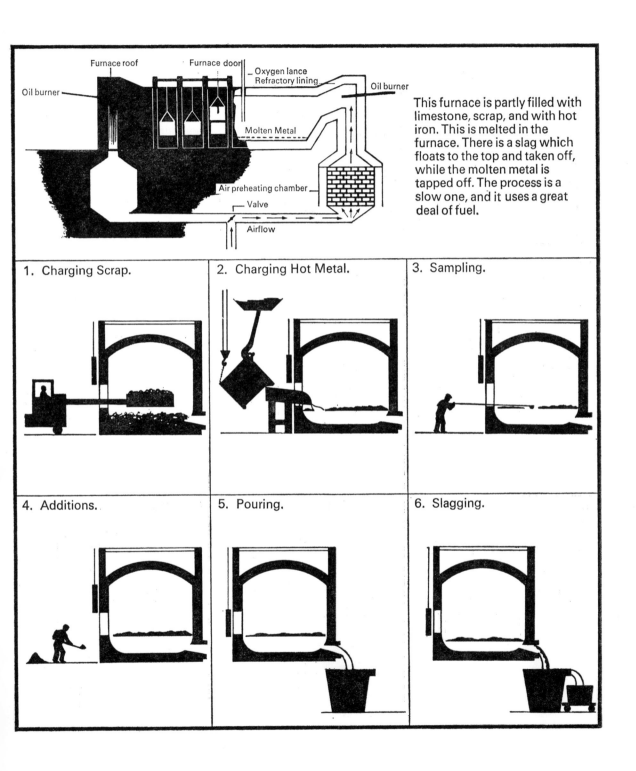

Furnace roof   **Furnace door**   Oxygen lance   Refractory lining   **Oil burner**

Oil burner

Molten Metal

Air preheating chamber

Valve

Airflow

This furnace is partly filled with limestone, scrap, and with hot iron. This is melted in the furnace. There is a slag which floats to the top and taken off, while the molten metal is tapped off. The process is a slow one, and it uses a great deal of fuel.

1. Charging Scrap.

2. Charging Hot Metal.

3. Sampling.

4. Additions.

5. Pouring.

6. Slagging.

Making Steel: (2) Electric Arc Furnace

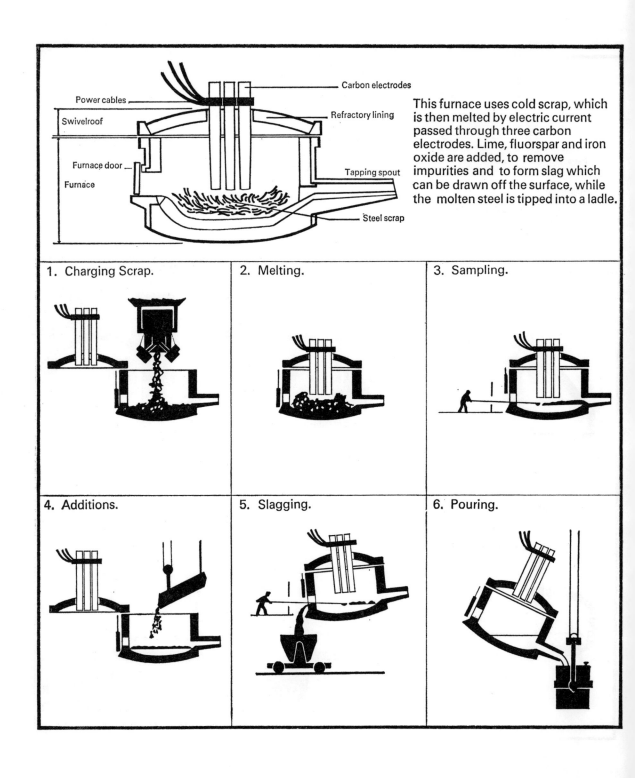

Carbon electrodes

Power cables

Refractory lining

Swivelroof

Furnace door

Tapping spout

Furnace

Steel scrap

This furnace uses cold scrap, which is then melted by electric current passed through three carbon electrodes. Lime, fluorspar and iron oxide are added, to remove impurities and to form slag which can be drawn off the surface, while the molten steel is tipped into a ladle.

1. Charging Scrap.

2. Melting.

3. Sampling.

4. Additions.

5. Slagging.

6. Pouring.

Making Steel: (3) Basic Oxygen Furnace

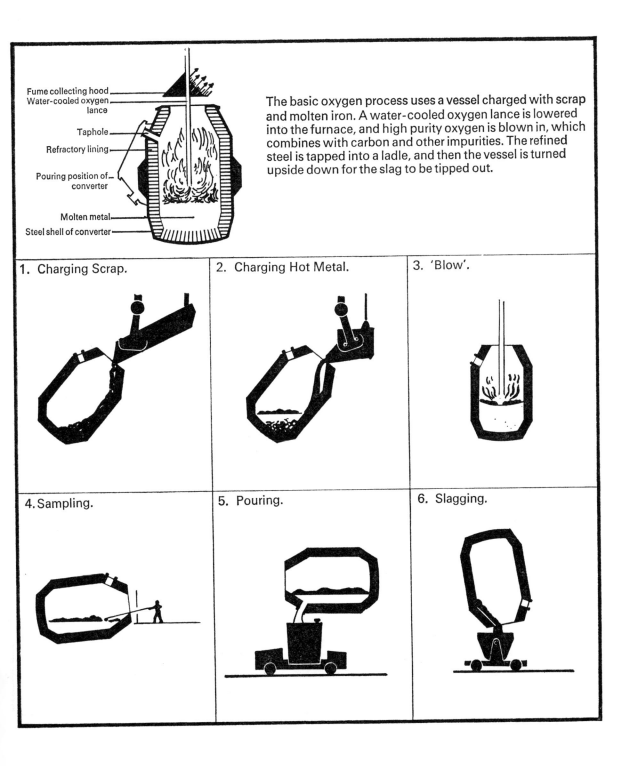

Fume collecting hood
Water-cooled oxygen lance
Taphole
Refractory lining
Pouring position of converter
Molten metal
Steel shell of converter

The basic oxygen process uses a vessel charged with scrap and molten iron. A water-cooled oxygen lance is lowered into the furnace, and high purity oxygen is blown in, which combines with carbon and other impurities. The refined steel is tapped into a ladle, and then the vessel is turned upside down for the slag to be tipped out.

1. Charging Scrap.

2. Charging Hot Metal.

3. 'Blow'.

4. Sampling.

5. Pouring.

6. Slagging.

2

The Difficult Twenties

For most people in the steel industry the 1920s were dismal years. They began with a full-fledged slump which, as will appear, was probably the most unfortunate single occurrence in the history of the steel industry because it was then that the optimists were proved wrong, and almost all their plans went astray. After the 1921 slump there was a brief revival – more a kind of convalescence than a recovery – followed by the catastrophic slump of 1929 to 1932. It was a decade that in retrospect seemed intolerable because of depression at home, and a serious loss of exports because of the overvalued pound. Help was not available from the government to reconstruct the industry, its firms suffered additional losses because they were heavily involved in the coal industry which was similarly afflicted by depression and loss of exports and had serious labour troubles as well. In the previous chapter it has been seen how the industry had come to be in a difficult position. Looking at the 1920s, it is evident that things got worse rather than better.

The first and major problem was over-capitalization and the second was excess capacity, largely as a result of wartime building. But, thirdly, much of the capacity was in fact not readily usable. It existed to produce products for which demand was falling, like steel rails, or it was so old that only at a time of high boom could it conceivably be used, or it was inconveniently located. This was a technical question, to which detailed reference will be made, but it could only be solved by a ruthless policy of scrapping and rebuilding. Such a policy was virtually impossible because of finance. And the financial situation was the key to almost everything. The firms had issued preference shares and debentures recklessly. Ebbw Vale, as late as November 1920, issued 8 per cent seven-year notes to the extent of £3 million. The result was that a good many firms were virtually unable to pay dividends on their ordinary shares – at one time or another in the 1920s this was true of over thirty major companies, and two of the leading historians of the industry list eleven firms that paid no dividend on ordinary shares between 1921 and 1931. Some firms were unable to pay their debenture holders; many firms did not pay dividends on preference shares. This put a considerable number of firms into the hands of the joint-stock banks –

Barclays, the Midland, the National Provincial, Martins and the Westminster are cases specifically cited in this chapter and the next.

In such circumstances firms were short of working capital, let alone money for extending or renewing their plant. It seemed a miracle in some months that there was enough in the kitty to pay the wages on Saturday and men were indeed laid off in very large numbers. Unemployment crept up to over a third of the insured labour force in 1922, and repeatedly exceeded that proportion thereafter; the real figures were higher since not all employees were insured.

Above all the industry faced renewed imports, accentuated by the revaluation of the pound and the return to gold in 1925, which made all imports cheaper, and especially steel since it came from countries, like France and Germany, which had devalued dramatically. As Peech of United Steel said in 1924: 'The franc having fallen from 67 to 84 today, the whole country is simply flooded with foreign billets and the prices of home billets have fallen to well below £8 delivered Midlands and the foreign price is under £7. With materials very little lower and wages on the up-grade it must be evident that firms taking under £8 delivered for billets must be losing very heavily indeed.' At the same time its exports suffered because of the revaluation of the pound. The attitude of the firms in the industry to each other and to their overseas competitors is of great importance in this context.

Concern was often expressed over foreign competition. Peech of United Steel, for instance, said: 'Many meetings also of the various Trade Associations in which we are interested have been held to consider what steps might be taken to keep in this country, the trade which appears to be going abroad. Many reductions in prices have been agreed upon, but these reductions are of little advantage in view of the foreign prices being so very much lower, but at least it is a step in the right direction. . . .'

There was an element of high politics at work. As Peech said: 'For many months now I have been of the opinion . . . that the international arrangements which were existing before the war would have to be revised in some form if we were to have our share of the world's trade in certain respects. It was apprehended that the French makers would have some difficulty in sitting round the same table with German makers and I was most anxious to ascertain if this was an insurmountable difficulty. To this end I thought it worthwhile to visit Messrs D.E. Wendel, the great steel-makers in Lorraine, and in a confidential conversation they gave me to understand that provided the suggestion came from another quarter, and they could join in with no loss of *amour propre*, they would be prepared to consider the revival of some such arrangement as existed before the war, and they felt they could arrange for the French firms to meet the German makers in connection with the matter.' And, in November Peech told his board: 'I have had many confidential interviews with the general managers of the various railway companies with a view to pressing them to place orders for railway material, but they all assure me that they are not likely to place large orders for several months.' Behind the troubles of the steel firms lay those very serious international and political matters.

These charges of dumping were of course made against a background of very tightly controlled price-rings in all commodities and branches of the trade. As well as from the records of the price-rings, the strength of the agreements may be judged by the ferocity with which those who broke them were attacked. 'Consett has reopened and are cutting prices unmercifully in order to obtain a "trial run"', United Steel minuted in 1925, and similar comments can be found widely in the records.

In this chapter, the response of the industry to the problems of the period is examined. It has been argued that the excess capacity, and much of the technical backwardness of the plant, was due to the firms which were in financial difficulties. To see why this was the case, first the managers and owners are considered, and next the men who worked for them, since it is the characteristics of the people in the industry which determined their policies. After certain general points have been made, a look will be taken in some detail at a number of the firms.

Steel firms were of many sizes and shapes. Some were conglomerates, like United Steel, some had extensive coal interests, some were effectively offshoots of shipbuilding or engineering concerns. 'Steelmen', therefore, often had their eyes on other parts of the industrial front. Moreover, the 1920s was the last decade in which major firms were customarily managed by one man without an effective managerial structure.

It will be seen that steel leaders tended to be 'dictators' – Frank Thomas positively called himself that. How far was this inevitable, and how far did it affect the nature and shape of the decisions taken? Let it be clear that often the dictator was a major shareholder; steel was in that sense a collection of 'small' firms, in that they were run as one-man firms. Day-to-day managerial capacity was obviously dreadfully low; there was no effective trained band of middle management, and the boards of companies represented shareholders, who were often distinguished men, like Sir Edward Boyle, but not trained managers. It was almost inevitable, then, that a dedicated temperamental managing director, especially if he were a major shareholder, would be able to use his 'experience' to take the strategic decisions almost alone. The head of the firm was usually very old. When Sir Arthur Dorman died in 1931 he had been fifty-five years on the board of Dorman Long, forty-two years as chairman; his successor, Sir Hugh Bell, who died a few weeks later, had 'sixty-nine years of service'. But an old man was sometimes a bold man. What is interesting is that boldness usually, ultimately, paid off; in the short run it often brought disaster – but that was because there was little financial expertise available and trade was so often bad. But when trade was good, a new modern plant was an asset of great value. Some of the dictators did build such plants. The problem, as we shall see, was to devise a structure of management and control that enabled bold decisions to be taken, without the day-to-day paranoid consequences of one-man rule, and which avoided periodic bankruptcy.

In this context, United Steel is an interesting firm, since after Harry Steel's death it was run as a coalition and not as a dictatorship. Clearly, the managerial styles that were being developed in other concerns, notably the newly amalgamated railways and banks, would be of interest, for the larger firm which was not a 'family' enterprise would require special skills. Especially, it will be seen, there was a lack of financial skill, and of technical expertise backed by scientific and engineering training. Firms paid their secretaries £300 a year, plus a house; his job was to take minutes. They had a book-keeper and a wages clerk. The technical skills came from men of experience, brought up from the shop floor, or sometimes 'poached' from neighbouring firms.

It is interesting that when new works were developed, more often than not the steel firms called in consulting engineers and, as will be seen, it was this that led Brasserts of Chicago to play so full a role in the affairs of the British steel industry.

Most surprising of all, in the papers of the period, is the lack of concern with marketing. This was because the firms had steady customers who stayed with them. Prices were fixed by local rings, and for most traders output quotas were allocated. United Steel took a slight interest in Austin, the Birmingham car manufacturer; but it was an interest, not a consuming passion. Their real worry was the market for steel products on the railways – and even in the early 1920s it hardly took much prescience to see that the motor car was the steel product of the future. Similarly with steel frame buildings, then being built in great numbers in America; the British were more interested in the Sydney Harbour bridge. Occasionally managing directors went on world trips to get business, but there is little sense of a passionate keenness to open up new markets.

Inside the firms, then, there was usually a father and his sons and brothers on the board, a few clerks, and perhaps an officer back from the Western Front and still using his military title to look after sales and labour relations. Interestingly enough, in these family concerns, the boss was often in his

Location of steelworks mentioned in the text

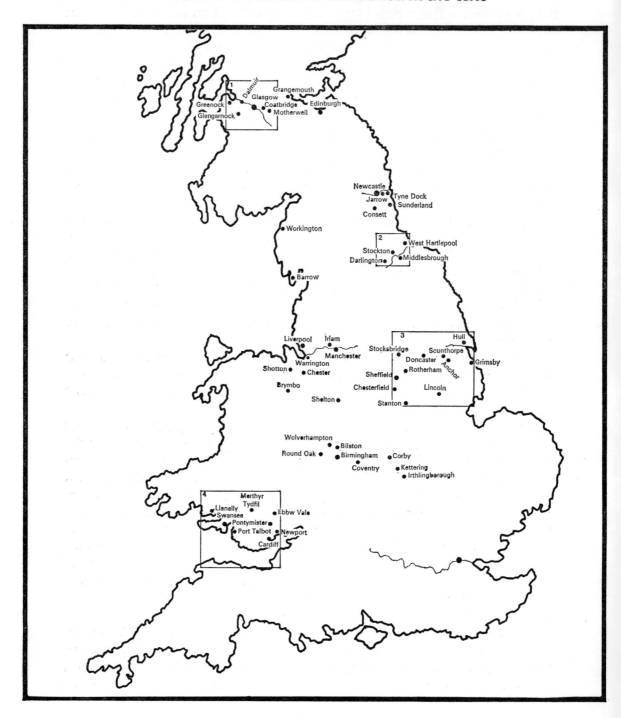

GLASGOW
1

Carron

Greenock

Dalmuir

Rothesay Dock

Linwood

Paisley

Glasgow

Blochairn

Beardmore

Gartsherrie

Coatbridge

Mossend

Clydebridge

Hallside

Motherwell

Glengarnock

Hamilton

Ravenscraig

Dalzell

Lanarkshire

Craigneuk

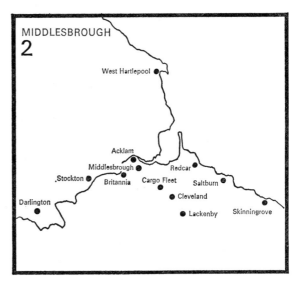

MIDDLESBROUGH
2

West Hartlepool

Acklam

Middlesbrough

Redcar

Stockton

Britannia

Cargo Fleet

Saltburn

Darlington

Cleveland

Lackenby

Skinningrove

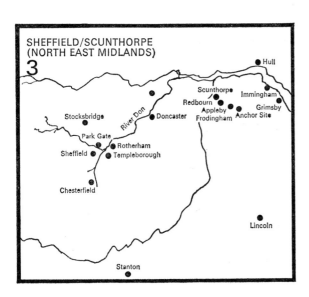

SHEFFIELD/SCUNTHORPE
(NORTH EAST MIDLANDS)
3

Hull

Scunthorpe

Immingham

Redbourn

Appleby

Grimsby

Stocksbridge

River Don

Doncaster

Frodingham

Anchor Site

Park Gate

Rotherham

Sheffield

Templeborough

Chesterfield

Lincoln

Stanton

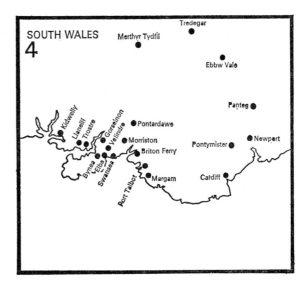

SOUTH WALES
4

Tredegar

Merthyr Tydfil

Ebbw Vale

Panteg

Kidwelly

Llanelli

Trostre

Pontardawe

Byrnea

Gorseinon

Morriston

Newport

Elba

Velindre

Briton Ferry

Pontymister

Swansea

Port Talbot

Margam

Cardiff

seventies or even his eighties. In a family business this was understandable because the assets belonged to him. But in a world where technology and markets were changing age was a serious disadvantage. It will be something to which this book will return since it was a habit that lasted until the 1960s.

The steel-masters had a reputation for being good employers. The evidence for this was that they and the men's representatives frequently said so; that wages were above the average for heavy manual work; and that strikes were few and far between. In part this reputation was obviously justified, yet it is in fact a slightly mystifying one. There is the fact, widely acknowledged, that the Iron and Steel Trades Confederation, under the leadership of John Hodge and Arthur Pugh, was heavily paternalistic and stood well to the right of the trade union movement. Why was this? Was it because it was so successful in arguing its members' case; or was it like the steel firms themselves caught up in some all-embracing 'steel' philosophy which made it difficult for them to be critical of what was going on?

The steel-masters, for one thing, may have been good employers; but the same firms owned large sections of the coal industry where they were regarded with virtually universal detestation. During the 1920s unemployment among registered steel-workers occasionally reached 70 per cent and never fell below 30; if casual labour had been included the percentages would have been higher. Standards of treatment of the men were different, of course, from what might have been expected to be accorded to others. Not a single ordinary meeting of the board of Richard Thomas occurred without a report of a fatal or a serious accident to a workman, and they were fatalities of an appalling kind – people crushed by falling rock in mines, decapitated by railway wagons, burned to death – and the compensation, if any, was negligible. Yet when directors died, as being of advanced years they tended frequently to do, lachrymose messages were sent to their relations. (Even in 1951, on King George VI's death the RTB board's minutes veritably sob.) At one meeting when hundreds of pounds were voted to non-executive directors, whose task it was to attend a board meeting once every two months, a pension of £1 a week was awarded with some self-congratulation to a man with fifty-one years' service. People were stood off at a week's notice as recently as the 1960s. In 1939, when the war began, managerial staff had their service pay and allowances made up to their usual salaries; for the wage-earners cases of hardship among their wives were relieved by a small sum set aside for the purpose, at a time when profits were soaring entirely because of the war. A similar arrangement was made at Lancashire Steel, where the board's proposal to deduct 3d a week (just over 1p) for each £1 of the workers' wages to found a hardship fund for workers in the forces was rejected by the workers. The board voted £50 a week for the fund.

Yet to write all this is to write with hindsight. Sufficient to say that the conditions of the weekly wage-earners and the management were radically different. Nobody ever consulted the workers about the opening or shutting of plants; the first correspondence about this that survives is from the 1930s when Members of Parliament like James Griffiths of Llanelli and Ellen Wilkinson of Jarrow raised matters in the press and in Parliament.

The problem still remains. If, by the early 1920s, the miners, their unions and their Members of Parliament – of whom James Griffiths was typical – were exceedingly radical and determined to improve their working lives, why were the steel-workers, often from the very same families, not at all radical?

To answer that question, several paths have to be trodden. The first concerns wages. The second concerns shop-floor management. The third concerns the union. In general, wages in the steel industry were relatively high. The reasons for this are not far to seek; wages were a relatively small part of total costs, and the steel firms needed a special kind of tough, reliable skilled man for the shift work that was involved with economical organization.

There is no evidence that steel firms differed from other colliery owners in their attitude to or treatment of the miners. It will be recalled that in the 1920s there were a series of strikes and lockouts in the coal industry. Relations between men and management never recovered from this period of the General Strike and the lockout of the miners who refused to accept lower wages and longer hours. As the Stocksbridge colliery manager reported to the United Steel Board on 21 September 1926, 'it is questionable whether Job would have possessed the requisite patience to deal with the trials of today'. But the firm needed coal and prices were good because of the shortage, so 'we must save up the punishment where any is required until our day comes'. On 26 September Walter Benton Jones of United Steel fully supported the other mine owners. 'The unanimous reply of the Coal-owners (which was unanimously opposed to Churchill's) cannot fail to carry considerable weight with the government and the general public.'

This implacable attitude certainly carried over to the steel-workers when they took part in the General Strike. Mackay, in charge of labour relations, reported to the United Steel board that 'the men, exercising confidence in their leaders, had been drawn into wrong action . . . as in the future we would have to work with trades unions, our policy should be . . . to meet the unions . . . impress upon leaders and delegates their offence, and get their written expressions of regret. . . . Thereafter we should . . . endeavour to make capital out of the incident in the direction of better and more amicable working conditions.'

It was accepted that the union was a reasonable one; 'Mr Hodge is resuming a closer grip on affairs as president, while Mr Pugh is chairman' of the TUC. Mr Hodge, it was said, was broad-minded. He was also in difficulties since his union lost virtually all its unemployed and many of its employed members, and the sliding scale agreement meant that the blast-furnace makers were earning only '10 per cent more over August 1914, but the cost of living was 70 per cent over'.

The expansion of output in the war years resulted in a rapid advance in blast furnacemen's wages. A general system of sliding scales was adopted. After 1920 the sliding scales of all classes of workmen began to fall. The management of the various firms saw no alternative to wage reductions. This policy met with resistance. For example, between August and October 1924 the whole of United Steel's works at Ickles, Templeborough and Stocksbridge were shut down by a strike of maintenance engineers.

Wages in steel, however, were relatively good. The firms employed men in small groups, many of them recruited in teams, and paid directly by the group leader. Consequently there was a strong pressure to conform to the norms of the small group. But, above all, the union had special characteristics.

The British Iron, Steel and Kindred Trades Confederation (ISTC) was set up in 1886 and it gradually absorbed many of the other iron and steel unions. In 1919 John Hodge who was president had been Minister of Labour in Lloyd George's coalition, and a Labour MP for Gorton, while Arthur Pugh was general secretary. It had 125,000 or so members, and it took part in a wide series of joint negotiating boards. In 1919 its authority was challenged by 'Direct Action' strikes to stop arms being sent to the Whites in Russia, and by unofficial strikes about wages and conditions, but the rising prices of iron and steel products led through the sliding scale agreements to rising wages for the members. But in the 1921 slump, employment, prices and wages slumped faster than the general price level. By March 1921 over 32,000 members were drawing unemployment benefit. The union, like the steel companies, had a large overdraft and it steadily lost members. A strike to alter the sliding scale would not have been practicable: the union had no money; the employers had little trade; and the union officials did not like strikes. An instance of this occurred at Consett in 1925, when E. J. George became general manager, and ordered the melters to work at weekends to keep up ingots output while a furnace was being rebuilt. The men struck; the union sent them back to work; and ultimately settled virtually on George's terms.

The General Strike of 1926 arose out of the miners' dispute. The ISTC

paid no benefit to its strikers, and had to pay out large sums to those unemployed in steel as a result of the coal miners' lockout. It lost members
steadily; by 1929 its membership was down to 53,000. The union described
'rationalization' 'as amalgamation of capitalist interests without plan or
regard for the human factor'. The Sankey Committee, set up with I S T C's
agreement, reported that British labour costs were higher than those on the
Continent; it favoured amalgamations on a regional basis, and 'the elimination of uneconomic units', and that the industry should possibly join the
cartel which controlled the continental steel industry, once it had put its
own house in order. The I S T C's counter-proposal was a publicly supervised industry, with special provision for help to labour. The resolutions
referred to 'conscious planning, organized control and the financial needs
for its rehabilitation and progressive development'. But that was as yet a
little time ahead. It does explain, however, the union's passivity in the 1920s.

The shareholders were more vociferous than the men. The suspension of
preference dividends was no light matter when the price-level was falling
and preference shares were a source of solid income to middle-class people,
who expected ordinary shares to be a source of profit and loss. In 1924 an
irate shareholder from Bristol wrote to United Steel: 'Up to now I have
received nothing in the shape of dividends for years for the use of my capital
invested ... I have caused enquiries to be made in Sheffield through my
brokers and, from what I learn they are most unsatisfactory and unless a
dividend on the preference 6 per cent shares is declared in the near future
I shall take action in connection with several other Bristol shareholders
whom I know personally to bring the matter to a head as no shareholder is
going to put up with such dastardly and villainous procedure any longer.'
A courteous reply was sent assuring the aggrieved shareholder that 'payment
of preference dividends will be resumed immediately circumstances justify
it'. A not wholly satisfactory reply, it may be felt.

So we see an industry with troubled management and dissatisfied shareholders. Above all, as we shall shortly see, the banks were fed up.

This pattern may be traced through a series of particular instances of
firms and areas which reacted in different ways to the state of trade in the
1920s. The output of pig iron in the early 1920s was almost the lowest since
1879. The North-East coast was in many respects characteristic, because it
was so hard hit, and because the industry was so fragmented.

In 1920 *the North-East coast* produced nearly a third of British pig iron
and about a fifth of British steel output. The Tees was a major importer of
foreign ore and exporter of Cleveland ore. It was the centre of a number of
old, well-established firms, like Dorman Long, Bell Brothers, Pease &
Partners, Bolckow Vaughan, Consett Iron, the Furness group and South

Durham. During the war a great deal of money was poured into new plant, notably at Redcar. Between them they had over eighty blast furnaces, of which sixty-nine were in blast in that year. The blast furnaces were for the most part exceptionally small and the equipment was particularly elderly. There had been a major shift out of the acid Bessemer process using a siliceous refractory into basic steel using a basic refractory of magnesite or dolomite making possible the use of high phosphoric ores and this had been accelerated by the wartime extensions of plant discussed earlier.

The situation was simple. On the basis of local coal and ore, and the local trades of shipbuilding and engineering, a great variety of iron and steel works and firms had been set up. All of them were badly hit by the slump, and as coal and shipbuilding were too, the North-East became the first and worst of the English depressed areas.

In 1918 Tees-side produced a third of British home ore. It was this that made it crucially important to the steel industry, but also some most important firms were situated there, or nearby, notably Dorman Long & Consett. The trend was for the works to move over from Bessemer to open-hearth production, and in 1920 all Bessemer production stopped.

The blast furnaces were, generally speaking, old and small. The United States average output for a blast furnace was 100,000 tons a year; if blast furnaces in Great Britain had been of the same size this would have meant about eighty blast furnaces all told, yet, in the North-East, where production was 2·6 million tons of pig iron in 1920, there were in fact sixty-nine furnaces in blast. The coal strikes, from 22 October to 3 November 1920, and from 1 April to 4 July 1921 caused a fall in output in the North-East and, at the same time, demand dramatically fell, both absolutely and as a proportion of the national total – from what had been more than a quarter to less than a sixth. The reason for this, purely and simply, was the antique equipment and the fragmented nature of the industry's organization.

The Cargo Fleet Iron Co. was part of the Furness group of firms, run by Lord Furness, a Lloyd George viscount, whose managing director was Benjamin Talbot. It worked closely with South Durham, which declared a 20 per cent dividend in 1917, as a result of high profits. In 1920 it was making a big profit on its coke, pig iron and, above all, its steel sections, but a loss on coal. It was a fairly typical middle-size family firm in the North-East. John James, who had run the iron foundry, became a director in 1920; his first big step on a ladder that was to lead to a dominant position in the trade for forty years. He and Benjamin Talbot, together with the works managers, ran the firm. It knew its place. Its coal production and prices was controlled by the Coal Control and then by the local Collieries Association; its share of steel output was allocated to it by the local branch of the

Opposite *Coke ovens at Ravenscraig use great quantities of coal.*

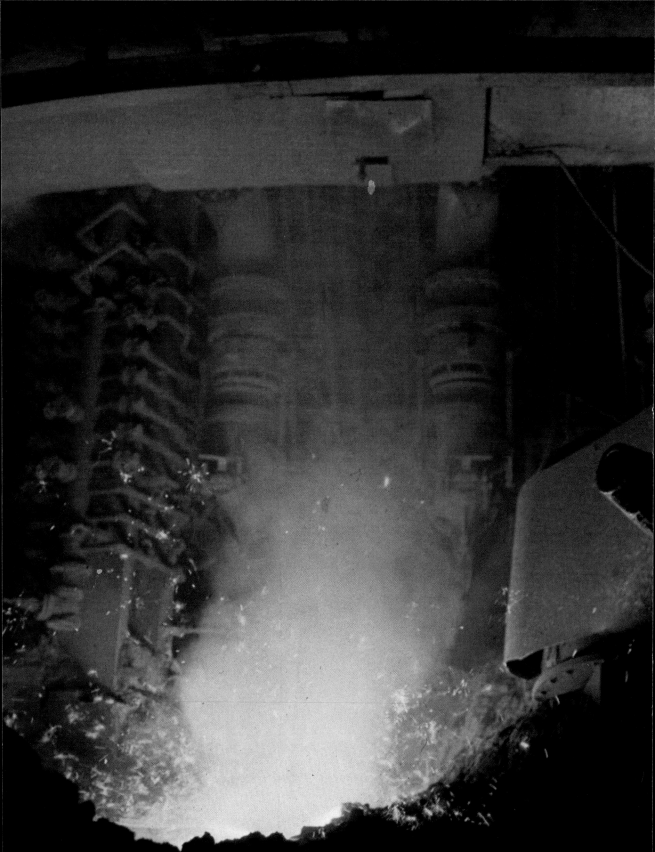

Rail Makers Association which also fixed prices. Even so, competition for particular orders was acute. In 1922 Talbot reported that Bolckow Vaughan had bought Redpath Brown, making competition in structural steel 'more acute', and Baldwin's and Partington were also competing, although they came from South Wales and Lancashire to poach locally. But the real depression did not hit until the summer of 1925, and by October the 'price of rails, joists and sections . . . are below the cost of production both in the home and export markets'. Then the General Strike brought all operations to a standstill. By 1926, the firm owed £197,000 to the Inland Revenue; the collieries were losing over £57,000 a month, and coal was imported to keep the steel works going. By 1927 the debts of the Sperling group of ship-builders (Fairfields Northumberland Shipbuilding and William Doxford) were such that they had to be written off in return for a guarantee that they would buy their steel from Cargo Fleet.

By 1928, it was agreed to merge with South Durham; and the Inland Revenue settled for £75,000 as against its claim which had now reached £203,000. South Durham, where Benjamin Talbot was also important, turned to welded steel pipe making in 1923, and A. N. McQuistan was made a director in 1926. McQuistan and Talbot fought a constant battle for the Furness firms, protesting against the Appleby plate mills, redeveloped with a government guarantee in 1926, and against Consett. The newly merged company was pushed by Barclays Bank to consider a merger with Dorman Long and Bolckow Vaughan in 1929. The merger, as we shall see, did not come off. The reason for that was longstanding hostility between Dorman Long and the Talbots.

Dorman Long at Middlesbrough, was run by the Dormans and Colonel Maurice Bell. They were construction engineers and bridge-builders, and they represented the diversified type of firm. In 1927, Reginald McKenna told Sir William Larke, who told Dorman Long, that 'a merger of interests of an operating company in the iron and steel trade might be desirable'. It was as a direct result of this that the merger with Bolckow Vaughan was undertaken, in negotiations that took two years, and were only concluded when both firms were approaching bankruptcy and needed a £4·7 million overdraft between them to keep going.

Consett is an interesting case that points this moral. It was an exceptionally well managed and well conducted concern, acutely conscious of its responsibilities to its work people and their communities. (The Pease family who originally ran it were Quakers.) It had nine major collieries, and it made plates, chiefly for Swan Hunter, in an integrated iron and steel works that had been brought up to date in the war, and it was expanding rapidly on wartime finance when the slump came. In 1921 it was a 'question of policy

Opposite *The blast furnace at the Abbey works.*

B

as to whether the works should be closed, pending better times, or whether whatever orders could be got should be executed and the works kept going as much as possible, with a view to keeping trade together and taking immediate advantage of any recovery'. Palmer's Shipbuilding of Jarrow cancelled a contract for 30,000 tons of pig iron; the £600,000 profit of 1920 was soon turned into a loss. But the firm kept on rebuilding its works, which were well inland in County Durham, despite advice that they should shift to the Tyne because they relied upon rich imported ore.

'During the period 1918 to June 1921, record profits have been earned in all departments . . . there has been undertaken and pushed on with considerable energy large capital undertakings . . .', the general manager E.J. George wrote, and got agreement to spend £3¼ million on three new blast furnaces, eight steel furnaces and a mixer, a slab cogging mill and two complete plate mills, with a public issue and the substantial backing of Lloyds and Barclays Banks. It was decided to scrap the old plant as it was 'extremely costly to work'. In the event their policy did pay off, and in the brief boom of 1924 they were able to issue a £1 million debenture at 6 per cent, and finish their new steel works and plate mills in 1925. But their collieries lost money seriously in the strike and lockout of 1925 and 1926, in which so many steel companies lost heavily and the firm's money and energy was absorbed by its collieries – its officials at one time were so intimidated that they dared not 'attend Masonic function' and police protection was needed. But it was a successful firm.

So when Clarence Smith, its chairman, and Edward George saw Baldwin, the Prime Minister, with other steel-masters and discussed the situation in the steel trade, their position was a strong one. Sir Frederick Mills at Ebbw Vale had proposed a merger of all steel firms. Benjamin Talbot of South Durham and Clarence Smith proposed a series of regional amalgamations, to begin with the North-East coast. Such an amalgamation, however, did not occur and the much-needed rationalization was far from being achieved.

Much the same was true of *Lancashire*. In 1920 Armstrong Whitworth bought the shares of Rylands Bros, wire-makers of Warrington and of Partington, their new government financed works at Irlam. Sir Glyn West of Armstrong's was the chairman, but the effective head was Sir Peter Rylands. The firm went ahead, at a small profit, and was building a big new bar mill. Its losses came from its colliery subsidiary, Moss Hall. By the end of May 1926 Price Waterhouse reported that the firm must have £190,000 by the end of June if it were to continue, and the Westminster Bank gave £550,000 as a first debenture. Sir Peter Rylands said to the general manager that he would be 'grateful if the bank would enable us to avoid the appointment of a receiver. . .'. So there was a scheme of arrangement; J. Frater

Taylor was put on the board by the bank, and A. S. Macharg came in as financial director to reorganize the finances with a scheme of arrangement while Brasserts were brought in to supervise the new Partington works. It was this collapsed firm, run by the Westminster Bank, that united with a colliery company to form Lancashire Steel, a 'rationalized concern' as will be seen in the next chapter.

South Wales suffered from many of the same problems, as shown by the case of Richard Thomas.

Richard Thomas was an old-established firm, first incorporated in 1884 but set up far earlier, in the South Wales tinplate business. In early 1919 the board consisted of some members of the Thomas family, notably Frank Thomas and Lionel Beaumont Thomas, Lord Bledisloe – who had controlled Cwmfelin Iron Co. – and H. C. Bond. The works had expanded in the war and grants were received from the government for munitions works to be converted to peacetime purposes, above all the Redbourn plant at Scunthorpe in North Lincolnshire. Nevill's and Redbourn's had been taken over. A perennial theme of this period is coal; the operation of the colliery subsidiaries took up a great deal of managerial time and absorbed a lot of working capital. The operation of the steel side of the company cannot be understood unless this central fact is appreciated.

As demand for steel grew a major issue of ordinary shares was made. At the same time, it is clear that though the shareholders were widespread, and though the board was largely a working board, the chairman in fact ran the business as a one-man show. 'The chairman referred to the difficulty he was experiencing in coping with the work. He, therefore, considered it necessary to have an assistant.' The ups and downs of the firm reflected the strengths and weaknesses of the leading man to a striking degree. The faith of the Thomas's in their firm was shown by the extent to which they took up the ordinary shares issued in June 1919 – nearly £250,000 by F. F. Thomas and his wife, for instance, and over £40,000 by the Bledisloes. The new money was partly the capitalization of reserves, but it was mostly genuinely new and was used to expand the business, though substantial sums were still being paid from the reserves in respect of wartime taxes owing for over three years. Another difficulty was the shortage of labour, so that the firm was operating well below capacity and not meeting demand. The building of Redbourn in Lincolnshire considerably exceeded estimates of its costs, by over £1 million, but it was expected that they would be able to meet the demand for tinplate with new, cheap facilities at Redbourn, and be the source of large profits. By the end of 1920 things began to go badly. F. F. Thomas's health collapsed and he resigned; there had to be a reshuffling of management and Henry Bond took over; and the firm realized that it might go under. 'Tinplates were now very difficult to sell owing to stringency in finance. Even rich firms were finding great difficulty in paying . . . it would be better to stop the works rather than sell at a loss.' It was proposed by the new management that the North Lincolnshire Iron Co. should be jointly owned by Richard Thomas and Stewarts & Lloyds as a possible preliminary to amalgamation. There was widespread panic at this and about the situation in which the money to pay for the new plant at Redbourn was tied up in unsold tinplate, and a delegation of ordinary shareholders, led by Sir Edward Boyle, went to demand Frank Thomas's return: 'Redbourn was the fruit of the genius of Mr Frank Thomas. It seemed to them disastrous that just at the time when those works are completed his powers should be withdrawn . . .', Sir Edward said on 2 June 1921; he also asked that the seductions of Lincolnshire and Stewarts & Lloyds should be abandoned.

Lengthy negotiations took place – 'the discussion was an extremely painful one to him', said Henry Bond, the deputy chairman at the board meeting on 23 June 1921 – and so it proved, for Frank Thomas said 'I shall lay myself open to the criticism that I am proposing to come back as dictator and not merely as chairman. Frankly that is the position . . . I cannot attend to the large questions of policy if I have to deal with carping criticism and giving explanations. . . . If I do resume the chairmanship I must have the right to control the policy and to dismiss any official who fails to carry out my instructions. . . . I do not require any salary, as the largest ordinary share-holder I have the greatest interest in the company's success.' Lord Bledisloe had 'claimed that he was the only independent director who represented the general body of shareholders and in effect has sought to exercise a veto on all my suggestions if he did not agree with them. Such a position was impossible', said the implacable Frank Thomas, so, not without difficulty, Bledisloe went and Sir Edward Boyle came. 'Many of my friends subscribed for shares on the faith of my name', Bledisloe grumbled, but Thomas was still the biggest shareholder, and, even more important, the wizard who would make the firm profitable. Even Beaumont Thomas, who had originally built the Welsh works up, was threatened, since he did not attend the meeting appealing to Frank Thomas to return on his own terms. Beaumont Thomas timidly explained that his wife was ill and he was going to camp with the territorials.

Frank Thomas immediately took charge and *pour encourager les autres* sacked (and then reappointed) Graham, the manager of the South Wales works. 'The board expressed their opinion very strongly that such a question as the appointment or dismissal of managers was entirely one for the chairman.' Thomas resumed his frantic reign and issued £1 million of debentures at $7\frac{1}{2}$ per cent, to finance ever more expansion despite the appalling state of demand for steel. On 14 May 1923 it was agreed to spend £700,000 more on Redbourn's blast furnaces and coke ovens. Grovesend Steel & Tinplate Co. was acquired, and so were several other concerns. At this stage W. J. Firth, a man who was to play a crucial role in the affairs of steel, first came on to the board. By this time, the firm was profitable, showing a 'works profit' of £368,000; the dividend was 9d (4p) having been 6d (2½p) the year before. The great financial disaster had not materialized; Thomas and his men were pulling through. But Redbourn, which had been the great hope of the company, was operating at a loss. 'The output of the blast furnaces had dwindled down to 2 to 300 tons per furnace per week . . . it might be necessary to close down the Steel Works if orders for Steel Billets and Tinplate Bars were not obtained at £7. 5. 0. (£7·25) to £7. 10. 0. (£7·50) before shipping on to the railways.' Firth was put on the newly constituted finance committee, and put in charge of the affairs of Redbourn, which was at last fully integrated with Richard Thomas. This interest in North Lincolnshire was to be important in Firth's later career. So, too, was Grovesend, since their proposed dividend of 25 per cent 'might be misconstrued by work people and result in their using it as a lever in their wages claims'. The Redbourn works were closed in the summer of 1924. As the collieries were also losing money the firm was resting entirely on Richard Thomas's own cash flow.

The firm of Redbourn was liquidated and the works remained shut; its losses were offset against tax on Richard Thomas's profits. The tinplate price-fixing agreement collapsed in May 1925, and Richard Thomas sought to reduce its prices and to reconstruct its works 'on American lines'. Then the coal strike began. This put the firm in difficulty; but Thomas's policy was to keep the plant up to date, so Redbourn was remodelled, yet again, and reopened, on the advice of Brasserts the American steel consultant engineers. But the financial affairs of the firm, despite a dividend of 2½ per cent, led to a special report by Sir Edward Boyle and a Committee, and this, in turn, led to Frank Thomas's second resignation. This time it was accepted though 'the board has been accustomed for many years to rely upon your great experience and exceptional knowledge . . . we realize too that this . . . must be of inestimable value to any important manufacturing concern and that our board will greatly miss the advantages of that knowledge . . . you have had a strenuous life and we sincerely hope that you will enjoy many years of health and happiness.' The episode recalls Lord Reith's dictum that the best form of government is despotism tempered by assassination.

Henry Bond succeeded him and W. J. Firth became deputy chairman. Within two years Firth had replaced Thomas as the effective head of the firm, exercising all his powers, and employing the same tactics of domination, except that he was not a substantial shareholder. But his power was absolute. In 1927 he said that either Redbourn must be finished, or sold. It had cost £4·2 million; it was worth in its half-finished state, £1½ million. If it were written off, the firm's capital would have to be written down, and that required Frank Thomas's agreement. 'It was mentioned that Mr Frank Thomas would be in this country in June and that his intention was to go to Vichy at the end of May.' The managing director, T. Ivor Jones, resigned, and so did other senior managers. The preference dividend was not paid. Redbourn continued to be remodelled and by November 1928 the blast furnaces were once more in operation, using the cheap coal and coke that the remodelled collieries owned by the company were now producing. So good were the results that on 17 January 1929 it was thought 'advisable to proceed to erect eight double tinplate mills and eight sheet mills in addition to existing capacity.

But already there were signs of over-production in tinplate. On 20 February 1929 a letter was sent to the Welsh Plate and Sheet Manufacturers Association, saying that there was 'cut-throat competition', and that 'the company should have a free hand in deciding which of its several works should be stopped from time to time in order to keep total output down to the allocated production.' Redbourn's output of billets and slabs was stepped up, but it was proposed to close Cwmfelin. This was in order to reduce costs, because economies of scale would enable steel to be produced at £4.17.6. (4·87½) a ton at Redbourn. By 21 November 1929 the chairman was reporting 'that the results of the business during the present year would show a substantial improvement on the past year'. The Redbourn tinplate and sheet mills were never built, as will be seen.

A different sort of reaction occurred to one major firm – Stewarts & Lloyds based in *Scotland*. Stewarts, the Scottish steel and tube-making firm, was a large producer in the steel industry. Even that statement is a controversial one, however, because as late as 1966 Tube Investments were denying that they were a steel firm; because tubes were made of steel, they were not a steel firm – they were engineers, just as the Duke of Wellington pointed out that everything born in a stable is not a horse. Steel is a very imprecise word and a most amorphous industry. But Stewarts thought of themselves as steel men, the biggest tube-makers in Scotland and in 1903 they merged with Lloyd & Lloyd, the biggest tube-makers in England. Lloyds were Birmingham people, who owned iron ore mines in Cumberland, Oxfordshire and near Corby in Northamptonshire.

Stewarts & Lloyds had a virtual British monopoly of small steel pipes; they exchanged directors, and markets, with Tube Investments, who made bigger pipes. It was mainly a Scottish firm centred on Clydeside, with extensive colliery interests. It is, indeed, striking that like several other big steel firms its major interest was from time to time thought to be coal; from 1908 to 1924 it controlled Robert Addie & Sons' Collieries, from 1923 to 1936 it controlled the Kilnhurst Collieries; in 1939 when the Stanton Ironworks was bought four more collieries were acquired. The main aim was to ensure supplies of good coking coal but since supply and demand within the group could never balance, it was selling coal to the market in general and buying additional coke as necessary.

Similarly, Stewarts & Lloyds sought to control its ore supplies. During the First World War ore became scarce and expensive. In 1918, therefore, the North Lincolnshire Iron Company Ltd was bought, and from it a respectable output of ore and pig iron was produced, as it was from Alfred Hickman, which was also taken over. Yet after the war and the immediate postwar boom, iron ore was plentiful, and the newly acquired assets seemed of relatively little use. Because the demand for pipes was rising, the steelworks in Scotland were able to meet a market, but met the raw material demand by buying Bessemer steel from the Continent. Bessemer steel – which was what Northamptonshire ores made – was useful for making pipes because it was easily welded. The Scottish works of Stewarts & Lloyds thereafter drew its open-hearth steel from nearby Clydesdale, and its Bessemer steel from Europe.

By 1918, when Samuel Lloyd, the founder and chairman, died there were a few small blast furnaces at Corby. Stewarts meanwhile, in Scotland, had coal companies. J. G. Stewart, the chairman of Stewarts, 'was a tube-manufacturer and not interested in commercial matters' as Scopes says; his concern was to produce better and cheaper tubes. Lloyd agreed with him, but he was concerned to reduce costs by getting cheap raw materials.

The North Lincolnshire purchase was significant because Corby, the biggest interwar steel project, grew out of those moves. Stewart, of Stewarts & Lloyds, was keen to develop a plant to produce cheap billets for his Scottish plant. These had been formerly imported from Germany. Eventually, after a great many comings and goings, a plant was begun in North Lincolnshire (near Richard Thomas's new plant at Redbourn), but only when the war was over. By the time it began to produce on a small scale, the boom was over and heavy losses were made. The management was changed and put under the Lloyds management, still without success. This was to be crucial because it still left Stewarts & Lloyds short of billets. In April 1930 they attempted to sell Frodingham to Richard Thomas: eventually it was sold to United Steel in April 1931 and Stewarts & Lloyds revised their whole corporate strategy.

Meanwhile the Clydesdale works of Stewarts & Lloyds had been developing its activities. Could it compete in making tubes with Dorman Long and with the Steel Company of Scotland? Clydesdale and the development of North Lincolnshire were seen together, and it was agreed that Clydesdale could not become a big works. Yet, by 1920 it was clear that a newly built big works in Lincolnshire would miss the postwar boom, so the firm bought Hickman's, an established tube producer of Bilston, Staffordshire, who owned a former Lloyds' subsidiary in Northamptonshire, to give them a source of ore. The firm also had several blast furnaces at Corby.

In the depression, Hickman's went under. Stewarts & Lloyds, to whose chairmanship A. C. Macdiarmid (later Sir Allan Macdiarmid) succeeded in 1926, was in a confused state. Its collieries were unprofitable. Several of its subsidiaries, like Hickman's and North Lincolnshire Ironstone, bought for expansion, were drains on resources and management. Its tubes were of an out-of-date design. Nearly £6 million had been spent on new plant at eight works, almost all of it unprofitable. The firm was heavily overdrawn, and though its Clydesdale, Imperial and Calder works were of good quality they were small. The home market was kept going, as Macdiarmid pointed out, by a price fixing agreement that was highly vulnerable to price-cutting. Its markets overseas, especially in Australia, seemed liable to disappear. At that stage, as Macdiarmid wrote, 'the public have the opinion now that Stewarts & Lloyds, whose shares they used to regard as a gilt edged investmet are just like the other iron and steel people, i.e. they have over-spent and are now over-capitalized'. They could either carry on or – and Macdiarmid favoured this – 'make up our minds what additional developments and plant and equipment are necessary and that we must find the finance for this purpose'. As it happened, in 1927 and 1928 trade picked up and Macdiarmid's get up and go temperament seemed appropriate to the circumstances.

The issue was a simple one. Basic open-hearth steel developed rapidly during the First World War. Basic Bessemer stayed stagnant and after the war its production collapsed. By 1925 it had stopped altogether. Yet a growing amount of this type of steel was imported from the Continent, chiefly in the form of pipes and wires. Stewarts & Lloyds, despite what the public thought, remained a relatively prosperous oasis in the depressed desert of the steel industry: above all it had an adequate cash flow. With the revival of trade in the late 1920s, before the great slump, Stewarts & Lloyds was able to look forward to what seemed like a steady growth of its markets. Moreover, with the coming of protection and the vigorous enforcement of the rules of the cartel, it could look out on a world where it was sure of the market at home for its tubes, but it was always worried by its dependence on foreign Bessemer steel for its raw material. It seemed as though a corporate strategy could be evolved which exploited the company's growing

Siemens (above left) and *Bessemer (above right)* were among the technological giants of the nineteenth century who made a major steel industry possible. The Bessemer process, seen below in Sheffield, was like a giant chemistry set, requiring metallurgical knowledge and mechanical skill.

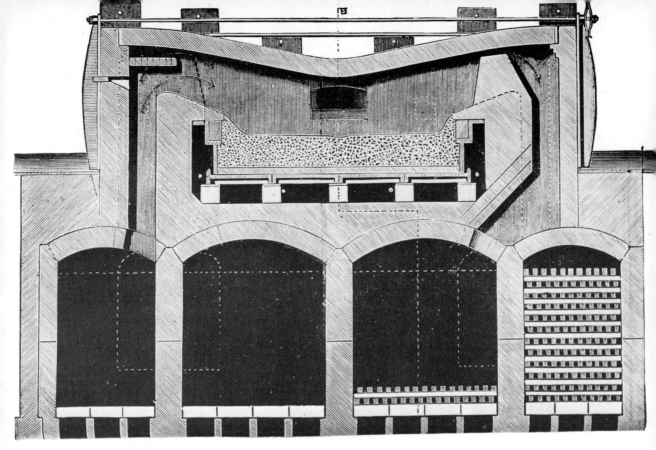

Siemens open-hearth gas-fired furnace (above) *was heated from below.
Iron was puddled* (below) *to remove its impurities.*

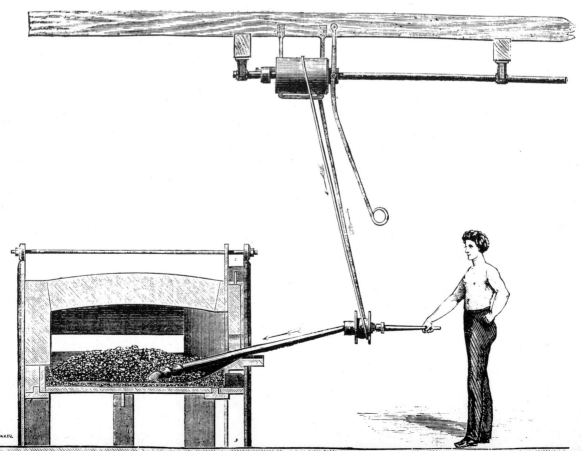

By 1907 Frodingham Ironworks, where these children are taking hot dinners to their fathers (above), combined the iron-making of the past thirty years in a standard layout. But (below) many processes still used human energy lavishly, as in this Lincolnshire iron-mine. Overleaf These Staffordshire ironworkers, in 1918, were skilled shinglers and puddlers, except for the sweeper and the boys.

Dorman Long's Britannia Ironworks (above) in 1920 was of an advanced design. But slagging a blast furnace (opposite) was still a disagreeable, tough job. The miners whose strike pay (below) is being delivered in Wigan in 1921, were severely afflicted by the downturns in the steel trade.

At Park Gate steelworks (above) hot metal is poured into a ladle from a blast furnace. The ladle had to be re-lined (below), another unpleasant job.

(and now protected) market, its good cash-flow position, its good quality coals, its iron ore reserves, and its Scottish rolling mill capacity. The missing links were two: the company's component parts still acted relatively independently, and so there was no integrated policy, and the iron ore reserves in Northamptonshire were little used to feed into the main steel-making activities of the firm.

The American firm of consultant engineers, Brasserts, was called in during 1928 to look at the company as a whole but especially to review the possibility of using home ore for tube-making. The solution, probably, was one that most of the directors already wanted. But an American firm could speak with authority because of the success of the great integrated works in America; and an outsider's advice is always welcome if it confirms your own prejudices.

In October 1929 Wall Street began to collapse. In February 1930 Brasserts, the consultant engineers, presented their report recommending an integrated iron and steel plant on the ore field at Corby, Northamptonshire, to produce Bessemer steel rolled into tubes. The plant was to cost £3 million and to produce 300,000 tons of semi-finished steel a year. Meanwhile the slump developed with ever-growing intensity and the greater part of the market for steel collapsed.

A major centre for reorganization was, therefore, Scotland. David Colville had been a major firm in Scotland for many years. Colvilles was essentially a firm that produced steel plates for ships as well as other goods. Its course of growth and amalgamation was set by two ambitious Colville brothers, who died suddenly in the First World War, leaving a brother, Lord Clydesmuir, who was not really interested in steel. The firm was acquired by the Pirries, who owned Harland & Wolff, and it was effectively managed by John Craig. Craig felt an obligation to the Colville trustees who retained an interest; at the same time Lord Pirrie found Colvilles a problem when trade turned bad after the First World War. In 1920 the firm was large, it had a big new works built for the Ministry of Munitions, and its output was big though its profits were small. 1921 and 1922 were spent trying to claim money from the government for the Ministry of Munitions extensions, which were still continuing. By 1923 the overdraft with the National Bank of Scotland was over £1 million who asked for security. This caused trouble with the Colville Trustees, who had prior claims, and in May 1923 Lord Invernairn suggested an amalgamation of all the Scottish steel firms. Sir William Plender, the accountant, was set to arrange it and Lord Pirrie called a meeting of the Scottish steel-makers to arrange an amalgamation.

The major breakthrough, technically, was made by the Clyde Alloy subsidiary, where Dr Andrew McCance was technically well ahead, and went to Detroit 'to consolidate the present good business relationships with the Ford Company', but the assets were given to the bank as a security. By this time Sir Robert Horne, the Chancellor of the Exchequer, was involved in the proposed Scottish amalgamation, on the basis of two reports by Plender. Negotiations were proceeding with other firms when Lord Pirrie died on 6 June 1924 and his family interests were assumed by Lord Kylsant. Lord Kylsant looms as an absentee landlord over the firm – he once asked the appalled Craig to move to London – until he was caught in a P & O scandal and sent to gaol. The firm continued to be run by Craig, but it was dominated by the family concerns of the Colville and Pirrie trustees, and the National Bank's worries about its overdraft.

By 1925 it was obvious that the Scottish negotiations were getting nowhere; in July 1925 Sir Charles Wright of Baldwins, in South Wales, proposed a 'fusion' of interests, and Dorman Long, of Middlesbrough, were also invited to join a concern, registered by Lord Kylsant as the 'British Steel Company, Ltd', which would control one-third of the steel output of the United Kingdom. This foundered on Dorman Long's prior commitment elsewhere. By October 1925 Sir Frederick Mills of Ebbw Vale (later to turn up elsewhere) was interested in a combine, and Craig opposed a purely Scottish combine 'as the makers were not fully equipped as a self-contained unit', and he too wished to link up with big firms in South Wales and on the North-East coast. 'The question of combining with the other Scotch makers to be considered only if similar groupings took place in other districts.' Politically, the industry sought to bring pressure to bear on the Prime Minister (Baldwin) and on Churchill, the new Chancellor of the Exchequer, who was reminded of his wartime promises from the Ministry of Munitions by Sir Charles Wright.

Throughout 1926, 1927 and 1928 David Colville made desperate attempts to merge with other steel firms. Lloyds Bank, as debenture holders, was selling Lanarkshire Steel, but wanted £200,000, while Colvilles would only offer £150,000; the Steel Company of Scotland would not play; F.A. Szarvasy, of the British Foreign and Colonial Corporation prepared a massive scheme for the mergers of all the steel firms in Britain by means of a holding company and had advanced £300,000 at 6 per cent to Scottish Steel. All the British firms (except, predictably, South Durham) agreed with Szarvasy's scheme. As we shall see, Scotland became a focus for rationalization.

But what of *Sheffield*, traditional home of the steel industry? Let us look at United Steel Companies, some of whose experience has already been quoted.

Harry Steel was the appropriately named chairman of Steel, Peech &

Tozer, the Sheffield steel-makers. His policies and career illuminate the way in which some successful firms were to face up to the problems of the 1920s. To his mind the secret was to take control of raw material and semi-finished supplies to feed into his open-hearth processes for making rails, railway tyres and railway springs, and semi-finished basic steel. The Templeborough works, begun in 1916 as an extension of the Ickles works, was very big – fourteen open-hearth furnaces, two billet mills, a rod mill nearby and continuous bar and strip mills, and it was to supply this large complex that security of supplies was sought. Harry Steel and F. S. Scott Smith of Samuel Fox, which was also a railway steel firm, combined their firms with wartime finance and produced over 0·4 million tons of steel a year. Since at peak periods steel-masters usually assumed that shortages of raw materials would be permanent, almost their first action was to buy the Frodingham Iron and Steel Company to get hold of Lincolnshire phosphoric ores through a half share in the Appleby Iron Company and the Workington Iron and Steel Company to ensure access to Cumberland hematite pig iron. They had hardly any coal mines, but in 1918 they bought the largest coke-makers, the Rother Vale Collieries, run by Sir Frederick Jones. This was to reduce dependence on foreign ore and coal supplies which, during the war years 'had been the source of very grave loss'. It was argued that 'the future success of the company was based very largely on home supplies of minerals'. Such supplies being one of 'the surest foundations and conditions of success'.

Even in the depression, when the firm was producing well below capacity, it was kept up to date by the steady repair and improvement of its plant. Indeed, in 1921 the company restarted a portion of its new Templeborough works, in spite of the fact that 'to a considerable extent this does not rest upon orders actually in hand. Two matters have influenced us, the one that it is so much easier to accelerate wheels that are turning than to start up those that are standing altogether; the other is consideration for our workmen.'

But the firm was not well run. Even as late as July 1925 the situation for some works was still very grave. The furnace and wheel mills at the Ickles plant were only working at 50 per cent capacity while the new tyre mill only worked at 16 per cent capacity. This low and sporadic working presented many problems, not least being the increase in ingot costs due to the cost of lighting up furnaces.

While plant managers were of course concerned with projects and efficiency, company policy was devoted to the development of new works – Templeborough in the 1920s and Appleby-Frodingham in the 1930s. After the First World War the company had two major developments in hand – the new Appleby Company steel works in North Lincolnshire and the Steel,

Peech & Tozer works at Templeborough near Sheffield. Throughout the 1920s the Appleby works had a somewhat chequered career. During the war the Appleby Company, at government request, undertook the construction of blast and steel furnaces along with a modern plate mill designed to produce 240,000 tons of steel plate a year. Because of the expenditure involved, £3·6 million, it was announced in October 1921 that these developments were to be postponed and resources thereby conserved.

Appleby-Frodingham is at Scunthorpe, in Lincolnshire, eight miles south of the Humber and near Immingham. It began as a source of iron ore and a little smelting began in 1865 soon after the ironstone was found in 1859. The Frodingham Iron and Steel Company began as a private concern of Lord St Oswald, and this firm amalgamated with the Appleby works in 1912; it had begun making steel in 1888. Half its interest was sold to the Steel Company of Scotland in 1914. Nearby, on the same ironstone field, was the Redbourn works at Scunthorpe, a central part of the firm of Richard Thomas of South Wales. Lysaght's Lincolnshire works, Normanby Park, was also close at hand. The complex of firms was to make the eventual development of the site as a whole extremely difficult, because once the quality of the Lincolnshire ironstone with its lime content was fully appreciated, and it could be quarried, then several firms were interested in developing their works there. Previously they had tended to be located near coal; the development of the South Yorkshire and Nottinghamshire coalfield brought good cheap coal within easy rail distance. The Northampton ironstone, without a lime content, especially near Lincoln, was also a valuable source of raw material, after 1909; it then looked as though British ores were the key to future low costs.

By September 1921 the total overdraft for the combine was over £½ million – £523,647 – due in part to the Appleby extensions which had already accounted for over £0·1 million. As a result, the firm told 'the Appleby management to suspend the new works at Appleby for six months', and 'in the meantime preliminaries of the proposal to amalgamate Appleby with Frodingham will proceed as far as they are necessary for the negotiation of further capital.'

The cash position of the combine steadily got worse. By the end of August 1923 the company had an overdraft of £1·4 million with the National Provincial Bank, and £0·4 million with the Midland Bank. The Midland Bank was displeased at the size of the overdraft and asked for promissory notes of £500,000 each from Steel, Peech & Tozer and Samuel Fox's to the parent company, which would then be held by the bank. This request was rejected and by March 1924 the company decided to transfer its Midland Bank account to the National Provincial.

The financial situation was now very grave indeed. In return for overdraft facilities of up to £2·3 million the National Provincial laid down severe conditions including first security on Steel, Peech & Tozer and on Appleby.

The position was that Appleby and Workington were running at a heavy loss and Rother Vale at a good profit. Under the Trade Facilities Act a loan of £0·3 million was raised for Appleby. But United Steel was still run by local Works Directing Committees, and the chairman of United Steel was merely chairman of the Control Committee. In 1928 the National Provincial Bank was to change all that.

Development on the Templeborough site on the other hand continued apace, and by 1925 it had cost the company nearly £2·5 million. The emphasis laid upon the Templeborough as opposed to Appleby works was in part due to the fact Steel's successor, Albert Peech, was mainly concerned, not with the business as a whole, but the branch that he had formerly managed, Steel, Peech & Tozer.

Here, then, was a major integrated firm, with a great deal of new plant, and combining two major traditions, which faced a virtually collapsed market. How did the firm survive? First, by not paying dividends, though the firm's records suggest considerable problems in financing the on-going production programme; second by dismissing large numbers of the weekly paid workers; thirdly, by deferring major investment projects.

It has been fashionable to analyze business behaviour as though firms had single objectives – profit maximization say. A cool unprejudiced look suggests that businesses have multiple objectives and the merit goes to Philip Andrews, the historian of United Steel, for advocating this view with a wealth of evidence. United Steel's chief aim during the 1920s was the survival and development of the business as a business. The shareholders got next to nothing. Though the firm was producing well below capacity, it was kept up to date by the steady repair and improvement of its plant. Its chief concern was to keep down costs. According to Albert Peech, 'the position is terribly handicapped by the cost of production, which is so very much in excess of the cost of our foreign competitors. . . . No employer wishes to reduce the wages of the workers for the mere sake of doing so. It is only the necessity of the position which forces it upon him; the worker of course resents it, but if he would only realize it his wages need not be greatly reduced.' There was also an 'overwhelming burden of taxation and government policies' which were 'putting a stop to enterprise and affecting the trade of the country very seriously'.

But, all along, the managers at Templeborough, at Steel Peech, at Samuel Fox, at Appleby-Frodingham and in Cumberland were keen to make their particular operations efficient. What rarely seems to have arisen was the lopping-off of one branch or other as a whole.

In 1918 Workington Iron and Steel Company, created in 1909 by amalgamation of four companies, became part of United Steel, to ensure a high quality steel-making iron for their Sheffield works. By 1929 the works was producing at such a heavy loss that closing down was considered, but instead it was decided to rebuild and remodel the works. This is significant because Workington had a long history of failure. Looking at Workington, two lessons may be drawn. The first is that in a loosely knit combine, only a ruthless chairman could have closed down a major component of the merged company. The second is that prosperity was always just around the corner. Workington had valuable iron ore; it had good coal; it was near Barrow; it might succeed.

An illustration also arises from the colliery interests. Walter Benton Jones was mainly concerned with them. He spoke at first for coal, rather than for steel. Coal is not a homogeneous product. Throughout the 1920s the price of coal was affected by several factors, and was highly unstable. For instance, in March 1921 there was an over-supply of small coal due to the short time worked at the coke ovens and a slump in the cotton trade. By June the cotton trade had recovered and consequently small coal and slacks were sold at as much as 10s. (50p) per ton higher than in March of that year, while there was a decline in prices attributed to a falling demand for shipping coal and to the fact that 'in the case of consumers with a bureaucratic system of management, e.g. corporations and public bodies, forward contracts are being made for as long as twelve months'.

'It is only during the last fourteen days,' Benton Jones said in August 1921, 'that normal working costs have been obtained and during this time substantial profits have been realized; but during the last ten days selling prices have fallen so rapidly and the prices likely to be obtained in the immediate future are such an unknown quantity, that it is impossible to say that profits will continue to be made.' By September 1921 Benton Jones suggested to the board that in order to avoid short-time working for the Rother Vale collieries all United Steel works should obtain the whole of their requirements of coal from Rother Vale. The board sanctioned an investigation into the various quantities of coal and slack used in the works. Peech said that the suggestion was one 'that carries out the intention with which this combine was entered into, and should receive sympathetic consideration from all concerned'.

In January 1928, R. S. Hilton (later Sir Robert Hilton), managing director of Metropolitan-Vickers, was appointed sole managing director of United Steel, while Walter Benton Jones became chairman. This was part of a major reorganization, which concentrated rail production at Workington, heavy railway products at Steel Peech, and special and alloy steels at Samuel Fox's. No sooner had the reorganization started than the great depression of 1929 began. Above all, however, the firm resumed work on the Appleby-Frodingham project.

It is interesting, however, that up to this time United Steel was run as a federation. Hilton, who became managing director, became a focus for reorganization. Walter Benton Jones, the chairman and Hilton's ally and successor, was a colliery manager from Rother Vale and had a deep concern for the collieries. But after their appointments – and as will be seen, after Clarence Hatry abolished the shareholders – the firm began to operate like a modern corporation, seeking to run an efficient and tidy ship. It was not decided to review the company as a whole, and to close down unprofitable parts. That was to come later.

The reconstruction of United Steel was part of a general movement of change in the steel industry that will be dealt with in the next chapter. But out of these vignettes of various firms certain general lessons may be drawn about the 1920s. What was lacking was a sense of purpose for the industry as a whole, and it had little financial expertise. As the slump was to show, both had to be found.

Steel production 1920-72

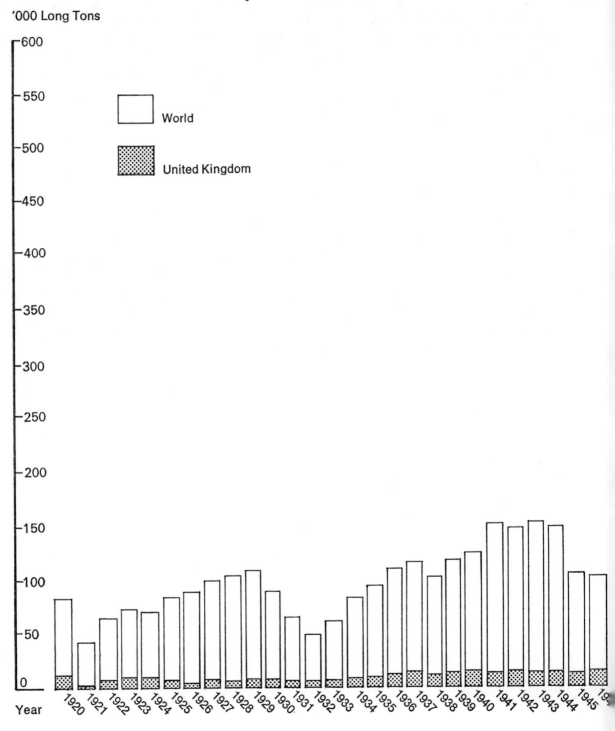

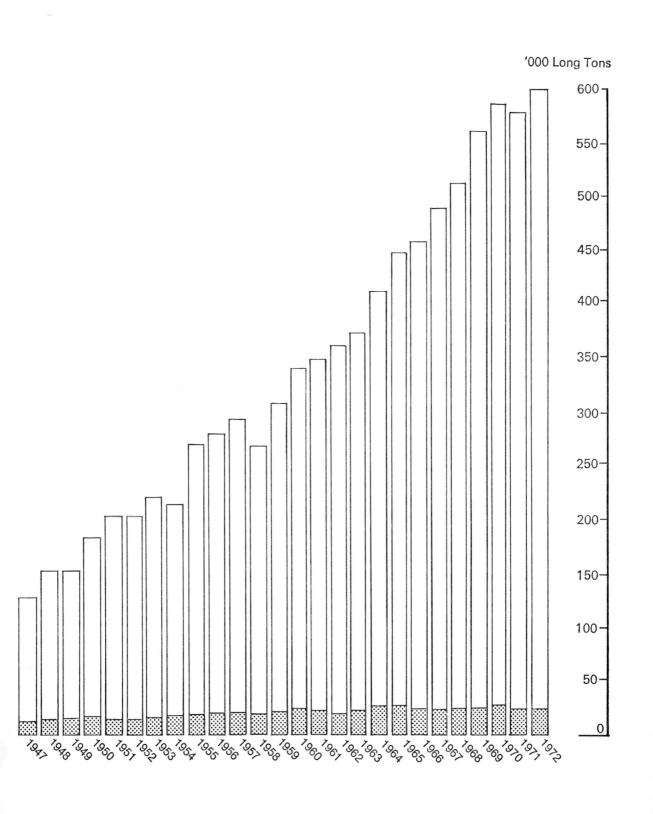

'000 Long Tons

3

The Watershed

The overvalued pound of the 1920s had dealt a serious blow to the export trades, and depressed demand at home kept investment low. Consequently the 'basic' industries, like coal, steel and shipbuilding, seemed to have a chronic over-capacity in the face of the demand for their products. Because the world was at peace, the armaments firms had little trade, and this particularly affected steel and shipbuilding. It was against this background that more and more people thought that rationalization of output in coal, iron and steel, and in shipbuilding, was the only answer.

By 1928, as has been seen, many of the major firms were in the process of reconstruction. The English Steel Corporation was formed to take over the steel interests of Armstrongs, Cammell Lairds and Vickers; Dorman Long took over Bolckow Vaughans on the North-East coast. The rapid rise of unemployment in the last half of 1929 accelerated in 1930; Guest Keen amalgamated with Baldwins, and Colvilles took over Dunlops. All this meant, in effect, defalcation on debt, and the writing-off of money capital. In this, as we have seen, almost every joint stock bank was involved.

There were three separate considerations. The first was the joint stock banks, the second was the Bank of England, and the third was the government; of these, the joint stock banks were the most important. In 1924 Reginald McKenna, the chairman of the Midland Bank and a former Chancellor of the Exchequer, was the leader of the bankers who began to foreclose on the steel firms. It had been a long tradition that joint stock banks did not provide long-term capital; those developments were financed from internal sources or from debenture issues. When overdrafts became substantial and extended over long periods, therefore, the banks sought to get their money out.

The City is a tight community. Ideas, notions, fancies spread quickly. In the case of steel, all the banks and many other institutions, like the insurance companies, were in trouble with the steel firms by the mid-1920s. It would be pointless to seek the origin of a point of view transmitted by nods and winks. Yet by reading the minute books and papers of all the major companies, it may be deduced that it was the Midland Bank that took the strongest view. It was they who precipitated the crisis in United Steel by requiring strong security for the Workington operations. In January 1927, it is reported, the chairman, Reginald McKenna, wanted one firm to run the British iron and steel industry. Barclays moved in on Dorman Long; the National Provincial on United Steel; Lloyds on Consett; Martins on South Durham. The Prudential and the Alliance loomed large. Inevitably, the Bank of England was involved. Certainly, by mid-1929 the deputy governor and the governor were deep in negotiation with several steel firms.

Vickers and Armstrongs were severely hit by disarmament, as were shipbuilding firms like Cammell Lairds. As a result their steel suppliers fell on hard times too. Armstrongs, by some accident of history, banked with the Bank of England. This led to Norman's involvement. Thereafter Norman found himself directly or through intermediaries picking up one industry after another. The protracted negotiations for the Vickers-Armstrong merger were based largely on the premise that the concern was 'essential to national defence', but Baldwin, the Prime Minister, did not give a guarantee that would enable either firm to survive, so that the Bank of England had to. But it was only able to do so if the reorganization were not seen as 'taking over' the armaments industry which was at that time subject to strong criticism, and was widely regarded as having been responsible for starting the Great War. So the reorganization was presented 'as an endeavour to bring about the rationalization of the iron and steel industry'. Meanwhile Duncan, formerly director of the Shipbuilders Confederation, coal controller, and now in electricity, joined the court of the Bank of England, and he wanted support for shipbuilding which was also particularly affected by disarmament. Company after company privately sought help from the City.

Montagu Norman insisted on a reconstruction of the management, and a scrapping of plant, in the cases where the Bank of England was involved. It was to finance the English Steel Corporation and the Lancashire Steel Corporation that he first became actively concerned. The grounds for Norman's views were partly a general belief that the troubles of the British economy were structural – that is, not connected directly with the state of trade – which they indeed were, and partly a special study of the steel industry which he commissioned from Brasserts. The structural argument absolved Norman, the City – and the politicians who shared their opinions – from the responsibility of the overvalued pound and insufficient public expenditure which in Keynes's and Ernest Bevin's judgement was the cause of the general unemployment of the economy; and though, in the case of steel and coal especially it clearly was true that the industries were obsolete and declining, it was equally true to say that correcting the structural defects would aggravate unemployment. Nevertheless the special study suggested a series of regional specialist firms, as part of its proposed remedies.

In 1928 the government as well as the banks were deeply concerned about iron and steel. In December 1928 Arthur Steel-Maitland, the Minister of Labour, proposed to Baldwin to set up a committee to enquire into the industry. Steel-Maitland noted that opinion seemed decidedly in favour of extensive rationalization and it was argued that the 'safeguarding' of the industry would only postpone the requisite amalgamations. But, the memorandum went on, 'the banks are partly responsible for the present situation. I hoped at one time that it might have been possible to get them to join in pressing the industry to reconstruct.' The reluctance of the banks to take the initiative was for fear of being accused of forming a money trust, but it was hoped that they would join in a proposal for reorganization. 'A stimulus has been sought as regards iron and steel in united action by the banks. It was precisely the kind of service that banks in Germany rendered very successfully. But enquiry has shown that it is not practicable here.' Steel-Maitland argued that 'it will further be remembered that for the success of the proposal – quite alien to British tradition as it is – the adhesion of all the five banks will be necessary. One abstention would vitiate the whole scheme. This unanimity of purpose would be difficult in any case, but the attitude of the Midland Bank is generally considered to make it impossible.'

Political factors, however, were felt to point to some public action. The major political factor in question was the imminence of an election – a policy of inaction would therefore merely give scope to those pressuring for safeguarding. As a result, Baldwin agreed to set up a committee, possibly under the chairmanship of Lord Weir, to look into the problems of the industry.

Lord Weir sent a series of notes to Stanley Baldwin saying that

Depressing as a survey of our basic industries may be, let us not lose heart and resign ourselves to apathy and inactivity. . . . Let me take the steel industry as an example, and consider whether in the basic essentials we are in any way handicapped against the rest of the great steel-producing countries. The ore for smelting, most of which comes from Spain, Sweden and Africa can be as cheaply and as easily landed at a British port as it can at any of the Continental or American steel centres. As for the fuel, we have it in abundance and at no greater distance than some, and very much closer than the leading American producing units. These factors alone are surely of no mean value. As for our men, we have always had and we still have today a body of skilled and intelligent workmen equal to any in the world.

Again I think I am correct in saying that we have contributed more to the metallurgy of steel than any other nation, and today the eminence of our technicians is everywhere acknowledged and respected.

With these tremendous advantages . . . surely our case is not so parlous as the pessimist would have us believe.

Weir recognized, however, that the industry was depressed. But 'no solution can achieve success unless we visualize our industry on an adequate scale – a scale comparable at least with that of other countries whose production costs have been lowered by the magnitude and completeness of their equipment and organizations.' In this reorganization, which the country needed, 'an infusion of youth into every board of directors in the country which would, I believe, be an invaluable catalyst. . . . I fully believe that youth unhampered by tradition and untrammelled by old association and prejudices will meet and deal with the problems more easily and possibly more wisely.' The directors of steel firms were astonishingly old.

There was mounting public pressure for state help to ailing industries, supported by Churchill, the Chancellor of the Exchequer, which Norman found 'an obnoxious expedient', as did Sir Horace Wilson, the official adviser to Jimmy Thomas, who as Lord Privy Seal was the minister responsible in the newly elected Labour government for attempts to reduce unemployment. For this reason, Norman pushed the Bank and the City to do the rationalizing – 'those in the City,' said Thomas, 'who have been studying this matter are convinced that a number of our important industries must be fundamentally reorganized and modernized . . . the City will be . . . ready to help, provided that the scheme under discussion fits in as part of the general plans for the industry in question. . . . ' Steel was top of the list.

The government inquiry was set up on 28 July 1929, under Lord Sankey, as a sub-committee of the Committee on Civil Research to inquire into 'the present conditions and prospects of the iron and steel industries'. It reported that opinion generally held high labour costs to be the cause of the industry's difficulties. The industry had sought fuel economies, rather than labour economies, in establishing larger units, but even so the firms were not as big as those overseas, and they were all in financial difficulty.

Like Brasserts, the committee found 'that the blast furnaces are the weakest part of the equipment of the industry', but the steel works also needed expenditure 'to modernize much of the plant'. The committee did not agree with the industry that wages were too high, though Continental labour costs were lower. The real cause of the problem was lack of coordination among steel-makers. Protection was not necessary till the industry had been reorganized 'in the nature of vertical combinations owning their sources of supply of raw materials and producing finished steel goods, and that each unit should, in the main, be confined to one district and should substantially represent the whole of that district.' They recommended 'five or six units', which should 'make arrangements with one another for the development of the industry on national lines'. The governor of the Bank of

England had said that the £15 million to £25 million needed for rationalization would be found. The governor's views were most influential.

Lord Sankey told Norman, when he gave evidence to the Sankey Committee, that rationalization was essential and he asked 'where is the money to come from?' 'I cannot get them money and I am never going to get them money, nor to help them get money for the most part,' Norman replied. 'But if . . . they from within will put their houses in order . . . then I say we will find them the money in London. . . .'

Norman, through Sir Andrew Duncan, found Charles Bruce Gardner (later Sir Charles) the managing director of Shelton Iron, Steel and Coal Company – a subsidiary of John Summers – to run Securities Management Trust, which was to run the Bank's industrial interests, and in turn Brasserts were commissioned to do a study of steel. Lord Weir, it will be recalled, had asked them to do the same for Scotland. Securities Management Trust then founded the Bankers' Industrial Development Company (BID – later the Finance Corporation for Industry) which was to make equity issues to reorganized firms, including those whose capital was reconstructed in connection with the Securities Management Trust. As a result of the Armstrong affair, the steel interests in Lancashire were the first to be seen to, the armaments manufacturers merged into English Steel, and their other interests into Lancashire Steel. Stewarts & Lloyds were encouraged to build Corby. GKN and Baldwins were encouraged to build at Cardiff.

Behind all this lay a six-page memorandum from Brasserts, in January 1930 (Norman believed, like Churchill, in half-page memoranda), proposing integrated plants in six regions, based on local ores in Northamptonshire and in Lincolnshire, imported ores in South Wales and the Clyde, and integrated works in the North-East and in South Lancashire. The difficulty was a 'multiplicity of plants, each producing too many products'. On this brief survey, the whole of Norman's policy until 1943 was based; and it lies behind the first development plan of 1945, which was in turn a reflection of the Franks Report. Its basis was technical – not 'financial consolidation', as proposed by most of the firms themselves – and the technical view was never really challenged.

Norman took a copy of the Brassert Report to the Sankey Committee: 'It is a report by a firm which I believe to be the best American experts . . . as to how it should be regionalized and rationalized and these people are willing to advise from time to time as to how the matter should be taken in hand and are also willing, and I am told competent, to provide not only the engineers for construction but the individuals for management, if necessary from abroad.'

The Brassert involvement is fundamental. Since American steel firms were so successful it was not unreasonable to assume that their success was due in large part to their management. Brasserts were consultants. Partly they were shrewd and highly competent advisers as their reports show and as their successful management of the Corby works was to demonstrate. But, partly, like all successful advisers, from doctors to lawyers, they told the client what he was already prepared to hear. Norman insisted that their advice be followed by any firm that his organization were helping. They gave advice to Colvilles, to United Steel, to Richard Thomas, to Stewarts & Lloyds, to Consett, to Lancashire Steel, and to other firms, and their experience led to their advice being passed, indirectly and directly, to the Bank of England. It had three common characteristics – first, it was technical, and rested upon a belief in new plant of American design, and then upon a view that an integrated operation was highly desirable. Lastly, it rested upon the assumption that big firms were likely to be more successful than small.

The Brassert Report given to the Bank of England was a hasty job. It proposed to set up six integrated 'pivotal' plants and to close down most of the rest of the industry. Workington was to be kept because of its local ore; new plants were to be built at Scunthorpe and Kettering, while Sheffield was to go; Dorman Long was to be the North-East coast firm; Partington in Lancashire was to replace the other Lancashire works, and in Scotland the seven major concerns were to be moved to a new site on the lower Clyde. The reasons given for each location were cursory, and the argument behind the report was exiguous. The report was marked by hyperbolic statements – Workington had the 'best ores in any part of the world', Durham had 'some of the best coking coal in the world', and Northamptonshire was compared to Lorraine. This kind of radical reasoning permeated Brasserts' other work, which was far more detailed.

The Brassert Report on United Steel was a thorough and a more typical document. It favoured amalgamations with other firms in particular areas – with Richard Thomas's Redbourn works in Lincolnshire and with Temple-borough Rolling Mills in the Sheffield area. It favoured technical development, two complete blast furnaces in Lincolnshire, and a massive development of coke and pig iron manufacture at Workington, based on imported ores, and leading to a new blast furnace there. It wanted 'the abandonment of old works and massive modernization . . . in spite of its present backward condition . . . Great Britain has a wealth of raw materials for producing iron and steel in close proximity to sea-coast harbours and great centres of population, and as no other country possesses.' (This opinion, reiterated by Brasserts from 1922 to 1937, was reflected as late as 1944 in the Ministry of Supply Report.) United Steel was the second largest

British iron and steel firm, producing 1½ million tons of steel ingots and nearly 3 million tons of coal. Its real strength lay especially, according to Brasserts, in its Lincolnshire ores, and generally in its control of raw material sources. It wanted modernization and bigger units, especially at the Lincolnshire site, if Redbourn could be acquired, with an integrated plant to produce sheets and tinplate. This would necessarily squeeze out Richard Thomas. Workington also had a great future, in its judgement, because of the juxtaposition of hematite ores with good coking coal; it would thus be the cheapest producer of hematite iron in the kingdom. All told, it was an optimistic report. It made recommendations for concentrating on fewer products and far better marketing, but above all it thought that cheap raw materials plus new massive and modern plants would spell success.

Three patterns of organization suggested themselves for the industry, but only one was fully thought out. Britain would support, it was felt, six integrated regional concerns – in Scotland, South Wales, the North-East including Lincolnshire and a 'Midland' group including Lancashire, Sheffield and the North-West coast – some specializing in tubes, some in special steels, but all of them producing most kinds of iron and steel. This was the implication of the report on Scotland, and on Lancashire Steel, and it was a model approved of by Montagu Norman. It was also the basis of the Sankey Report to the Economic Advisory Council, which was presented to the cabinet in May 1930.

The second model was less well thought out, but it involved a central holding company like United Steel, with diversified interests expressed through the original firms which would maintain their identities. This was the pattern followed in 1949 when steel was first nationalized. In 1927 Reginald McKenna of the Midland Bank had told Sir William Larke that 'a merger of interests in the form of an operating company in the iron and steel trade might be desirable', and Larke said that Baldwins', United Steel, Colvilles and Dorman Long were agreeable. 'The banks were said to be anxious with regard to the extent of their commitments in the iron and steel industry and Mr McKenna's suggestion was prompted by this feeling.' In the spring of 1927, F.A. Szarvasy circulated a questionnaire to the firms to get a scheme going. The support for Hatry's proposal sprang, it seems, from this background, as may be seen from the situation in Scotland.

By 1927, the Scottish steel companies, but especially David Colvilles, were in chronic trouble. Colvilles was effectively a subsidiary of the Belfast shipbuilders built up by Lord Pirrie, while Scottish Steel was owned by a consortium of Clyde shipbuilders of whom the Stephen family were the leaders. All the firms were in grave financial difficulties. Lloyds Bank was insisting that Lanarkshire Steel should be merged with other firms; the

These Sheffield men (above) have helped to produce steel tyres for railway engines. The blast furnaces at Workington (below) in 1930 were working mainly for the railways.

JUDGE AND "MOST APPALLING FRAUDS"

Daily Mirror

THE DAILY PICTURE PAPER WITH THE LARGEST NET SALE

No. 8,171   Registered at the G.P.O. as a Newspaper.   SATURDAY, JANUARY 25, 1930   One Penny

HATRY SENTENCED TO 14 YEARS

Clarence C. Hatry, who was sentenced yesterday to fourteen years' penal servitude, photographed with his wife in a schooner.

Edmund Daniels, sentenced to seven years' penal servitude.

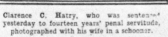

John G. G. Dixon, who is to serve 5 years' penal servitude.

Mr. Justice Avory, who passed the sentences. The trial lasted five days.

Albert Edward Tabor, sentenced to three years' penal servitude.

John Gialdini, who, said Hatry's counsel, suggested the duplication of stock.

Hatry's house in Stanhope-street, W., which is to be sold.

The luxurious main hall of Hatry's house.

In passing sentence on Hatry at the Old Bailey yesterday Mr. Justice Avory remarked: "You stand convicted of the most appalling frauds that have ever disfigured the commercial reputation of this country—frauds far more serious than any of the great frauds on the public which have been committed within the last fifty years, according to my personal experience." Other sentences, to run concurrently with the principal sentences, were passed on all the accused on other counts. Hatry, a picture of sartorial perfection, remained outwardly calm during the Judge's scathing remarks. When he heard the sentence he closed his eyes for a moment.

Montagu Norman (above), the Governor of the Bank of England, tried to reorganize the steel industry during and after the great slump. Clarence Hatry (left) tried too, but got caught himself in the great crash. The real victims (overleaf) were working people, like the Jarrow marchers, who went to London to get government support for their work.

CHANGEING. GUARD. APPLEBY. IRON. CO. APR
STRIKE. DUTY.

The Appleby Ironworks was guarded by police during the 1926 General Strike (above).
During the reconstruction of the steel industry the Trent Ironworks was dismantled (below).

Sir John Craig (above left) *was the great Scots steel-master. Reginald McKenna* (above right), *Liberal politician and chairman of the Midland Bank, wanted a fundamental reorganization of the steel industry and helped to enforce it by financial control. In Middlesbrough* (below), *appallingly hit by the slump, the bankers and others thought this complex of steel and ironworks cried out for rationalization.*

Consett (above left) *in the North-East began to revive in the mid-1930s. A new steelworks and tubeworks, with bank support, began at Corby in 1932* (above right), *and by spring 1933 the supporting blast furnaces were well under way* (below).

National Bank of Scotland was increasingly concerned about its advances to Colvilles and was requiring stronger security for them; and Szarvasy, the financier, was proposing a merger of all steel firms, supported by H. C. Bond (of Richard Thomas), the chairman of the National Federation. In this connection, the financial editor of *The Times* asked Bond to meet the deputy governor of the Bank of England to discuss the steel industry: 'It was quite evident that the banks and other financial houses were anxious to see combinations among the steel-makers.' Szarvasy, however, ran into 'unsurmountable difficulties in certain directions', and Sir Harry Peat, the accountant, was asked 'by leading financiers in London' to arrange for mergers. By this time Colvilles had mortgaged a great deal to the National Bank of Scotland, causing deep difficulties with the Colville family trustees. Talbot, of South Durham, as president of the National Federation, met Bond and Craig to get mergers all round; but the trouble was that each firm was negotiating with a different group of allies, and one move depended upon another, so that little got done.

By June 1928, Sir James Lithgow and Lord Invernairn, the shipowners, were trying through Lord Weir, to get 'American finance', from Sir Harry McGowan of the Anglo-American Finance Corporation, to support a Scottish merger because the problem was that a merger that brought new money was fairly easy to arrange, whereas a merger of semi-bankrupt concerns involving writing off capital, especially debentures, was emotionally and legally difficult. By the autumn of 1928 Mitchell of Stewarts & Lloyds was discussing a 'combination' with Colvilles and Beardmores. In December, 'Lord Weir, who admitted he was in close touch with leading members of the government . . . indicating that government money may now be available at a low rate of interest provided a suitable combined scheme was submitted. . . . Stewarts & Lloyds . . . were sympathetic to a scheme of amalgamation.' Craig told Colvilles' board that Sir William Larke had spoken of 'his interview with the Chancellor of the Exchequer [Churchill] which . . . confirmed the views expressed by Lord Weir'. Peacock of the Bank of England confirmed Weir's statement, and in February 1929, after agreement that a merger should go ahead, Lord Weir engaged Brasserts of Chicago 'to make this investigation immediately'. Boynton of Brasserts (who later appears at Lancashire Steel) made two reports, of which the major one was on pig iron. They seem to have recommended the expansion of capacity, new blast furnaces, and an integrated works on the Clyde. In the meantime Clarence Hatry 'had approached certain North-East coast makers and possibly also, a maker in South Wales', and Craig met Hatry on 16 May 1929, who 'proposed to extend these negotiations' (about United Steel 'now practically completed') 'with a view to forming a large combine to control about one-half of the total output of the trade'. Craig and Kylsant said they would await the Brassert Report, but otherwise were sympathetic.

The Brassert Report was unacceptable except to Lord Weir. He was 'in close touch with leading members of the government' who were disposed to 'grant a measure of government support, and the Governor of the Bank of England said that Beardmores and Lanarkshire Steel would not be allowed to impede a scheme'. Dunlops and Lithgows by this time, under pressure from the chief general manager of Lloyds Bank, were keen to agree on a scheme. The point at issue was that Brasserts had recommended a large technical development – a new works on the Clyde – and Colvilles pointed out that a merger of steel firms must precede such a project. The difficulty was to agree on the terms of the merger. Stewarts & Lloyds, who were to keep their tube capacity, wanted to keep on making iron and steel; Beardmores sold their plates, sections and rail activities to Colvilles; Stephen, of the Steel Company of Scotland, hedged his bets. By the summer of 1930, with the National Bank, the Colville trustees, and Lord Kylsant all seeking security, the Bank of England actively intervened in the person of Charles Bruce Gardner who was 'being consulted by the cabinet as regards the feeling of the industry any government action that might be proposed'. In the upshot, Dunlops merged with Colvilles, Stewarts & Lloyds decided to move to the Midlands though their tube interests which remained in Scotland were supplied with steel by Colvilles, Lord Kylsant went to gaol, Colvilles Ltd was separated off from Harland & Wolff, and immensely complex negotiations for a further series of Scottish amalgamations followed. This was not achieved until 1934, when the National Bank accepted 15s. (75p) in the pound for its overdraft, and McKenna of the Midland Bank agreed to issue £4½ million of shares. In the event they were issued by Cazenove's, as McKenna's terms were too hard, but thus ended the extraordinary saga of the reconstruction of the Scottish steel-makers.

Implicit in all these reconstructions by merger was a third model, originally postulated by the TUC in 1934 and the Fabian Society, and probably evolved by the industrial and city commentators of *The Times* and *The Daily Herald*, that steel would be run as 'ten or a dozen' product divisions, based not on a geographical contiguity of plants but on a similarity of final product. These divisions would have been vested in a public corporation as 'Ingot' (Sir Richard Clarke) proposed in his book in 1936. This is, of course, the model adopted, finally, in 1969 by the British Steel Corporation with a smaller number of divisions, and it is similar to ICI's structure.

It will be seen that the individual schemes for the industry as they came up for consideration were judged sometimes by one criterion – regionalism –

and sometimes by another – product specialization. But, from day to day, the actual problem was putting your hands on actual money. Plans come and go, but the bankruptcy court is really there.

This is where Hatry comes in. Clarence Hatry was born in 1888 and went to St Paul's School. He had an early bankruptcy in 1909 from which he was exonerated because it was caused by his father's sudden death. But, in a subsequent successful career, he always had a slight cloud over his reputation, and the cloud became larger when he had unexpected success in making a big position for himself in the local authority loans market, where local authorities raised cash for their short- and long-term needs. This market had long been the preserve of the City establishment, and Hatry's bank, the Commercial Bank of London, which had been concerned with lending chiefly on trust deeds but which entered more general business as opportunity arose, was not welcome in it.

He comes into this story because his biggest deal, and the one he was caught out on, concerned steel – the second biggest steel company, United Steel. As has been seen, United Steel did not pay a dividend on its ordinary stock after December 1920 or on its preference stock after December 1921. The reason for this was simple. Its enlarged plant which was the source of many problems was commissioned in and just after the war and came into operation when the market had collapsed. It had been financed with high interest loans. The management of the combine was remote and acted as a holding company and not as a force for technical rationalization. Using the model of Imperial Chemical Industries, and other major combines, it was almost self-evident that to avert collapse a capital reconstruction was necessary followed by vigorous action to reorganize the production side of the company.

In December 1926 the general manager of the National Provincial Bank, who had become the firm's sole banker after the Midland had left, advanced £500,000 to restart the pits and furnaces which had been stopped by the General Strike and coal lockout. To Sir Frederick Jones's horror, he insisted on doing this as a debenture which gave the bank rights over specific assets, rather than as an overdraft. Throughout 1927 there were bad technical difficulties with the Strip and Bar Mill and with the new Templeborough works. The firm found itself unable to service the debenture; the bank was also concerned that the Appleby works was mismanaged. The constituent companies also still owed large sums for wartime taxation. By late 1927 each branch had to finance its own current operations as the firm's loan account was strained.

In December 1927 the bank insisted that Peech should be removed, that Walter Benton Jones should be chairman, and R.S. Hilton brought in from Metropolitan Vickers as managing director. J. Ivan Spens was put on the board as the bank's watchdog and a scheme of financial arrangement was made to restructure the company's debts.

Through Spens, Hatry approached United Steel – or it may have been the other way round – in late March 1928, and they had a meeting with Benton Jones and Hilton. In June 1928 United Steel sent Hatry's firm, Austin Friars Trust, a most glowing letter about its prospects. Their fixed assets, they wrote, had been written down from £16 million to £6·7 million. The assets were worth, however, £11 million, and over £7 million had been spent since the war on new plant. No mention was made of the technical problems associated with all the new plants. The troubles, United Steel said, had been due to 'the Continental inflation', the coal strike, and the burden of capital commitments. Future profits were 'conservatively' estimated at £1·13 million a year. The arrangement that was made was for a firm called the Steel Industries of Great Britain to take them over, and shortly to absorb three-fifths of the steel capacity of Great Britain.

Clarence Hatry had successfully floated a light engineering firm, Allied Ironfounders, which merged twenty-three family firms in the iron industry. Hatry's firm, Austin Friars Trust, bought all the debentures and shares of United Steel, for nearly £5 million, and advanced nearly £3 million for working capital as a basis for a heavy steel combine. This advance was made after a difficult experience in raising money from merchant bankers for a bridging loan. The Austin Friars holdings were then transferred to Steel Industries of Great Britain, which raised a further £1·6 million in debenture, and reconstructed the capital of United Steel in June 1930. But, meanwhile, in 1929 Hatry had found one of his other firms was short of cash; rumours spread, and because the slump had begun he was unable to advance the money required by the original deal. The bridging loan found him strapped for cash. It was then that his agent was found uttering forged securities for the Borough of Swindon and other authorities and, amid considerable scandal, he was brought to trial, convicted and sentenced to fourteen years in gaol. He had appealed to Montagu Norman for help with the bridging loan and had been refused. According to Lord Grantley, Norman summoned every merchant bank involved in financing Steel Industries of Great Britain and warned them of Hatry's reputation.

Hatry thought that Norman was personally hostile to him for moving into the local authority loan market; others think that Norman was doing his duty as governor of the Bank of England in warning the City of the problems ahead. Neither foresaw the coming slump and certainly Hatry's scheme for steel ran completely counter to Norman's evolving ideas on the industry.

The upshot, then, was that United Steel belonged to Steel Industries of

Great Britain, which effectively was a legal fiction; it was financed by the Bank; and managed, ultimately by and with the consent of Montagu Norman. It became a pure example of a 'managerial firm', with no shareholders; it was now profitable since Hatry had removed its indebtedness; but it was not the nucleus for the Hatry amalgamation which would have been called Steel Industries of Great Britain. Approaches were made to Stewarts & Lloyds and an agreement was reached about linking output but not about a merger. This was because Allan Macdiarmid was an individualist; he would not be taken over. Approaches were made to Lancashire Steel. In the event, it was Hilton, helped by Walter Benton Jones, whom Norman put in to run United Steel. Hilton, as his letter books show, was a gruff but amiable man with considerable managerial skill. Benton Jones was, as has been seen, from the colliery side of the business, but his skills were 'managerial', as were Hilton's; both were concerned with graduate recruitment, marketing, with cash-flow and with modernizing the organization of the firm.

As the depression intensified, firm after firm fell into severe financial troubles which made the 1920s seem an era of relative prosperity. Hatry was but the first of a series of financiers who became involved in the affairs of the steel industry. The extraordinary figure of Major Pam of Schroders loomed large over the Mersey. By the time the slump was over many of the leading people in the industry came from the world of accountancy and finance – Andrew Duncan, and a whole host of others – brought in directly or indirectly by the City, to tidy up the finances of steel.

In 1928, as has been seen, Stewarts & Lloyds, Colvilles and the other Scottish firms, were in doubt as to their future. At this stage most of the big Scottish steel firms agreed that Lord Weir should commission Brasserts to study the Scottish iron and steel industry. Their report showed that Scotland's own original ore deposits were exhausted, and that pig iron had to be imported. They therefore proposed a new greenfield steel works in Scotland, at the mouth of the Clyde, financed by the Scots firms. Now, regionally, this made sense. But, clearly, in such a scheme the major parties would be Colvilles and the Steel Company of Scotland. So Macdiarmid of Stewarts & Lloyds decided to ask Brasserts to study the tube-making situation. He set about acquiring small tube works, closing them down, and making an agreement with Tube Investments to share the market and work jointly, but not amalgamate, since amalgamation would have involved his stepping down in favour of Arthur Chamberlain, the chairman of Tube Investments. Small precision tubes went to Tube Investments; gas, water and steam tubes went to Stewarts & Lloyds. Thus, by the time the slump began Stewarts & Lloyds was not primarily a Scottish steel-maker, but a tube manufacturer with some works in Scotland linked with the other big tube-maker. In this respect Stewarts & Lloyds, already beginning to plan its Corby works, was uncharacteristic.

It has already been seen that most of the firms were to a considerable extent conglomerates; that is to say, they included a great many activities, like coal mining and shipbuilding which, though linked with were not the same as steel-making, and 'steel-making' itself was a term for a heterogeneous series of activities. In addition, the firms had works scattered up and down the countries. A total merger of all firms – such as was to be achieved by nationalization in 1950 and 1967 – would have removed at least some of the legal and business difficulties to a major reshuffle of management and assets and a change of the entire managerial structure of the industry, not to speak of a surgical operation on the souls of almost every entrepreneur.

This is, indeed, what the trades unions and the Bank of England (for different reasons) sought to do. But any rationalization of steel implied major changes both in firms and in localities, with a great deal of hardship on all sides. Thus to give ships to Scotland (and what of Tyneside ?), wire to Lancashire (and what of Sheffield ?), and tubes to Northamptonshire (and what of Scotland ?) suggested a knowledge of geography but not of capitalism, psychology or politics, or even, perhaps, of the steel industry.

There was great resistance to the loss of individual identities. Thus, as the depression intensified, Cargo Fleet and Dorman's on Tees-side, in the hardest hit North-East, did not amalgamate; Firth-Brown's in Sheffield did not join the other firms; the situation at Scunthorpe was not rationalized.

Indeed, looking in detail at particular firms, it is interesting to see how slow they were to realize what had hit them. In 1929 Richard Thomas was doing fairly well. Redbourn was beginning to live up to expectations. All sections of the firm were profitable and a preference dividend was once more proposed to be paid. W. J. Firth was put directly in charge of Redbourn, and began a policy of closing down other parts of the firm. But then Lloyds Bank found that it had to call in some of its finance: 'We hope,' they wrote, 'that this may be the beginning of a new era of successful trading and that your anticipations for the resumption of dividends may be accomplished.' The state of trade was such that minimum price agreements were abolished in November 1930; Redbourn works was 'closed down' in November 'in view of the existing state of trade'. In the last week of November 'the trade had worked 48 per cent'. On 19 February 1931, 'the board decided that, having regard to the present depression, it was desirable to make every effort to reduce the overhead charges so far as this could be done. It was decided to reduce directors' fees by 20 per cent, directors' salaries by 15 per cent, salaries of staff in receipt of £1,000 per annum and over by 10 per cent, and so on.

In April 1931, the firm discussed making 'full finished sheets for motor car manufacturers', a market dominated by Lysaghts and Baldwins, and operating only at 38 per cent of capacity. In October 1931 H. C. Bond retired 'in these difficult times', and accepted a £5,000 a year pension, and W. J. Firth became chairman. He promptly sacked five senior members of the managerial staff and appointed three men – T. F. Davies, T. O. Lewis and A. W. Kieft – as his managers. From this time on, the board was made up basically of Firth's managers, together with Sir Edward Boyle. Firth was knighted in the summer of 1932, and as Sir William Firth took his place among the leaders of the industry.

1930 and 1931 were years of amalgamations. Lancashire Steel was formed with Partington Iron and Steel and its half-finished works as its largest asset. English Steel combined Vickers Armstrongs and Cammell Lairds steel interests with several works in Sheffield and Manchester. Guest Keen & Nettlefold linked up with Baldwins. David Colville took over Beardmores and John Brown amalgamated with Thomas Firth in Sheffield. In 1933, a little later, Dorman Long amalgamated with South Durham Iron and Steel Company and in 1936 with Bowesfield Steel at Stockton. These were all attempts to put the financial affairs of the companies straight. Incidental to this was the attempt to rationalize output, both by product and regionally.

Cargo Fleet and South Durham were merged in 1928 but their losses continued, largely because of Cargo Fleet and the collieries. In the autumn of 1929, C. F. Goodenough, the chairman of Barclays Bank, told Benjamin Talbot to make a close working arrangement with Bolckow Vaughan and Dorman Long. A joint advisory committee was formed; but it was brought to an abrupt stop when Mitchell of Dorman Long fell out with Talbot. In 1931 John James, who had no real place in the merger, left for Lancashire Steel; and by 3 June 1932, after two years of seriously bad trade (Cargo Fleet working at 40 per cent of capacity in 1931, and South Durham at 21 per cent), the steelmen met Sir George May of IDAC. Mitchell of Dorman Long was made chairman of the North-East committee, with George of Consett and McQuistan of South Durham and Cargo Fleet. Barclays Bank and the Bank of England's solicitors, Freshfields, proposed scheme 'Y' for merging all the firms – a scheme agreed, without Consett and with great reservations, in 1933.

In 1933 Charles Mitchell, the chairman of Dorman Long, asked John James of Lancashire Steel to prepare information on South Durham and Cargo Fleet, to pave the way to amalgamation. In this he was actively helped by Montagu Norman and Brasserts. The background to this was a catastrophic story of Dorman Long. They had merged with Bolckow Vaughan in 1929 after two years of negotiations, when an overdraft of £4·7 million was necessary to avoid a complete stop to the business. The Sydney Harbour Bridge was their biggest project, but it cost far more than intended on a fixed price contract, and other international schemes did equally badly in a world of unstable currencies.

As a result the Dormans, who ran Dorman Long, took Roland Kitson, Ben Walmsley and two others on to their board. By March 1930, they had got £2 million from Barclays and rather less than £1 million from the National Provincial, the Midland, and Williams Deacons. Charles Mitchell was put in as managing director, despite the urgent request of the Bank of England that he should work for Securities Management Trust. The merger with South Durham would, it was thought, save £1 million a year, and the Bank offered Dorman Long £3·3 million to buy South Durham and Cargo Fleet outright. In 1931, Sir Arthur Dorman, who had been fifty-five years on the board, died, followed by Sir Hugh Bell, who 'had given sixty-nine years of service'. Mitchell succeeded to the chair, sacked the executive directors, and put in a management committee. A very tight policy was followed; when the Miners Welfare Committee offered to pay for pithead showers if the company would pay for the drainage, the request was refused. Throughout the autumn of 1932 Barclays became increasingly worried; in February 1933 the chief accountant was found to be defrauding the company, and in May 1933, the insurance company (the Alliance) and the Bank insisted on the capital being written down from £17·7 million to £8·5 million, and a merger. At this point, the shareholders of South Durham refused to agree to the merger – the nominees of the financial interests were to be 'not directors but dictators' it was said – and the court (Mr Justice Maugham) agreed with them. A receiver was appointed for Dorman Long, Mitchell and Ben Walmsley departed and Lord Greenwood was brought in as chairman. Within a few years he had found an accountant to run the business. Thus ended one attempt at self-regulation.

Consett had come through the 1920s with a modern, integrated plant. It planned in 1928 to start yet another big new extension to its works. Inevitably Brasserts were asked to advise but their advice was not taken. The firm was adequately financed and the directors heard with interest of Winston Churchill's proposals to give government money 'for balancing and re-conditioning existing plants', listened to Clarence Hatry's proposals to merge Dorman Long, Bolckow Vaughan, South Durham and Cargo Fleet, and watched carefully the abortive negotiations between South Durham and Dorman Long.

By the autumn of 1930 Charles Bruce Gardner had become the head of Securities Management Trust, and he came to the North-East to discuss three possible stages of a reconstruction of iron and steel. The first was an area amalgamation, such as that proposed for the Middlesbrough firms; then a regional amalgamation which would include Consett and Appleby; and the third would be a national arrangement based either on a 'physical' amalgamation or on 'working arrangements' between districts. Consett did not need money, though it felt it might consent to a national working arrangement. In October 1930 it refused to merge with Dorman Long since 'Consett is already a completely "rationalized" and almost fully modernized undertaking. . . .'

Interestingly enough, as with some other firms, Consett's problem arose after the worst of the slump was over. True, in 1931 the preference dividend was passed, but they resisted all attempts to merge and to restrict their output until in June 1932 Lloyds Bank insisted on an overdraft reduction, and by the early summer of 1933 the bank had insisted on a debenture holders arrangement, which was to result, in November 1933, in E. H. Lever of the Prudential arranging to take over $£2\frac{1}{2}$ million of the debentures at 6 per cent, and for the first time Consett was no longer master of its own destiny. Like other firms it had failed to 'go it alone' and was ripe for 'rationalization'.

The difficulty was threefold. The first was that the firms were heterogeneous, both in products and in location. The second was that the managerial and entrepreneurial skills of the industry were not high. The third was that the plant was for the most part very old, and that any attempt to rebuild it required finance, which was only available in small quantities, as well as closing down works at a time when registered unemployment was over 3 million and unregistered unemployment even greater.

English Steel was a typical example of the problems of a merger. It combined the River Don works, the Holme Lane works, the Grimesthorpe works, the Cyclops works in Sheffield, the Penistone works at Penistone, the Whitworth Street works and the New Street works in Manchester, and Taylor Brothers. A drastic capital reorganization was necessary, and over £5 million of shares were written down. Forging and armament plate was concentrated at the River Don, steel casting and springs at Grimesthorpe, while Grimesthorpe's other sections were closed and Whitworth Street was dismantled, together with New Street. Penistone was dismantled, and tyre, wheel and axle production concentrated at Taylor Bros.

The Lancashire Steel story is fascinating, not least because the accepted version is so truncated as to be misleading. There were several firms in Lancashire and at Warrington – the Wigan collieries controlled by the Earl of Crawford and Balcarres and his family, and the wire works run by Peter Rylands and his family. The constituent firms were all in a bad way, and under Brasserts' guidance they had embarked upon a large reconstructed

D

Partington works at Irlam, for Pearson Knowles of Warrington. As a result of financial difficulties, the firms were amalgamated into the Lancashire Steel Corporation at the end of July 1930. J. Frater Taylor was put in as chairman, and a preliminary reorganization undertaken. Major Pam of Schroders worked with Montagu Norman and Securities Management Trust to raise the funds to complete the new works, and to start up some of those that were closed. Almost immediately, Securities Management Trust instructed Frater Taylor to resign, and Bruce Gardner refused to advance the cash to buy Whitecross, the wire works which would have completed their local combine.

Lord Crawford was put in as chairman, and on 31 October 1930, Brasserts were asked by Bruce Gardner 'to report on the desirability of amalgamating United Steels [*sic*], Stewarts & Lloyds and this Company.' The Brassert Report recommended that United Steel and Lancashire Steel be 'rationalized' but that Stewarts & Lloyds be developed as a separate unit, to supply surplus Bessemer steel to Lancashire Steel. 'Mr Brassert had seen the governor of the Bank of England on the morning of 16 October 1930', it was reported and 'the governor had seemed worried concerning the Lancashire Steel development owing to criticisms as to its local nature, but Mr Brassert had advised the governor that the Lancashire Steel scheme of development was quite sound, and that, moreover, were the Lancashire Steel and the United Steels now one, he would still make the same recommendations with regard to the Irlam development as he had made in March 1928. Mr Brassert stated that the governor was quite satisfied with his explanation and agreed with him that the Irlam development scheme should be pushed on.'

The directors then chose a coke oven design for Irlam not approved by Brasserts. On 28 November 1930, A. J. Boynton of Brasserts was made a director to supervise Irlam. He wanted Woodhall-Duckham to build the coke oven but the directors accepted the lowest tender by Koppers. On 11 December 1930, 'Major Pam had stated that the decision to select the coke oven contract which was not recommended by Brasserts was very serious and that he had been requested by the governor to represent the viewpoint of the financial interest. . . . They had assumed that the Lancashire Steel Corporation would accept Brasserts' advice on all matters of outstanding importance.' Lancashire Steel then revised its decision. Major Pam saw Lord Crawford on 20 January 1931 and asked for a scheme for 'rationalization of steel companies in the Midlands'. In the spring of 1931 'Lord Crawford reported conversation and correspondence with Mr Montague [*sic*] Norman . . . and announced that, at the instance of Securities Management Trust Ltd, Mr John E. James, of the Cargo Fleet Iron Co. Ltd, was

64

to be appointed chairman and managing director of this corporation.'
Three directors resigned 'as a protest against the continual interference of
the SMT', but on 26 June 1931 John James was in the chair he was to
occupy for over thirty years, and Crawford and Rylands, whose family
firms had merged to form Lancashire Steel, were there still.

Schroders advanced £1·25 million at 7 per cent, and Brasserts continued
with their new wire rod mills and other developments at Irlam, and in
December 1932 Major Pam allowed them to buy Whitecross. The mosaic
was complete. On 1 June 1934, it is recorded that Major Pam toured the
works at Irlam and 'expressed his satisfaction'. In November 1934, he
relaxed the stringent conditions on borrowing that had been imposed; John
E. James had worked his passage and Major Pam, botanist, zoologist and
polymath, was satisfied.

The firm was a major coal producer, a steel producer and, above all, a
major wire producer. James set about rationalizing all three sides of the
corporation's activities. Irlam was a major steel producer and Wigan –
especially with its new Nottinghamshire pits – was a major coal producer.
The corporation therefore sold household coal, and steel billets, surplus to
its wire-making requirements.

As a result of bankruptcies and other developments, therefore, nominees
of the Bank of England and the joint stock banks controlled all the firms, and
Richard Thomas, John Summers, Dorman Long, South Durham, and
Lancashire Steel especially closely. Allan Macdiarmid was head of Stewarts
& Lloyds's tube combine. Sir Charles Wright was at Baldwins. Sir James
Lithgow was Scotland's leading industrialist and was involved with Colvilles.
James and Lithgow joined Richard Thomas's board. Macdiarmid of Corby
joined the United Steel Companies board whose chairman was Sir Walter
Benton Jones who joined the board of Stewarts & Lloyds; and Lancashire
Steel was to produce rolled products at Corby, and then John E. James
joined the Corby board. United Steel invested in John Summers, so R. S.
Hilton joined Summers's board. By 1937 Richard Thomas at Ebbw Vale
and John Summers at Shotton owned the only two mass steel sheet plants
in Britain – producing two-thirds of British output. John Summers had
two United Steel directors on the board; Richard Thomas got other
nominee directors. We see, therefore, a pattern of mergers and linked
directorships. But the majority of steel firms were not actually merged with
each other.

Indeed, apart from the major firms that fell into the control of the
financiers, there was no great demand for rationalization. What the steel-
masters wanted was rigid price agreements and a stiffer tariff. The price
agreements were vigorously enforced but certainly frequently broken. The

tariff depended upon the election of a protectionist government. And, indubitably, a stern system for allocating output to different areas suggested some far more effective system of central control which might itself be counter-productive in terms of efficiency. What did this mean in practice? To answer that, a little more must be said about the reorganization proposals that were under active discussion.

It will be recalled that Brasserts gave the Bank of England a short report, proposing regionalization. The Bank of England report was reproduced, to a considerable extent, by an official body, originally a sub-committee of the Committee of Civil Research, chaired by Lord Sankey, a great one for reorganizing industries as his Commission on coal had shown. The proposal was to spend over £15 million on making the industry more efficient in closing down out-of-date works and building new ones. Stewarts & Lloyds in Northamptonshire were to be the chief part of this proposal for a major new tube and steel works on a home ore field. But the central feature was to be bank-financed regionalization and scrapping of old plant.

As with Sankey's earlier proposals for coal, all that this scheme lacked was political realism. Herbert Morrison as Minister of Transport was re-organizing London's buses and trams, including one of Hatry's companies, the London County Council trams, and the General Omnibus Company. In 1921 the railways had been regionalized. But coal and steel, like agriculture, seemed to be in a different class. They were very large employers in the distressed areas. Above all, though they looked hopeless to outsiders, to individual dynamic people in growing firms, like Stewarts & Lloyds, the prospects seemed bright. In their view, the first thing was to stop the industry falling into the hands of bureaucrats like those who ran the cartel, or civil servants who would treat firms equally and share the markets equitably, but who would not allow individual breakthroughs to take place. This was the penalty of the cartel system though, let it be said, not a penalty that seemed to have been paid in Germany or Belgium but which had been paid in the North-East and in Sheffield.

Though the slump reached its depths in 1932, the bottom of the industry's output was reached in 1931. Devaluation in 1931 protected the home market, and the government deficit and falling interest rates stimulated demand and so investment. Nevertheless the industry's output as a whole was well below that of 1929.

The Labour government had presided over a period of great distress. Its own policies had disastrously failed. Some Labour members had proposed a surtax, to balance the budget – which would itself have worsened the depression by reducing consumption. Yet the industry's reaction was that there was a shortage of savings, as *The Iron and Coal Trades Review* commented: 'Evidently new investments are only made out of aggregations of revenue derived from investments already made. If the state takes away a portion of this revenue, there remains less to be invested in new undertakings, hence, whatever the amount levied under the surtax, it must mean as much taken away from fresh capital investment in commerce and industry. . . . A surtax will reduce still further the millions of trade capital required to set at work the thousands of the younger generation who are knocking at the factory doors.'

The solution sought by the industry was not state control, but tariff protection, because the real problem seemed to be international trade. It seemed that for many firms the difficulties arose from dumping. But if there were a tariff, then benefits would fall on the just and the unjust alike. Even after devaluation by the national government in September 1931, when Britain abandoned the gold standard, tariffs were introduced. In the early 1930s certain countries, notably Germany, were selling steel abroad at prices substantially below their home prices. Most steel countries imposed substantial tariffs on imports of iron and steel products. These tariffs, usually 20 per cent *ad valorem*, varied from about 10s (50p) to £3 per ton, according to the value of the imports. Up to 1932 the British industry in contrast found itself with an unprotected home market, and shut out from any export markets. As a result 'we were, therefore, driven to play the same game and with government help and a discriminatory tariff system the British industry was placed in a stronger position to fight back. Thus our action in the 1930s was largely defensive, to deal with the unfair trading methods of certain other countries, particularly Germany.'

This then was the aim. How did it come about?

As a consequence of the election in 1931 not only was the pound devalued, but import duties were imposed. The double action gave considerable protection to the industry. An Import Duties Advisory Committee under Sir George May was set up which in March 1932 recommended duties of $33\frac{1}{3}$ per cent on most steel and 20 per cent on the rest. The quid pro quo was the reorganization of the industry. The reorganization was to take the form of limiting capacity, cooperation between different firms, and some form of closer link with overseas cartels, as Sir George May spelt out at a meeting of the chairmen of steel companies on 3 June 1932.

After a third of a century the Import Duties Act 1932 gave iron and steel most of what its spokesmen had asked for, just as the overvalued pound (the basic cause of the troubles of the 1920s) sank to its proper level. At the same time, too, the revelations of the state of the industry, made by the Ministry of Munitions in the First World War, sprang to life again in the proposals for reorganization. The trades unions, and members of the Labour party (now in a tiny minority in Parliament), held that the reorganization should take place under public ownership and control. The Import Duties Advisory Committee, which the Act established to advise the government, required reorganization as a condition of the extra protection, over and above the general level of 10 per cent, that the industry was given at its own request. In June 1932 Sir George May, chairman of the Import Duties Advisory Committee, who had been chairman of the Committee on Expenditure whose report had brought the Labour government and the pound sterling down, arranged a meeting of the boards of firms in the industry, to require them to set up a National Committee to propose a plan of reorganization for the industry. Initially the difficulty that arose was that there was formally no such thing as an iron and steel industry. There was a congeries of fifty or so groups of producers. Many of the members of those groups were, of course, the same firms, so that the diversity was more apparent than real. Nevertheless the bigger firms were often engaged in a wide range of activities and they did not necessarily regard themselves as heavily involved in what is now called the iron and steel industry. It took lengthy negotiations, therefore, to establish the British Iron and Steel Federation, which from 1934 to 1967 was the body representing the firms in the industry.

It is fair to say, at this distance of time, that the governmental intervention continued without cease for thirty-five years, culminating in the second nationalization, and that the issues raised at this meeting were to be those that were central to the industry's policies till the present time. They were the relations between the government and the industry, whatever its ownership; location; the right level of capacity; investment decisions; pricing; and imports and exports.

4

Revival

The 1930s, after the worst of the slump, was a period of reconstruction and new developments. When the slump began the steel families still controlled much of the industry. By the time the revival began a new breed of director was seated at the boardroom tables. Not to put too fine a point on it, the industry was divided between steel-men, on the one hand, and financiers on the other. The problem was for the steel-men to believe that the financiers could behave reasonably and for the financiers to think that the steel-men knew their jobs. Ironically, as events showed, the financiers were easily assimilated and often became more like steel-men than those reared among blast furnaces and rolling mills were themselves.

The key to this period is the emergence of a strong central organization of the industry. It was brought about largely through the efforts of Montagu Norman, the Governor of the Bank of England, helped by the men in key positions in the major firms in which the banks and the insurance companies had dominant or large holdings.

The foundation of the British Iron and Steel Federation was important in itself since the Federation, directly or indirectly, formed the effective spokesman and forum of the industry for a third of a century. It negotiated with government. It provided personnel, policies, data and ideas for the Board of Trade, the Ministry of Supply, the Iron and Steel Board and the two nationalized corporations. But the foundation of the Federation had another significance. Some firms all of the time, and many firms some of the time, were against the Federation, or doubted its value, or did not think it worth the money. It would not be too much to say that it was accepted reluctantly as the price of government defence by means of tariffs.

The result of Montagu Norman's activities was later summed up by a city editor: 'Steel is an outstanding example in Britain of a tightly controlled industry in which competition is regulated and prices are fixed. Its development along cartel lines has been encouraged by the government and aided by the Bank of England.

No steel-maker could get busy on a major scheme of expansion without first obtaining the Federation's approval.'

Yet, to get to that position, three years after the Import Duties Advisory

69

Act was passed, a great many tricky passages had to be negotiated. Part of the trouble was that individual firms seized the opportunity provided by the protection of the devaluation and the tariff to expand their trade and lay down new capacity. Any capital plan, initiated by a cartel, was likely to penalize the adventurous high-investment firms. The Federation, it was clear, was thought of by people like Sir George May, chairman of the Import Duties Advisory Committee, and Montagu Norman, as a body that would buy up and get rid of out-of-date equipment. But the price-fixing bodies already in existence, and the Federation, as various schemes emerged, seemed designed to penalize excellence and to keep elderly and inadequate plant in service. The reason for this is easy to see: most firms were equipped with out-of-date plant that it would have been difficult to scrap, so that at meetings of steel firms the majority was always in favour of geriatric steel policies. Yet, paradoxically, almost each firm in some respect thought that it had the secret of survival, expansion and profitability. So their attitudes to industry-wide schemes had two directly opposed sources of suspicion.

While the Federation was beginning to be negotiated the firms not only carried on with their plans but carried through amalgamations. Colvilles, for instance, became virtually the Scottish monopolist producer. In South Wales, Richard Thomas expanded while Guest Keen & Baldwin's began a major reconstruction of their works in Cardiff. Each firm continued, that is, as before, on its own course. In these cases the policies were those approved of by the banks. But even so, other proposals were less acceptable, and alternative solutions to the industry's problems were being put on the table.

It had been hoped that the Federation would finally emerge as a Federation of most of the specialist bodies which had been in the industry till 1934 – price-fixing and labour relations groups, for the most part – and though it would have had little independent power, even over its affiliated bodies, it would be able to fix prices, production quotas and impose levies to close down redundant works. In the event, it was constituted as representative of companies and it was only after some years that the other bodies became affiliated. It is clear from the minutes of the price-fixing bodies that have been examined that there was no change in their composition or modes of behaviour. The Federation's constitution was therefore very permissive and voluntarist, not differing significantly from the manufacturers' National Federation of Iron and Steel Manufacturers which was very active in drawing up the constitution of the new B I S F, and whose director, Sir William Larke, became director of B I S F.

But the B I S F's significance was enhanced by appointing as an independent chairman a fifty-year-old Scots solicitor called Sir Andrew Duncan who had worked successively before and after the war for the Shipbuilding

The building of Ebbw Vale in the 1930s symbolized the revival of steel, and of South Wales.

In the revival of the 1930s, the industry became a mixture of old and new techniques. Above is an old 'Batho' type open-hearth furnace, while below is an oil-fired furnace for an axle-rolling machine. English Steel at Sheffield (opposite), a reorganized company, cast giant ingots for heavy forgings for the rapidly growing electricity industry.

Colvilles, in the Glasgow area, began a major expansion of which this re-rolling mill (above) was a part. Meanwhile at Shotton hand-rolling (below) continued.

As trade revived in shipbuilding and automobile manufacture John Brown's shipyard on Clydeside (above) gave orders for steel. So did the Nuffield works at Cowley (below).

As trade revived, the industry started up old plant. Opposite are two furnaces at Dudley, one mid-nineteenth century, the other about 1900, restarted in the 1930s. Cargo Fleet (above) in 1936 was relatively modern, and Corby's Bessemer converter (below) was new in 1934.

H. A. Brassert (above left) was Montagu Norman's expert consultant and his advice was required for most new steel plans. Allan Macdiarmid (above right) of Stewarts & Lloyds, got Corby built, while Sir William Firth (below left) built Ebbw Vale against opposition from almost every quarter. Sir Andrew Duncan (below right) was put in to reorganize the steel industry.

Employers' Confederation, as coal controller at the end of the war and then as chairman of the Central Electricity Board. He was a director of the Bank of England and among those around Montagu Norman who thought that the right response to the slump and the continuous troubles of British industry was self-regulated reconstruction by planned limitation of capacity and strategically placed new investment.

Duncan was a remarkable man, with highly developed skills as a negotiator, innumerable contacts in the City and Whitehall, wide experience at the top level in business, and a powerful, though quiet, personality. He soon came to dominate the somewhat lesser figures in the steel industry. By his persistence, and the accident of the war which required a strong central control, in 1939 he recreated the BISF in something like its original intended form, as conceived by Norman and May.

Throughout the 1930s governments sought to regulate industries affected by the depression. The forms of regulation varied from country to country. But in Britain the self-controlling industrial body, with independent firms, responsive to public needs, was conceived to be the appropriate body. What did the government want to achieve through the BISF?

The government had several policies which affected the industry. In the first place it was concerned to rescue it from the worst effects of the depression. Whitehall was still firmly in the grip of the Treasury doctrine inherited ultimately from Peel and Gladstone, that the government should intervene as little as possible. But the national government had adopted Montagu Norman's philosophy that the major depressed industries should be re-organized by their own collective action, with the support of the banks and other city institutions There had also been a major reversal of British policy on foreign trade by the adoption of protection and the abandonment of the gold standard, which gave the industry a privileged position in the domestic market and made its exports dependent on international negotiation.

A major purpose of the tariff was to enable Britain to take part in international arrangements. To look forward a little, as a result of this government action there was, by 1935, in each of the major European steel-producing countries a national cartel or price-fixing trade association, each a member of the international steel cartel (*Entente Internationale de l'Acier*). The main purpose of this international trade body was to control the export trade by fixing quotas and price controls for each of the main classes of steel products. Under the 1935 agreement between the BISF and the other members of the international cartel, United Kingdom export quotas were fixed on their share of trade in 1934. The other cartel countries accepted in return an import quota to the United Kingdom of 525,000 tons per year, although in actual practice expanding British consumption made it necessary to import more than the agreed quota in most years. By 1935 the imports of most iron and steel products into the United Kingdom were subject to import duties, though those from Empire countries were admitted duty free and those from 'quota' countries were admitted at a special low tariff, usually 10 per cent *ad valorem*. All other imported products were then admitted at a higher rate of tariff, varying from 25 to $33\frac{1}{3}$ per cent *ad valorem*, according to the type and value of the steel product.

But this tariff protection, substantial though it was, left the question of the industry's structure still to be determined. Scotland and Lancashire had been 'rationalized'. Stewarts & Lloyds had been sent to Corby. Other firms, however, carried on as before.

There were those in Whitehall and the City who, remembering the experience of the Great War, thought that the only way of bringing the industry to an efficient condition was by ruthless scrapping of equipment and merging of firms. This view was held in those departments concerned with defence procurement. It was strongly held by people like 'Ingot' – 'Otto' Clarke, later Sir Richard, a *dirigiste* civil servant – and other outside critics of the industry. Some sources of this view lay in the concern with the regional problems that the slump had accentuated. The parts of the steel industry most seriously affected by the depression lay in the depressed areas, and attempts to 'rationalize' the industry by scrapping obsolete plant accentuated the problems of unemployment. The needs of the depressed areas, too, found expression in demands for new plant to be located where unemployment was most severe – Ebbw Vale, for instance – rather than on the home ore sites, like Corby.

Location policy was perhaps a central feature of government involvement, though rearmament was soon to overshadow it.

But in the meantime, as public policy evolved, a major new steel works was being built. Steel is an industry that suffers from manic-depression. When demand is low, costs of productions are high and people become extremely depressed. As demand rises, costs fall and they plan new works. Corby illustrates this, and as a major integrated steel works it became an exemplar of what many people inside and especially outside steel thought could be done if steel-men really tried.

Stewarts & Lloyds continued its serious study of the Corby project from 1927 onwards. In November 1932 it was finally agreed to go ahead with the plant. The only mystery about the project was its timing. For once – well, perhaps not quite once, but rarely – the project was well-timed. It was built at minimum cost, when prices were falling and firms were competing with each other for work. It came into operation as the economy moved out of the deepest part of the slump, which had been in 1932–3, into the small boom of 1937, which was followed by rearmament and the Second World War when the demand for steel was limitless. Foreign ores were to be virtually unobtainable and it was a great boon to be able to use home ores. Because of the depression, labour-intensive projects like the building of a steel works were strongly to be desired. Yet, when the go-ahead was given, little of this future could be known. It is often said that Corby was built for one set of reasons but succeeded for another.

What was known was that the demand for tubes kept up, chiefly because of the housing boom that was the national government's response to the depression. Stewarts & Lloyds took over the Scottish Tube Company in 1932 and so there was a reduction in competition, a process continued by the purchase of John Spencer in 1935, and of another firm in 1936 – British Mannesman Tube Company. British Mannesman had been nationalized during the First World War because it was German-owned, and it was taken over in 1919 by a private syndicate. It built the Newport steel works and in 1921 was taken over by Baldwins, so that Newport was linked to Margam. Yet again, in 1926, the German Mannesman firm took over Newport, which was reconstructed, and a growing part of trade was captured. In 1936 it was this firm which was bought jointly by Stewarts & Lloyds and Tube Investments who, as we saw, shared the British market between them and divided their export markets.

Stewarts & Lloyds, as tube manufacturers, was short of modern capacity. They had a dynamic, aggressive chairman, Allan Macdiarmid. In August 1929, just before the slump began, he commissioned H. A. Brassert to do a complete report on Stewarts & Lloyds. The Brassert recommendations on Scotland had not been fully accepted (though they were to be thirty years later); and Brassert, who seemed knowledgeable beyond anybody in Britain, was retained by Stewarts & Lloyds to build any new works he might recommend. It follows, as a matter of simple logic, that he and Macdiarmid must already have decided to build a new works in August 1929, before the slump began. The question, therefore, was what sort of works, and where? That, it was already clear by September, as Atha wrote, was to be Corby, as C. G. Atha and Macdiarmid had recommended in September 1927 to the Stewarts & Lloyds board.

The reasons for Corby were simple. First, it was not in Scotland where Macdiarmid had just declined to join a consortium of steel-masters. He proposed in 1927 to transfer the head office from Glasgow to London. Next, it was on an appropriate source of ore, which would have had to be shipped to Scotland. It was fairly near the Midlands coal fields. It was not associated with the catastrophes of North Lincolnshire. There was a large site. The main market for tubes was in the South and Midlands and it was this, plus the low ore charges, that made Corby the least-cost site. That it was not the least-cost site for British industry as a whole is very probable; but Macdiarmid was convinced that it was for Stewarts & Lloyds and he called in Brasserts, as any firm may call in consultants, to confirm his judgement.

The Corby scheme was recommended by Brasserts in February 1930, when the slump had begun. Negotiations with the Bankers Industrial Development Company ensured that its output was to be for tube mills alone, and not for a wider range of products as originally envisaged. In particular, sheet steel for the motor car trade had been strongly urged by Brasserts. The reason for this concentration on tubes was that Montagu Norman, in rationalizing the steel industry, had other proposals for other products in mind. Initially, indeed, his advisers wished to merge Stewarts & Lloyds with Lancashire Steel, which the Bank of England controlled. But Macdiarmid's scheme for tubes was the first realistic proposal for a new works based on a major product for the East Midlands, and Brassert's immense authority convinced the bankers that they should put up the £5 million required. Sir Andrew Duncan, a confidant of Norman's and head of the Electricity Board supported Macdiarmid, especially when Brassert asserted that 'the three cheapest producing pig iron locations in the whole world were (a) Alabama, USA, (b) Alsace-Lorraine and (c) Corby District' – assertions that were characteristically direct and brief.

The agreed proposal was for 435,000 tons of steel a year, divided between basic Bessemer and open-hearth, with two blast furnaces and a blooming mill, together with other ancillary equipment. To add to the confusion, one of Montagu Norman's other advisers, Lewis, proposed in the autumn of 1931 to add sheet steel capacity to the Corby plan in order to get greater economies of scale. Macdiarmid, who had originally wanted this, found himself in the paradoxical position of arguing for a plant limited to tubes. He did this because he realized that the protection promised by the national government was contingent upon a sharing of the steel market; he and Tube Investments had tubes and so Corby's market was assured, but if he moved into general steels his market would be exposed to the attacks of his rivals, who already deeply distrusted his schemes, and had regarded his defection from the Scottish scheme with outrage.

Stewarts & Lloyds retained Clydesdale, which gave them a share in the Scottish quota, but only on condition that the other firms did not make tubes, and Stewarts & Lloyds did not 'enter their steel market'.

Macdiarmid had thus secured his Scottish flank. He feared United Steel at Appleby and Lancashire Steel at Warrington, both well poised to enter tubes, and both alarmed that Corby's costs of production might be so low that Stewarts & Lloyds might seek to enter their markets. Macdiarmid therefore agreed to a demarcation agreement and cooperation in which 'every endeavour should be made to form an alliance'.

Underlying all this was Macdiarmid's strong personality and excellent judgement. He felt that if Corby were not pushed through, Stewarts & Lloyds would be merged with other firms as a subsidiary and he would work under Chamberlain of Tube Investments who was senior to him. He had Brassert's expertise at his disposal; his scheme was well worked out and eventually it found favour with Montagu Norman. The slump made a new works seem a ludicrous addition to capacity virtually all unused. 'We so adjusted [the scheme] as to be able to assure the BID and our own board that, even if the tonnage available should remain at the level obtaining during the lowest point of the depression, it did ... represent a sound piece of economics. We allowed the BID to understand that it was purely a tube scheme and that we had no intention of destroying the Bank's frozen credits or putting out of action other steel-makers' plants by encroaching on territory not hitherto within our province. ...'

In the event Corby was built and managed by Brasserts. It was a remarkable story. Corby was preferred to other sites such as the Thames estuary, Newport and Humberside because of the high-quality ironstone reserves, which were suitable for Thomas steel. The works were to have three large-scale blast furnaces, three open-hearth Bessemer converters, and three mills. It was opposed, both as to site and as to size, by virtually the entire board of Stewarts & Lloyds, on utterly reasonable grounds. Work started in the spring of 1933 and the first blast furnace was commissioned in the spring of 1934. By the autumn all three were in operation. The first Bessemer converter was in operation before the end of 1934. Nearly four thousand staff and workers were recruited and a special new town was built for them.

But by 1935, with trade booming, the situation was different. The international tube agreement began to crumble. The other steel firms were reactivating capacity and building new plant. Sir Andrew Duncan sought to rationalize. Stewarts & Lloyds was seen as part of a possible Midlands amalgamation, with United Steel, Richard Thomas and Lancashire Steel. Macdiarmid's view was that it was vital for Stewarts & Lloyds to expand Corby in order to have extra low-cost steel to undercut his ruthless rivals. The demarcation agreements were breaking down. 'Our present position is not only weak in offensive power and in the power to establish quotas, but it is even very vulnerable. Our *intrinsic* position is very strong. We know that we can produce steel cheaper than any other firm. If we stay as we are, the advantages in our favour will gradually diminish. ... The Midland grouping, either on Benton Jones's idea or on Firth's or Duncan's is being pressed. We shall be in a much stronger position to negotiate when we are making 450,000 tons of steel at the lowest cost in the country. . . .'

The 'Midland grouping' arose from the meeting held by Sir George May, chairman of IDAC, with major steel firms, on 3 June 1932, when he proposed four groups – Scotland, the North-East Coast, South Wales and the Midlands. In July 1932 a letter was published saying that United Steel, Lancashire Steel and Stewarts & Lloyds had agreed to a mutual sales policy, to eliminate unnecessary competition between them, and jointly to agree new capital expenditure. An unpublished letter – Letter 2 as it was known – made this agreement more specific and binding and fixed its term for thirty years.

The groupings were apparently to be more financial than physical. As Hilton wrote to E. J. George about May: 'We did by far most of the talking. . . . I fear Sir George has not much sense of humour . . . he did not consider that physical amalgamation was essential, that it might be desirable for certain districts while in other districts it would not be helpful. . . .'

Lancashire Steel was developed carefully under John E. James, with the careful supervision of the Bank of England and Schroders, acting through Charles Bruce-Gardner and the egregious Major Pam, the founder of Marmite, and possessor of gold medals from the botanical and zoological societies. In 1936 James went to the United States to choose a rolling mill to be used at the plant that was to be constructed at Corby in conjunction with Stewarts & Lloyds.

Meanwhile, paradoxically, United Steel – once a source of grave scandal – flourished. Walter Benton Jones became chairman in 1928, and Robert Hilton was brought in by the Bank of England from Metropolitan Vickers to be managing director. A vigorous programme of centralization and rationalization was introduced. Brasserts made a report on the reorganization and, apart from other proposals, two big developments sprang from the consultations that led to and followed the report. The first was the development of a pig iron and an open-hearth process at Appleby-Frodingham, which was to supply steel slabs to a new plant at Shotton built by John Summers to roll wide sheets. Though the Appleby-Frodingham steel was in the event not usable for this purpose, United Steel took shares in John Summers, increasing its range of diverse interests into a rapidly growing market. John Summers was a family concern in which the Bank of England had a controlling interest so that its benevolent respect for Brasserts' judgement of United Steel's future allowed it to make an exception to its policy of regionalization. The reason for this was that the policy was built around a new works, Appleby-Frodingham, and a new market, wide sheets for motor car bodies.

After its formation United Steel was run as a loose federation. Different parts of the group made losses at different times, but Workington, Samuel Fox and parts of Rother Vale were more often in serious trouble than other sections. It was not until the late 1920s that the firm was looked at as a whole, and by that time the Hatry catastrophe had occurred.

At that time, too, there was no urgent need to make a profit, since there were no shareholders and, from the point of view of the management, what mattered was the survival of the firm. Since the depression was general, there was no reason to suppose that any one part of the combine might be more likely to be valuable than any other. In any case, there were always several possibilities open. One was a Midlands group of steel firms. To this end, approaches were made in September 1931 to Lancashire Steel, only to be stopped by 'a principal shareholder in Steel Industries of Great Britain' – the Prudential Assurance Co., and by the Bank of England on the advice of Sir Alfred Lewis of the National Provincial Bank. Even so, in June 1935, an offer was made to buy Lancashire Steel. Just after the approach to Lancashire Steel, approaches were made to Stewarts & Lloyds which led to an arrangement in which the two companies agreed 'to cooperate in the policy of enterprises in steel production and avoidance of uneconomic duplication of plant' and to cooperate in sales policies and in research and technical development. Hilton attached particular importance to the Midland Regional Committee of the National Council for the Heavy Steel Trade in arranging possible amalgamations. In late 1935 discussions with Firth were occurring about Redbourn Hill (as it was known) where the Appleby-Frodingham scheme was underway.

In August 1930 Hilton wrote to Gerald Steel that 'I have been asked to prepare a rationalization scheme for the Midland area . . . which will take in all the Lincolnshire works, probably Park Gate, Steel, Peech & Tozer and Templeborough etc., and Partington, will have part of its regional area in North Lancashire and Cumberland.' In this scheme Lancashire Steel was to be the engineering section, without blast furnaces.

In this context of amalgamations Cumberland has to be seen as a heterogeneous group of collieries, hematite ore mines, and pig iron and steel works, some of which made losses and some of which made profits. The aim was to float them off as a separate company, combining all the iron and steel interests in that area, and repeated discussions took place with other firms. United Steel thought of itself as a Midland group; by the time its various merger proposals in that area were completed, Workington was once more profitable.

Furthermore, it must be remembered that Benton Jones was from the coal industry. All through the 1930s, Sir Ernest Gowers and the Coal

Commission were trying to merge the South Yorkshire colliery firms into a regional group, a scheme on which Benton Jones alternately blew hot and cold. When United Steel was refloated it was announced that it was intended to run its major interests through subsidiaries, which could have meant that Benton Jones would go to coal, Hilton – already elderly – to the Midland Steel group, and Workington would continue on its own. But in the event that did not happen. Increasingly Benton Jones came to the fore and in particular he was concerned with sales.

Hilton was a centralizer, and he became a powerful figure in the BISF. In 1939, when he stopped being managing director, there were difficult times for United Steel, since the management had been so autocratic. His chief monument, however, was a tight control of the finances of a major steel company, and a big new plant at Appleby-Frodingham. As Hilton had grown in public importance, and since he was in any case elderly, Benton Jones played a major part in the making of United Steel's policy. He resembled in some respects another major figure in steel, Firth.

Sir William Firth was ubiquitous and outspoken. He built a new steel works, too, but it was not as favourably remarked upon as Corby had been. Ebbw Vale or not, that was a question that dominated South Wales in the early 1930s, because Sir William Firth, of Richard Thomas, had devoted his considerable energies chiefly to Redbourn. An agreement was made with Whitehead's to move their capacity from Tredegar to Redbourn, in Lincolnshire, which was reopened in 1933. Firth travelled the world – Australia, Canada, America – in search of profitable business and new ideas – making agreements with Broken Hill and other overseas firms like the Canadian Tinplate Company.

In October 1933 Firth was discussing future acquisitions in South Wales and L.D. Whitehead was made a director. The firms concerned were the Briton Ferry Steel Company and W. Gilbertson & Co., and the acquisitions were to be financed by £3 million debentures at 4¼ per cent, partly in repayment of existing 7 per cent debenture holders. This scheme was proposed by Sir Edward Boyle, a director. The Briton Ferry scheme fell through, but the Gilbertson deal was completed for £350,000. The Gilbertson brothers became directors, and on 22 March 1934 it was agreed to issue £450,000 debentures at 4¼ per cent. The capital structure was reorganized in late 1934 and early 1935. It is clear that Major Beaumont Thomas and Sir Edward Boyle took a leading part in these matters, and that the financial affairs of the company, in relation to the stock market and to the banks, were largely in their hands. Firth was concerned with management and planning, down to the smallest detail, but money he left to other and more financial brains. By early 1935, Cyril Watts and A.W. Kieft were

Opposite *The Bessemer process at Ebbw Vale.*

made assistant managing directors to relieve Firth of the 'accumulation of work and the strain of effort to overtake arrears', resulting from 'the number of international and national trade committees on which, in the interests of the company, he had to serve'. In fact Kieft's job was to plan the Redbourn hot and cold strip plant, and to buy land in Northamptonshire for iron ore mining, while Cyril Watts was to act as company secretary. Kieft was to fall almost immediately and Watts to soldier on.

Sir William sought to build a strip mill at his firm's Redbourn site in Lincolnshire on home ores. Meanwhile Welsh and Cumberland interests spoke out strongly about the decline of the industry in their areas. It is said that Stanley Baldwin, in 1935, as Prime Minister, felt able to argue that Ebbw Vale should be bought by Richard Thomas and new integrated sheet rolling works opened there. Not a shred of hard evidence supports this view. More was in it than met the eye of course, as will be seen below, since among the assets acquired were the profit-making coal (anthracite) mines which helped Richard Thomas's cash flow position, especially under the coal marketing scheme. Yet there is a possibility that, as will be seen, public policy played a part in helping to affect Sir William Firth's mind in his changed decision.

The South Wales scheme was an interesting instance of the complexity of the situation that Sir Andrew Duncan had to deal with. Firth constantly manoeuvred to take over Baldwin's, in order to reduce the costs of South Wales tinplate by rationalization. He was cordially disliked by the Baldwin's directors, and Stanley Baldwin shared this distaste. When Firth proposed to build a new plant in Lincolnshire, to get the finance for this he had to go to the banks. This was Montagu Norman's chance. Acting with May and Duncan it was agreed to finance the Ebbw Vale scheme. They would not finance Redbourn, which was in the middle of the Scunthorpe belt of works – Appleby, Frodingham, Lysaghts and Redbourn – and was not suitable by itself for a large development, while Richard Thomas was not in the Midland group. Redbourn could be kept to supply billets across the country to South Wales. They would support a scheme in South Wales.

The plan to merge the Lincolnshire works was sponsored by United Steel, and it was proposed that Redbourn Hill should be acquired by United Steel and Stewarts & Lloyds after details of costs had been collected by Brasserts. On 24 July 1936 Hilton wrote that he had 'run across Firth. . . . I told him we had in mind a wide strip mill and that it seemed Lincolnshire was the proper place to put it down, possibly in connection with Redbourn . . . we had a long talk about the amalgamation of Richard Thomas and ourselves. . . .' United Steel found the need for a strip mill in the Midland area was satisfied by the agreement with Summers to build one at Shotton.

Opposite *Open-hearth furnaces at Ebbw Vale.*

E

The Ebbw Vale offer came suddenly and, with the agreement of Sir Edward Boyle, a deal was done with Sir John Beynon, the Ebbw Vale chairman, and agreed by a full board on 31 October 1935. The Ebbw Vale scheme and the Redbourn scheme needed close supervision. Kieft's retirement left a managerial emergency. G.A. While and H.R. Ayton were appointed assistant managing directors. Offices were rented in Shell Mex House for the very large firm that Richard Thomas had now become. By June 1936 Sir Robert McAlpine & Sons were beginning the new Ebbw Vale works, and Ralph Freeman and Sir Alexander Gibb and Partners were supervising their building. It was agreed on the advice of Rothschilds to issue £7 million of debentures at 4 per cent and 3¾ million ordinary shares at 13s.4d (67p). The total cost was to be £7½ million for Ebbw Vale and £1 million for Redbourn. This was financed by £7 million of 4 per cent debentures and 3¾ million ordinary shares issued at 13s.4d (67p), giving £9·16 million and a bank overdraft of £2 million. In December 1936 'Sir Edward Boyle, Bt., proposed a vote of thanks to the chairman for the able way in which he had conducted and completed the negotiations for raising the new capital.' The stock was taken up by the Prudential Assurance Company, with a requirement that the development programme should not be varied, in letters exchanged in July 1937. This was a critical step. Firth sought to ensure that all was well by appointing a committee to supervise the new works (at £2,000 a year each) of L.B. Thomas, Sir Edward Boyle and C.T. Thomas. But the committee was not able adequately to fulfil its duties, and by 28 April 1938 the firm was to all intents and purposes insolvent, according to Lloyds Bank, its bankers, who engrossed the debenture, and so handed the firm's assets over, as a mortgage, to the Prudential. In the event, the costs of building had been more than expected, and the market for steel began to collapse in the 1937 depression. On 5 July 1938, the banks lent £6 million, through Securities Management Trust, a subsidiary of the Bank of England. J.E. James, S.R. Beale and Sir W.C. Wright were appointed directors. As a result, the Bank of England, through Securities Management Trust, effectively took control of the debenture holders' interests, and so gained control of the company.

It was Montagu Norman, therefore, who put in S.R. Beale, chairman of Guest Keen & Nettlefolds, John James of Lancashire Steel, and G.H. Latham, director of Whitehead's Iron & Steel Company, to represent his interests. Their view, increasingly that of Norman, was that Ebbw Vale had been a mistake; they worked uneasily with Firth on a Control Committee.

The reason for this was not far to seek. While building Ebbw Vale, Firth had run directly counter to the interests of the City and of the B I S F, notably Duncan. In mid-1936, Firth was seeking to expand his empire.

Walter Benton Jones of United Steel wrote privately to A. O. Peech, on 24 July 1936: 'After dinner Firth asked me if I would wait and have a chat with him and we had a long talk about the amalgamation of R. T. and ourselves. He is insistent that if R. T. and ourselves were to be amalgamated we would manage an extremely strong position in the steel trade.

'I know that any such proposal would not find favour in certain quarters.' That was certainly true, as Firth was to discover four years later when he was sacked.

In December 1938 Benton Jones proposed to merge United Steel with John Summers but after discussions with the Bankers' Industrial Development Company and the Governor of the Bank of England the proposal was dropped. Instead, directors were exchanged between the firms and United Steel bought some of Summers' ordinary shares. Earlier, the attempt to buy Lancashire Steel had been indignantly stopped by the Bank of England.

John Summers were a firm with two major plants, one at Shotton for sheets, and a steel-making concern at Shelton. In 1939, of 2 million ordinary shares, over 900,000 were held by those with the surname of Summers and 260,000 by a family named Jones. It had extensive overseas interests, and after a long and unhappy relationship with the American firm of Armco, it began to build a strip mill at Shotton in 1937. The original estimate of £2 million soon rose to £4$\frac{1}{2}$ million, and a financial crisis caused the firm to be largely controlled by the Bank of England, and to exchange directors with United Steel. The strip mill at Shotton came into operation in the spring of 1940, and took its steel partly from United Steel.

While Firth had been manoeuvring, and building Ebbw Vale, Duncan had been consolidating his position and strengthening the Federation. Crucial to this was the cartel.

Germany had had a cartel since the beginning of the century, and its international ramifications had become notorious. The evidence comes chiefly from United States Senate hearings and de-Nazification proceedings, but there is some independent material in the British archives. Broadly speaking, the cartel was an extension of the German Kartell. It allocated markets, and quotas in those markets, fixed prices and drew up quota schemes for output. After the imposition of import duties and the devaluation of 1931, it seems the European Steel Cartel, after some reorganization, revised its attitude to the British market, and Continental firms sold steel at prices lower than those generally prevailing.

This practice was generally called 'dumping', though discriminatory pricing was universal in all steel markets and had a theoretical justification, that marginal costs were substantially lower than average costs. It was a practice, too, that was clearly in the short-term interests of customers of the steel industry, since it gave them steel at lower prices. But it was agreed by the government and by the industry that 'dumping' should be stopped. The Federation's first task was to negotiate with the cartel to alter the arrangements for the British market. As part of these negotiations threats to raise tariffs were freely used, and the threats were partly implemented in March 1935 when IDAC's recommendations to the government to raise tariffs from 33⅓ to 50 per cent were accepted. By April 1935 agreement had been reached between BISF and the cartel to limit imports from the Continent, and the duties were suspended. In July 1935 a five-year agreement between the federation and the cartel was concluded, fixing a maximum tonnage of steel in various categories to be imported at a duty of 20 per cent and giving Britain a share of total European exports.

In this narrative two major points emerge. The first is that the BISF established itself as the body which effectively negotiated on behalf of the industry both with the cartel and with the government. From a loose, distrusted consultative talking-shop it had become a major independent force. The crucial relationship in this matter was that between Sir George May, of IDAC, and Sir Andrew Duncan, who shared a common view of the way that industry should be reconstructed, through a strong central body that had the trust of the government, and who were able to act jointly, using tariff proposals and market share arrangements as bargaining counters.

Secondly, however, Britain effectively joined the cartel as a junior partner, and entered into its discussions. But for the outbreak of the Second World War this would have had formidable consequences.

In practice the arrangements with the cartel required almost immediate adjustment. The adjustment was facilitated by the central negotiating position that the Federation held between the industry, the cartel and the government. The Federation had become a quasi-autonomous partner, though of course there were links between individual firms and their subsidiaries or allies on the Continent, and individual firms were independently powerful in Westminster and Whitehall. Baldwin, for instance, was once more Prime Minister, while Colvilles had close connections with a major German firm. So the Federation was certainly not all-powerful, or even as influential as Sir Andrew Duncan suggested, but it was of great significance in relation to imports. The quotas admitted under the agreement with the cartel were bought by the British Iron and Steel Corporation, a subsidiary of the BISF. This gave BISF a role that was to be of great importance in 1939.

But, meanwhile, the cartel was almost universally welcomed. As G. H. Latham, of Whiteheads said: 'It is gratifying to know there is every prospect of America joining the international agreement. Meanwhile the Continental cartel, by its regulation of production in France, Belgium and Luxembourg, has once more shown insight and determination to prevent the flooding of the world's markets with quantities of unwanted steel.'

The essential point to remember by the mid-1930s, however, was that trade was reviving. Partly this was due to the upturn in world trade, partly to changes on the sterling exchange rate and protection, and partly to rearmament.

It is hard for generations accustomed to forty years of high military expenditure and perennial fears of armed conflict or actual experience of it to appreciate the extent to which the whole world was first disarmed and then unarmed between 1920 and 1936. Since armaments had had a high steel content from the time of swords and armour onwards it followed that war was 'good' for the industry, and peace created problems for it. The sinister interpretation of this, as expressed for example in the trial of Krupp at Nuremberg, was that it was in the steel industry's interest to foment war. It was a principal argument in Shaw's *Major Barbara* that this was so, and Vickers' armament interests were a major reason advanced for its rationalization. However, in the archives so far studied there is no evidence to support the hypothesis that British firms put forward arguments for a warlike policy.

The three parts of the steel industry specifically and directly affected by disarmament were sheet steel, tubes and wires. Tubes were the responsibility chiefly of Stewarts & Lloyds, wire of Lancashire Steel, while sheets had several major producers. All of them had to have special help to tide them over sixteen disarmed years.

The revival of trade led to the establishment of new works, of which Corby was one of the best examples, as well as others like Ebbw Vale, Shotton, and Appleby-Frodingham, and also to a realignment of the industry in regions like the North-East, and in Scotland and Wales. The revived industry, however, though it contained fewer firms than those that had entered the First World War, showed similar fissiparous tendencies, which alienated those who sought to give it help.

One of the major changes in the 1930s was the gradual restoration of the position of the main union. As has been seen, the union had lost membership and influence during the years of heavy unemployment. Arthur Pugh retired in 1936 and was succeeded by John Brown; by this time the membership was nearly double its 1931 level. By the time the war came the union was playing its full part in wage determination and was being consulted widely on the future of the industry.

On the North-East coast the situation was as complex as ever. The South Durham and Cargo Fleet shareholders had rejected the proposed merger with Dorman Long partly because of likely unemployment in Hartlepool but mainly because Dorman Long was bankrupt and ill-managed.

As the story is unravelled it becomes deeply fascinating. In 1931 Dorman Long became subject to a Management Committee, installed by Barclays Bank, with instructions to arrange a merger with the other North-East coast firms, and by 1933 Ellis Hunter of the accountants Peat Marwick was reorganizing the capital structure and negotiating with Cargo Fleet and South Durham. The arrangements were bizarre. Mitchell of Dorman Long was to be chairman of the merged company, and Benjamin Talbot of South Durham was to be a consulting expert at £5,000 a year, net of tax, with the right to draw a pension at the same rate on immediate notice. The irate South Durham shareholders rejected the scheme which linked them 'to a firm in whom we have very little faith indeed' and where the nominees of financial interests were to be 'not directors but dictators'; the court upheld the shareholders and the merger was stopped.

Consequently, Barclays insisted on Mitchell's and Ben Walmsley's removal from the board, and put in Lord Greenwood as chairman. Dorman Long's troubles had sprung from their attempts to build big bridges all over the world at prices below their costs. It was this firm that Ellis Hunter succeeded in reconstructing. Meanwhile the South Durham and Cargo Fleet firms, united when Benjamin Talbot died, did extremely well. By the spring of 1934 they were operating at 72·45 per cent of capacity. Even so, the pressures to merge with Dorman Long and Consett were extremely strong. Andrew Duncan and Brasserts proposed a big expansion in pig iron output; Brasserts' view was that if Britain could not produce a further $2\frac{1}{2}$ million tons of basic Bessemer the cartel might break down as the government would have to allow an increase in basic steel imports. In their opinion Cargo Fleet was the best place in the North-East for a £2$\frac{1}{2}$ million development (whether there was an amalgamation with other firms or not) to produce 600,000 tons of ingots, most of which would be an addition to capacity. Lord Aberdare had a syndicate that was prepared to clear the Jarrow site to produce 300,000 tons of basic Bessemer, and Consett was supporting it. South Durham and Cargo Fleet opposed the Aberdare scheme.

But even Consett, which was extremely well run and up to date, was now in the hands of the Prudential. This was ironical because by the time that it happened in the autumn of 1933, the conditions of trade had radically improved. Even so, the banks insisted that Brasserts should be called in as technical advisers, though Consett managed to keep Brasserts at arm's length, consulting them, at Sir Andrew Duncan's request, only about the reconstruction of Palmer's iron works at Jarrow. The future had already signalled the close of the 'Brassart' [*sic*] era – as Consett's careful minute-taker for once Freudianly slipped up – because in November 1934 came the first request by the Admiralty for a return of the capacity and output of steel plate, steel sheet and steel sections. Rearmament was about to begin, and in the autumn of 1935, when Cammell Laird, Vickers Armstrong and Guest Keen exchanged directors, the armaments industry was once more becoming an important customer for steel. By 1936 trade had recovered so much that the capital of Consett could be reconstructed and a new share issue made.

It was at this time that Jarrow loomed so large in public discussion.

Here, as in Wales, was another instance where the BISF took the occasion to exercise its influence over location schemes. The proximate cause of this was Jarrow and the Jarrow hunger march led by Ellen Wilkinson, Jarrow's MP and subsequently a minister in Churchill's and Attlee's governments. The major employer in Jarrow, Palmer's shipyard, had finally closed and over four-fifths of Jarrow men were on the dole. It was proposed that Consett build a plant to produce pig iron and Bessemer steel on the shipyard site. Eventually the scheme fell through, chiefly because of hostility from Dorman Long and Cargo Fleet who refused to let the new firm have a share of the market that was divided up by the producer groups.

As a result of the row, which reached considerable proportions in and out of Parliament, Sir Andrew Duncan and IDAC felt obliged to seek a submission of all new expansion plans to the Federation, with a view partly to examine markets and costs, but chiefly to see how far expansion plans were likely to conflict with each other.

The board of United Steel, despite Hilton's important role in the Federation, was unwilling to submit their proposals to expand to the Federation. Even Consett, anxious to proceed with a plant for bright steel bars (at the request of the Governor of the Bank of England) found the major bureaucratic delays of the Federation and the Bankers Industrial Development Co. extremely frustrating, so that the new Jarrow plant was not begun until 1938. In the papers of the Federation it is clear that there were three main motives in the minds of Sir Andrew and his staff: to build up the BISF into an organizing and planning body; to avoid over-capacity; but, above all, to seek BISF control or supervision over the producers' market-sharing and price-fixing groups.

Underlying the problems of the industry and the policies adopted for growth and development was a complex structure of costs and prices. It is this structure of prices which was to be the major bone of contention for many years and it gives a good idea of what the struggles between the Federation, the firms, and eventually the government, were about. From

1870 onwards Britain had been a relatively high-cost producer – or, at least, foreigners were accused of under-cutting British firms at home and abroad. From the 1890s onward prices were fixed in a series of local specialist price-fixing rings. In the 1920s the difficulties of the industry arose from the low prices of imports which drove profit margins down to vanishing point and British firms to break their own price agreements. In the 1930s, in return for import duties, the industry agreed to regulate its prices at least partly by agreement with public bodies, and it sought to improve its productivity by new investment.

After the introduction of protective import duties on iron and steel in 1932 it was decided to formulate a policy designed to stabilize prices in the face of fluctuating trade conditions. This policy was framed so as to give a reasonable return on capital at a 'normal' level of production. It followed that when output rose to near full-capacity levels, the profits would be super-normal. Responsibility for the scheme lay not with the existing price-rings, which continued, but with the newly constituted British Iron and Steel Federation established in April 1934 under the chairmanship of Sir Andrew Duncan.

Before the BISF was set up the various sectional associations in the industry already had price-fixing arrangements which established *minimum* prices by simple agreement between the producers concerned. Many of the minutes of these price-rings survive. Their techniques were unsophisticated, but the results were effective. There was not much price-cutting. Under the BISF policy, representative producers in each section were selected for cost investigation in order to revise the industry's prices on the basis of production costs, as ascertained by independent accountants, plus a mark-up for profit and depreciation. Originally the scope of this price review, undertaken at the Federation's request by the 1932 Import Duties Advisory Committee (IDAC), was limited to the primary products, pig iron, steel ingots and billets. Following the advice of the IDAC, BISF then adopted a system of *maximum* prices based on monthly audited costs of production obtained from the 'representative' firms selected for investigation. The final cost taken for pricing purposes was a weighted average cost of the firms investigated.

An important part of the Federation's pricing policy was the establishment of a 'stabilization fund', the objectives of which were to assist and expand the finding of markets for steel, to help research and development and to maintain, on a 'care and maintenance basis' in less busy periods, plants which might well be necessary to meet peak demands of busy periods. The fund sought to do this by establishing greater equality of delivery charges in connection with scheduled prices, and in order to make provision for eliminating redundant or inefficient plants it had to maintain a 'reasonable' price level by making grants to meet the position of certain high-cost plants whose output was considered essential in busy periods but whose costs were too high by which to determine the price level.

It will be seen that this was a policy, based on respectable economic arguments long advanced by Alfred Marshall, and later presented by P. W. S. Andrews in his study of the steel industry, which rested upon a concept of long-run optimum costs including 'normal' profits. But the steel industry was one where boom and slump alternated, so that periods of severe loss and high profit were endemic in the scheme.

It was originally intended that expenditure to support high-cost plants should be met by raising £1 million from a levy on the output of steel ingots. However, by 1937 a shortage of pig iron and scrap developed so that the stabilization fund was temporarily suspended to permit the creation of a 'spread-over fund' to provide for extra imports of these materials while enabling stable prices to be maintained. In 1937 the BISC was formed to carry out the necessary importation and distribution. Initially its activities were financed by advances from the banks on the security of agreements made by the Federation with its steel-making members who undertook to pay a levy of 5s (25p) per ingot ton on all steel produced.

This stabilization scheme became a major part of the mechanism by which Sir Andrew Duncan drew the 'steel barons' into the day-to-day affairs of the BISF. His policy reached its culmination, as will be seen, in the war.

Yet the BISF, to establish its links with the industry's policies as a whole, as had been foreseen by Montagu Norman, had to engage in other complex negotiations. It was these negotiations, a prelude to the war, that lead into steel's wartime experience. But, before the narrative turns to that period – one of the most fascinating in the history of this complex industry – it may be worth recalling that an election was due, at latest, in 1940 and it was possible that the Labour party might be returned to power. The Labour party was no longer what it had been when Ramsay Macdonald had been Prime Minister. It had what seemed to be well thought-out proposals for the nationalization of armaments, steel and coal. In the event, in 1940, Labour ministers joined the government and some of those people who had drawn up the paper schemes for nationalization were in the civil service, drawing up plans for the industry's present and future.

5

The War

The shadow of the war loomed across Europe from 1935 onwards. Inevitably, as governments began to rearm, steel was needed and the steel-makers found their order books lengthening. At Consett, for example, the Admiralty made enquiries in November 1934 as to the output of and capacity to produce steel plate, steel sheet and steel sections. By the time that Edward George and Clive Cookson became the team that ran Consett, in December 1935, Consett's order book was picking up dramatically. Cammell Lairds, Vickers Armstrong and Guest Keen exchanged directors in September 1935 as part of a project to provide adequate capacity to meet the rearmament programme.

This effect of rearmament is seen most strikingly at English Steel. This company had been formed in 1929 to take over the steel-making capacity of Vickers Armstrong (chiefly gun forgings) and Cammell Laird, which made armour plate and bullet proof plate. They were also involved with John Brown and Thomas Firth whose business had suffered severely from naval disarmament. The early years of the corporation were marked by a radical restructuring of the output of the combine, moving plant to Trafford Park, closing the Cyclops works, reconstructing the River Don works, and the management had the melancholy task of dismissing and compensating many hundreds of loyal workers with years of service, with the legal opinion that 'the company was not entitled to give the workpeople anything in the shape of pensions'. After four years the corporation was a much slimmer and much more efficient producer than had at one time seemed possible. By the autumn of 1933 the first enquiries from the service departments were coming in and a major new drop forge and stainless steel plant were being built at a cost of nearly £700,000. In 1935 the 'Admiralty may require armour plate beyond the 9,000 tons that the Corporation has undertaken to be ready to supply . . .'; the firm was going ahead reopening its Darlington plant and it was making guns for Vickers Armstrong, and 'aeroplane propeller blades' for the R A F. By 1936 English Steel was once more paying dividends, and it was spending over £3 million on new plant for all these services. It would not be correct to see the process of rearmament as a single upward sweep; in 1936, for instance, English Steel resented enquiries by the War Office to other suppliers about gun forgings, lest their goodwill be lost when rearmament was over. But by mid-1938 the firm was assuming that the era of preparation for war was a permanent one.

By the time of Munich, in the autumn of 1938, all the North-East makers had major developments under way. Consett was remodelling its integrated plant and investing heavily in the new Jarrow Bright Steel Bars plant. Its 10 per cent ordinary dividend in 1938 represented a return to the prosperity that had marked the end of the First World War. Cargo Fleet and South Durham were spending substantial sums out of their own cash flow – no less than £6 million on such things as ingot soaking pits and the Irchester ore mines. Similar developments can be seen elsewhere – £3 million at English Steel, £2½ million at Colvilles where, in 1938, Sir James Lithgow was approached by the Admiralty to become their Scottish representative in developing armaments facilities. The Colville developments were financed entirely out of internal cash flows.

Other major developments in the industry were those of Richard Thomas at Ebbw Vale in South Wales and of John Summers at Shotton in North Wales – the first big British strip mills, primarily producing sheet steel for motor cars. These developments are dealt with elsewhere.

By 1938 steel was booming, partly because of rearmament and partly because the economy was itself enjoying a modest boom. Effectively, the major firms were now run by 'City' men, rather than by 'steel' men. Indeed Keynes did say that 'the captains of industry are dead and the office boys rule in their mausoleums'. But this was unfair. A great deal of modernization was under way and the firms had been reorganized. And those who ran the industry included men with flair and men with judgement. It is instructive to take two extreme cases to illustrate this point. One is William Firth and the other is Ellis Hunter.

Sir William Firth was an autocrat. In defiance of a good many important people he had built Ebbw Vale. In early 1939, W. R. Brown was made general manager of Richard Thomas & Baldwin. The minutes of Richard Thomas record on 13 April 1939 that 'Mr S. R. Beale [who was a Bank nominee] stated that while he would accept the chairman's [Firth's] view of the matter . . . he felt that in fairness . . . he would feel happier if it could be recorded in the minutes of the meeting that the appointment of a general manager had been made by the chairman on his own responsibility and in accordance with his rights.'

Later, in May 1939, the financial director, Adamson, complained that he had not been consulted about the purchase of 70–80,000 tons of foreign steel bars – 'the purchase of so large a quantity and the starting up of so many works was a matter of policy, a point on which he as financial director and the board should have been consulted. The chairman stated that . . . it seemed to him to be normal business transaction.'

Beale and his allies, Wright and Adamson, were removed from the board on 3 August 1939 by Securities Management Trust, and replaced by the more powerful group of steel-men, Lord Dudley of Round Oak, Sir James Lithgow and A. C. Macdiarmid of Stewarts & Lloyds. But even they found Sir William Firth uncontrollable. Lord Dudley rarely attended a board meeting because at the beginning of the war he was made the Midland regional defence commissioner and Lithgow and Macdiarmid had their own very considerable work to do in their own firms. They tried to get agendas and reports issued in advance of meetings; they tried to make themselves available to be consulted; but Firth did not consult them. On the outbreak of war the headquarters moved to his house, Hatchford Park, Cobham, Surrey, and he lived with the firm in a most direct way. He was, like his predecessor Thomas, a 'dictator'.

In April the blow fell. An extraordinary meeting of the directors was held on 18 April 1940, with John E. James of Lancashire Steel in the chair, and it was reported that on 15 April Securities Management Trust acting as the holder of the whole of the 'A' shares, had removed Sir William Firth 'forthwith' from the board of directors. Lord Dudley was appointed chairman. Firth's allies and appointees followed him, notably G. A. While and F. S. Padbury, who had just agreed to serve for £3,000 a year for the war, plus allowances and directors' fees. The staff returned from Cobham to Shell Mex House.

From August 1940, E. H. Lever of the Prudential Assurance Company was made chairman, at a salary of £12,500 a year plus expenses of £2,500. His job was to be finance director as well, and he was appointed by the Control Committee, acting for Securities Management Trust, of which Montagu Norman was chairman. Firth's reaction was predictable. The steel barons were being replaced by insurance agents and financiers. He made this point forcibly at the Annual General Meeting, attacking John James and G. H. Latham in particular with some vigour. Lord Dudley was shouted down at the annual meeting on 30 July. 'A shareholder asked Lord Dudley and Mr James if it were true that they were not personally shareholders in the company. They admitted that it was so. "Good heavens," cried Mr Russell, "is this a mad house?"' 'About two years ago in very dirty weather some pirates pushed us on to the rocks, disguised as "national interests" men', Sir William said. He referred to the Control Committee, chaired by Montagu Norman, with Lord Greenwood and E. H. Lever as members, leaving 'money idle in the bank'. The directors in charge of the firm were not shareholders or steelmen but representatives of outside financial interests. The Ebbw Vale works was not working at anything like capacity, and output was being stepped up at other works in which directors had shares. The papers show that Sir William's facts were correct; the implications he read into them were not necessarily so. After various peremptory and registered letters, threats of litigation and other comings and goings, Sir William accepted £50,000. 'Thanks not a little to the public spirit of Sir William Firth', the South Wales *Evening Post* reported on 13 June 1941, 'all outstanding matters between him as the deposed chairman and the company have been settled.' His supporters, notably Barnabas Russell, stopped collecting subscriptions for a fund to bring an action against the management of the company. 'If Sir William Firth were a member of this union he would be receiving victimization benefit,' Mr Ivor H. Thomas, a Welsh trades unionist, said to Swansea Rotary Club.

That was, effectively, the end of Sir William Firth in steel, though he was later once more to enrage his former colleagues by supporting the nationalization of the coal industry. He had been a strange combination of modernizer, rationalizer and tycoon.

Firth's type was replaced more and more by people like Ellis Hunter. Ellis Hunter was an accountant, born in 1892. His firm, Peat, Marwick & Mitchell, formed in 1928, were accountants to Dorman Long, which had recently merged with Bolckow Vaughan.

Dorman Long was an amalgamation of several firms including the Bell iron firm. It was a conglomerate of works, not closely related to each other, nor really capable of efficient operation as a single unit. The works were scattered along the banks of the Tees, six on the south and one on the north, between Middlesbrough and Redcar, what Charles Wilson calls 'a haphazard collection of firms'. They had embarked upon a programme of expansion in the First World War that was to give them chronic excess capacity, exacerbated by the amalgamation with Bolckow Vaughan in 1928. The firm was unable to pay its debenture holders, and Ellis Hunter became, first, secretary of the Debenture Holders' Association and then deputy chairman and managing director in 1938.

Sir Arthur Dorman, chairman of Dorman Long, died in office in 1930, aged eighty-two; he was succeeded by Sir Hugh Bell who was aged eighty-seven, and who died in 1931. So when Ellis Hunter succeeded in 1938, he was a mere youngster of forty-six. Yet he in his turn remained chairman until he was sixty-nine.

The state of the firm had been dreadful. The BID offered £3·3 million in 1930 to enable the firm to merge with South Durham, but after protracted negotiations this had come to nothing. The new chairman, Lord

Greenwood, brought in Viscount Davidson, Baldwin's confidant, and Goodenough from Barclays Bank, as well as Ellis Hunter.

Dorman Long was reorganized financially, and its production was rationalized – coke at Cleveland, light sections at Middlesbrough and plates at Redcar – and the management structure changed. Graduates were recruited, and a major new works was begun at Lackenby.

Ellis Hunter was responsible for writing off £9 million of capital. He initiated a programme of rationalization, which was radical at the time. It has to be recalled that Dorman Long was a big firm, in 1938 producing 4 million tons of coal, 2 million tons of ore, $1\frac{1}{4}$ million tons of pig iron, and $1\frac{1}{4}$ million tons of steel. By 1952 the greater part of its profits (and probably the greater part of its turnover) were derived from structural and other engineering activities. During and after the war, Hunter's managerial team planned the Lackenby works which was to be based on imported ore as local ores ran out, and which linked the existing works at Cleveland and Redcar. We see in Ellis Hunter, then, the prototype of the new 'managerial' businessman, keen to organize the assets efficiently; determined to keep the finances straight; and with a broad and liberal concept of managerial responsibilities to the firm, the workers and the public. Hugh Beaver at Guinness, and others, were to be figures like him.

It must not be forgotten, however, that people like Lord Dudley were still important. Lord Dudley 'owned' Round Oak, in the sense that his family had a controlling interest. Up and down Britain in firms big and small, the 'family spirit' survived. John Summers, for example, though it was controlled by the Bank and was closely linked to United Steel, was a 'family firm' in this sense; even Lancashire Steel, also a Bank of England firm, was still a Rylands family concern, because they had been making wire in Warrington for so long and remained on the board.

Colvilles had an admirable and effective arrangement whereby Craig was largely responsible for financial control, relations with the finance interests and the government while McCance, a Fellow of the Royal Society, ran the steel interests with superb technical competence. The three families – the Colvilles, the Pirries and the Lithgows – were all interested, but they ceased to 'own' the firm.

With the outbreak of war on 3 September 1939, the industry came under the direction of the Ministry of Supply Iron and Steel Control. Moreover, while it is true that this development imposed upon the industry controls 'which owed their existence not to any natural evolution but to the exigencies of the war itself', the fact remains that many of the wartime developments reflected an acceleration of a process started with the 1932 Act, the foundation of the BISF in 1934 and the BISC in 1937.

The War

The outbreak of war was obviously a major watershed in the evolution of the steel industry. In the first place, the British Iron and Steel Federation virtually in its entirety became the Iron and Steel Control of the newly established Ministry of Supply which took over responsibility for the steel industry. The people stayed in their own offices in Tothill Street and Sir Andrew Duncan, with some diffidence, accepted a post somewhere about the assistant secretary level at a sixth or so of his former salary, which was of course made up, but initially the move – accompanied in November 1940 by a physical evacuation to Ashorne Hill near Leamington – was in the direction of industrial self-regulation, rather than of direct civil service control. Three steel-masters were brought in as Duncan's deputies – Sir Charles Wright of GKB (deputy controller); McCosh of Bairds and Scottish Steel (raw materials); and Alsop of Consett (iron and steel supplies). In February 1940 Sir Andrew Duncan became President of the Board of Trade; he later became Minister of Supply, and alternated between those offices in Churchill's coalition government. He was succeeded as controller by Sir Charles Wright, and then in 1942 by Sir John Duncanson, of Scottish Steel. Control of steel remained, throughout the war, the direct responsibility of senior members of the boards of steel companies. But, as will be seen, their environment altered radically.

Looking at the war as shown in the affairs of the individual steel firms, some trends become evident. The atmosphere changes and the way the firms behave, while never ceasing to be characteristic of themselves, alters perceptibly.

Lancashire Steel during the war was run by John James. His chief ally was one of the original directors of the firm, Sir Peter Rylands, who was seventy in 1938, while John James was a mere sixty-four. The Bank of England never relaxed its tight control. When Lord Crawford died in June 1940, the Bank of England put in Robert Crichton (knighted summer 1948), the managing director of the Workington branch of United Steel, and in February 1942, Earl Peel and L.E. Mather. In 1942 James, Benton Jones of United Steel and Macdiarmid of Stewarts & Lloyds joined the board of a heavy engineering firm, Davy & United Engineering, which supplied equipment to their firms, while in October 1942, in common with other firms, Lancashire Steel was extending its coal interests to safeguard the future. The war did exceedingly well by Lancashire Steel; in 1943 its profits were so good that it could float its first preference and ordinary shares, and by 1944 its cash surplus was embarrassingly large. The tributes to Norman on his retirement, and James on his seventieth birthday, which almost coincided, were indeed heartfelt.

Initially it has to be realized that the steel firms were doing better than

93

they had done for nearly twenty years. Their old plants were coming into production again, their 'extravagant' new installations were beginning to work nearer the capacity for which they were designed, their collieries were not so chronically depressed, and they were paying dividends again. But politically, of course, the weather was stormy. Had there been an election in 1940 Labour might have won it and one of the most important issues would have been armaments, an issue on which the steel industry could not win, because either the country was grossly undefended due to their lack of patriotism, or else they were helping to produce armaments from which they made gross and bloodstained profits. Nobody will understand the way in which the industry behaved unless it is realized that from about 1936 onwards the steel industry was still the object of widespread and often mutually contradictory public criticism.

But, then, too, it must be remembered that the running of a steel firm from 1938 onwards was very difficult. Men joined up or were called up. Raw material supplies were switched, demands for output, increasingly peremptory, came upon firms unexpectedly. Air raid precautions, air raid damage – of which there was surprisingly little – increasingly complex government regulations, all put a great strain on the administrative structures of firms. The impression that arises is of people living from day to day, dealing with crises as they arose, and dealing extremely well with them.

These problems may be illuminated from a variety of firms. All steel works had to undertake anti-glare precautions which caused a deterioration in working conditions. Young men were called up for the forces or volunteered. Attempts were made to get them back, generally unsuccessfully. In the case of the coal mines, where service was obligatory under the 'Bevin boy' scheme, major problems of discipline and absenteeism developed. Women were recruited for heavy manual jobs in steel and there were major problems over shift work as the labour shortages became acute.

Senior executives were called to the public service – Sir Charles Craven from English Steel for example. Some people were killed in air raids which were so severe at Sheffield that the gas supplies were cut off. Firms like Consett which relied upon imported ore suffered severely. Its ships were sunk; Franco nationalized its Spanish iron ore subsidiary; it faced major technical problems, as did Colvilles which had to substitute home for foreign ores.

The first task of the Iron and Steel Control was to keep up steel output and to redirect it to wartime purposes. This required great economies in manpower, as labour became progressively scarce, and a major attempt to replace foreign ores by home ores and by a scrap drive. This last problem only became serious after the loss of Norway and France in the spring of

Opposite *The growth in the number and size of electric arc furnaces altered steel-making after the Second World War.*

1940, and home ore output was increased during the war by some 7 million tons – or by nearly two-thirds on its 1938 figure – chiefly from Lincolnshire and Northamptonshire. The establishment of BISC to buy ore was fundamental to this process of changing raw material sources.

But since the ore used was different from what was thought to be ideally suited for production, some kinds of steel were relatively easier to obtain during the war than others. Many of the acute shortages of steel arose from shortages of low phosphoric ore, needed for special steels and alloys. The use of home ore also imposed a serious burden on the hard-pressed railway systems, since it had to be transported for long distances.

The shortage of coal also raised serious problems. It increasingly concerned the steel firms, both because of their own needs for coal of special quality and because they were major coal producers.

The first stages of the war were not serious, in almost any respect, but the fall of Norway, the low countries and France, in April to June 1940, not only brought the imminent risk of defeat but, almost simultaneously, cut off a major source of iron ore, of coal, and most major export markets. The decisions which had been implicit until then became explicit. Britain was to wage the Second World War with its own steel industry, but not to expand it. Billets and ingots were to be imported from America. The growth sector in Britain was to be at the engineering end of the industry, on the finishing side.

The original Iron and Steel Control was the BISF incarnate. It paid most of the salaries of its members who joined the Control until August 1941. It had direct access to Sir Andrew Duncan when he became a minister and this affected not only steel but coal. United Steel much welcomed his personal interest in the coal industry. By the autumn of 1940, the raw material and labour shortages focused attention on the need to control the use of what pig iron could be produced, and it was at this stage that the Control exercised its power most ruthlessly. There was always a serious shortage of hematite pig iron, produced from low phosphoric ores, and in late 1940 a tight rationing scheme was imposed.

But the firms continued as before. An enlightening episode occurred at United Steel where, in January 1941, the managing director, C.J. Walsh died. Rollason, of John Summers, was made managing director. Montagu Norman, still the Governor of the Bank of England and the effective controller of Summers, caused 'difficulty' and so in June 1941, Walter Benton Jones became managing director, helped by Gerald Steel on the iron and steel side, and Ward Jones on the coal, coke and chemicals side. The aim of the Rollason appointment had been efficiency; the objection was that it might

Opposite *The basic oxygen process, here at the new Anchor plant, was a major development of the 1960s.*

F

lead to a merger. Which was more likely to help the war effort, people asked themselves?

The impression had grown up that the acute shortages of the right types of steel, notably plates for tanks, were only partly due to raw materials problems. It was felt, perhaps unfairly, that the BISF people were more concerned with the problems of the steel industry, and its constituent firms, than with the needs of the war economy. The difficulties arose in two main directions – steel prices, and rationalization of output. Later, as will be seen, they arose also out of the consideration of the long-term plans of the steel industry.

Throughout 1941 the machinery of central control was expanded. In November 1941, as a result of discussion in and out of Parliament, the then Minister of Supply, Lord Beaverbrook, decided that the functions of control should be separated from the BISC and the BISF and the personnel of the Control appointed to the civil service. This was unlikely to have been Lord Beaverbrook's own decision, but rather Sir Walter Layton's, the head of the department, and Harold Macmillan's, the Parliamentary Secretary. The Control was to be responsible for production, the meeting of requirements, licensing and price regulation; the corporation on the other hand became responsible for the purchase and distribution of imported materials, the collection of Central Fund levies and the administration of the Central Fund on Ministry of Supply account. For these duties the corporation was paid an annual fee by the Ministry of Supply.

The activities of the BISC were further extended through the creation of a number of subsidiaries. In June 1940 BISC (Salvage) Ltd was formed to recover iron and steel scrap from wrecks round the coast. By 1943 some 364,000 tons of ferrous scrap and 147,000 tons of non-ferrous metals had been salvaged at an overall net cost of £7 per ton of ferrous scrap. This compared well with £9.10.0 (£9·50) per ton for American imported scrap. Virtual cessation of imports of scrap from the United States at the end of 1941 made the operations of this company even more essential to the war effort. BISC (Scrap) Ltd was also formed in June 1940. This subsidiary, however, was not a trading organization in the same sense as the corporation itself or its salvage subsidiary. Its main purpose was to direct scrap into the hands of scrap merchants, who paid direct for it at scrap controlled prices. Up to February 1943, the total tonnage dealt with by the company amounted to 954,241 tons. It was partly the need to control the use of pig iron that led to a reconstruction of the Iron and Steel Control in 1941, when Duncanson became controller, but under the close supervision of the Ministry of Supply's deputy secretary in charge of raw materials, Professor O. S. Franks. It was in this connection that the civil service, largely staffed by temporary civil servants recruited from academic life, took effective charge of the Control, and the functions of the Iron and Steel Control and the BISF began manifestly to diverge.

A major difficulty was prices and profits. Inevitably, as output rose, economies of scale operated and the firms began to make very large profits. The reason the profits were so high – so high that they attracted public attention – was the price-fixing system adopted before the war by the BISF.

The BISF had been built up almost against the wishes of the industry before the war; it had sought to control prices and profits; in the war the staff of the BISF moved into the Ministry of Supply and almost immediately implemented their prewar policies in full. The increase in profits for the industry as a whole in the early war years can be attributed to the fact that prewar prices allowed an element to compensate for the maintenance of capacity in excess of normal conditions. With the outbreak of war, however, this capacity, which primarily existed in the lighter trades, became fully utilized. The industry was thus enjoying major economies of scale on fixed capital. This problem of excessive profits was further aggravated by the fact that during the prewar standard period the prices of many of the fringe products excluded from the 1937 BISF policy, but originally accepted as reasonable by the IDAC, were set on a guaranteed cost-plus basis for individual contracts. Under this procedure overheads were normally assessed on the basis of cost estimates modified by past trading results. With the wartime expansion of output these prices gave considerably more profit than that earned in the period when the overheads were fixed. This was unacceptable to public opinion. It was also unacceptable to the BISF theorists because such prices were not necessarily related to current costs, but to a notional figure for past capital costs.

The costs at which the prewar prices of primary products were fixed included a levy, made by the Federation on all members of the heavy section, calculated at a fixed rate per ton of ingots produced by each member. The main object of this levy was to provide a fund from which the 'excess cost' of imported materials – that is the margin of cost over and above the price of similar home produced materials – could be met, with the result that the price of home materials could be stabilized and those firms which for various reasons had to work on imported materials would not be placed at a disadvantage.

At the beginning of the war this levy amounted to 5s (25p) per ton. It was soon apparent that the cost of imports would rise substantially owing to increases in freight rates and insurance, and so on, and at the same time extra costs would be incurred in securing home supplies of scrap and other materials from unusual sources. It was therefore decided to use this existing levy (the 'spread-over fund') for home purposes generally and to provide a further levy called the central fund to meet import costs. As the cost of imports rose, the central fund levy was increased in February, July, November 1940 till it reached the equivalent of 49s (£2·45) per ingot ton.

The increase in the levy was arranged chiefly because it was expected that the British industry would have to rely to a great extent on high-priced imports, chiefly of American pig iron in order to fulfil its war orders, since it had been decided not to increase British iron-making capacity to any great extent.

These levy increases became then a principal factor in the rise in steel prices during the early war years. For example, between November 1939 and November 1940 the price of pig iron rose by nearly a fifth, and rails by nearly a half. By November 1940 the situation was again reviewed and it was decided to stabilize selling prices at the level then reached, regardless of any increase in costs. In order to make this stabilization possible, in spite of cost increases, it was decided to set up a price fund which, according to a Treasury report of 1942 was 'based on the fact that it is essential to keep all firms in production however high their costs, and that the high cost firm has to sell its products at the general stabilized standard prices. In brief the scheme provides for the distribution of some of the profit earned by the lower-cost producers in aid of the high-cost producers, and it has avoided giving increases in price in order to secure at least a minimum return on their capital to the high-cost producers.'

Or, at least, so it was hoped. But there were already major divergences of view about the whole policy of the industry. Many people felt that it was doing a fine job in difficult circumstances. Some of the newly enrolled civil servants in the Ministry of Supply and their friends in politics and journalism suspected that it was being paid extremely well to do a reasonably good job, others, also in Parliament, the civil service, journalism and the industry, suspected that the 'steel barons' (most of whom were extremely mild-mannered accountants) were looking after their own interests.

The records seem to suggest that the middle position was probably the correct one. The lamentable catalogue of losses and of financial difficulty was succeeded by a healthy boom which seemed surprisingly quickly to be taken for granted. The government advanced the capital and allowed the resources for a major United Steel development at Appleby-Frodingham in 1942. The work was advanced with great difficulty, but the board of United Steel had its eyes very carefully on the need to limit the company's financial commitment to a project that might be a liability, not an asset, after the war.

Already people were thinking of the war's end. In February 1943 United Steel extended its coal interests in order to keep coal resources in the hands of the firm; the coal mines already took a tremendous proportion of the firm's managerial time. Yet it was prepared to venture further into that troubled industry. At the same time, Benton Jones and his board at United Steel revived the proposal to set up a Midland group – a combine of steel firms, United Steel, John Summers, Lancashire Steel and Stewarts & Lloyds. Montagu Norman's Bank of England controlled two of the firms – Summers and Lancashire Steel – and he turned the scheme down flat when Macdiarmid and Benton Jones went to see him on 20 January 1943. This was partly a proposal based on wartime needs, but mainly based on a view of the future of the steel industry. As will be seen, alternative views were also being propounded. Despite Norman's rebuff, the four firms made an arrangement for joint working which soon became an essential part of their corporate strategies.

But meanwhile the 'excess' profits of steel had been brought under control. In 1941, much the most immediately important fact was that under the existing price arrangements certain branches of the industry were earning abnormally high profits. For example, wire rope manufacturers were earning a return of 26·5 per cent on their book capital in the early war years as compared with a mere 8·8 per cent in the prewar standard period. Similarly, profits from drop forgings were estimated at 26 per cent as compared with 18·6 per cent, while profits on cold drawn tubes were as high as 42 per cent compared with a prewar average of 27·5 per cent.

In the light of these figures the advisory accountant to the Iron and Steel Control made recommendations for changes. Subsequently, Andrew Macharg, the then price controller of the Iron and Steel Control, said that 'it was ultimately decided to apply a block rebate system under which the profit results of the two industries would be ascertained and an overall percentage rate on turnover fixed which would be paid by each firm by way of levy to the Ministry. This voluntary levy arrangement was accepted. . . .'

In order to determine whether prices required adjustment, regular monthly costs of production for the basic steel products were obtained from a sample of representative steel firms responsible for some 80 per cent of all primary production. These costs were then weighted on the basis of tonnages produced and the need for any price changes assessed on the basis of the profit implications of movements in this weighted cost. In May 1943 the Ministry of Supply wrote that 'the policy in dealing with iron and steel prices has been to fix at a fair level standard prices for the whole range of iron and steel products and to ensure stability of such prices over a period. . . .'

The Ministry suggested the very strong advantages of this standard price policy, when compared with fixed cost pricing on individual contract. They were enumerated under four headings.

The first concerned the efficiency of the firms. Because producers worked to the same price there was, therefore, a greater incentive to efficiency than when separate prices were fixed to meet the individual costs of each producer. This implied higher profits for the more efficient – the supernormal profits at full capacity that were mentioned earlier. But, next, since prices were publicly notified, delay and uncertainty in settling prices were likely to be avoided. Thus in 1939 the BISF replaced the more rigorous IDAC policy of special cost investigations at stated intervals with a procedure whereby running costs were regularly ascertained and verified and the trends exhibited by these costs reviewed to consider the need for price changes. In the light of this change the time lag between investigation and announcement of the new prices was reduced from four months to a couple of weeks. It might not be popular for prices to rise but it was desirable that people should know where they stood as soon as possible. Thirdly, because the approved prices applied to civil as well as direct and indirect government work, control of a wider field of steel prices was possible than under contract costing. This, finally, suggested that the checking of the reasonableness of a standard list of prices covering the whole output of the trade could be done more accurately, and more simply, than a process of costing numerous separate contracts each representing a comparatively small part of each firm's total output, which would have required an army of clerks to do the checking.

Under the later wartime controls strenuous efforts were therefore taken to ensure that consumers were protected from having to pay 'unreasonable' prices. No doubt such concern was strengthened in large part by the fact that nine-tenths of the steel produced during the war years entered war production.

Prices, then, were a major aspect of wartime steel problems and policy. But prices were part of the means of achieving certain ends, notably increased output, control of demand, and greater efficiency. It will be seen that in the desire for high output, the government accepted responsibility for improving management and productivity. This step, which would have been unthinkable to the industry in 1939, was to become a major leap in the relations between publicly responsible bodies and the firms.

Looking at individual firms towards the end of the war, it is apparent that they were working flat out in the national interest. They were making good profits but dividend distributions were not high; most of the profits were retained or were used for the renewal of plant, more of which was done than is usually supposed. The industry made its own arrangements for closing down plants and concentrating production; a process made easier by the practice of interlocking directorships and the seconding of eminent members of the firms to key government positions. The firms were all eager to do more but they were not allowed to do so because of shortages of raw materials and of new plant and equipment. As it was, the evidence is most striking that, with a diminished work force and with a management considerably attenuated by the demands of the armed services and the civil service for managerial talent, the firms made tremendous efforts to respond to national needs, not just when they were told, but by enterprise and initiative to anticipate those needs.

This was a major characteristic of the firms that determined much of their postwar attitudes, since they took it for granted that patriotism took the form of pulling together and they worked closely with the civil service, with ministers and with the trades unions. Two major points need to be made, however. The firms did not reconstruct themselves by amalgamation and reorganization. This was fundamental, since the postwar proposals for development projects came from the firms constituted in the form that they had been after the upheavals of the slump. The proposals might have been different had, for instance, the Midland grouping proceeded as the firms wished. The other point is that the shortage of young and middle-aged men at managerial and board level left the senior posts in the hands of men of considerable age. The tendency for the industry to appeal to experience and length of service, rather than to youth and drive, was reinforced by this fortuitous circumstance that the younger people were largely absent. The firms where the boards were younger seem to have had a different atmosphere from those where the leading men were in their sixties and seventies. But the major factor that marked the war was the close alliance between the firms and the central organization of the industry. In terms of its objectives this organization was reasonably successful. This in itself made for acceptance of greater central supervision once the industry regained its independence. Prices remained relatively stable – although there was, it is true, some resentment against the low-profit ceilings fixed on heavy products.

Some 86 million tons of steel were produced and handled during the war; of this 14 million tons were imported, $13\frac{1}{4}$ million tons from the United States, $\frac{1}{2}$ million from Canada, and $\frac{1}{4}$ million from Australia. At the same time the industry mined and used over 100 million tons of iron ore and approximately 5 million tons of scrap were obtained from three major collections – the national survey, which produced $3\frac{1}{2}$ million tons, steel scrap recovered from 'blitzed' buildings, which provided approximately 600,000 tons, and railings which also amounted to about 600,000 tons. During this period the statistics covering the relationship of demand against supply show that in 1941 deliveries met 92·6 per cent of allocations, in 1942, 96·1 per cent and in 1943, the highest consuming year (15·9 million ingot tons) 100·8 per cent, while in 1944 the figure was 98·1 per cent. Closer examination of the uses to which this output was put discloses that some 60 per cent went directly to the provision of munitions of war. Most of the rest was absorbed in the maintenance of essential war industries and services such as merchant shipbuilding and repairs, maintenance of railways and war factories. Only about 3 per cent was utilized for purely civilian needs. This is certainly a record of which any industry could be proud.

Corby's blast furnaces (above) *blazed with light and were a target for bombers. As the First World War had shown* (overleaf) *steel was essential to produce munitions.*

Ebbw Vale

Hochofen- und Stahlwerk „Richard Thomas & Co. Ltd."

Genst. 5. Abt.   Dezember 1

Länge (westl. Greenw.): 3° 12′ 00″   Breite: 51° 45′ 45″

Mißweisung: − 11° 56′ (Mitte 1940)   Zielhöhe über NN 380 m

Karte 1 : 100 000

GB/E 27

Maßstab etwa 1 : 22 500

500   0   500   1000 m

This German aerial photograph of Ebbw Vale (opposite) was taken to help the Luftwaffe's bombers. Emergency blast furnaces (above) were hurriedly built in 1940 to replace bomb damage, like that to a mill building (below).

The shortage of scrap led to the confiscation of garden railings in 1940 (above), and King George VI and Queen Elizabeth (seen with Sir Richard Summers at Shotton) visited steelworks to help keep up morale (below).

The oil pipeline across the Channel, laid after the invasion of Norway, was a big technological venture (above and below).

Sir Ellis Hunter (above left) *was one of the accountants who came to dominate the steel industry. Sir James Lithgow* (above right) *was another powerful man. Sir Walter Benton Jones* (below left) *ran United Steel after Captain R. S. Hilton* (below right) *had reorganized it.*

6

War and Peace

The firms made plans for their postwar redevelopment as the war progressed. The war itself was a time when the plant was often run flat out and so it began to wear out, though more was done to reconstruct than is sometimes imagined – English Steel at River Don, United Steel at Appleby-Frodingham, and Stewarts & Lloyds at Corby, for example, were sites of substantial new capital expenditure. But in general the war helped to wear out the plant which was in any case not in too good a shape after the slump. Again that statement must be qualified because on three occasions some firms had undertaken big investment programmes – just after the First World War when many wartime schemes had been completed, in the brief period of quasi-prosperity between 1926 and 1929, and from 1936 to 1939. So firms like Consett, United Steel, English Steel, Richard Thomas, John Summers and Stewarts & Lloyds had modern and up-to-date plants. Technology had not advanced so rapidly, either, that the plants were obsolete. Though there were technical improvements throughout the 1920s and 1930s, especially in alloys, tinplate and sheet steels, there seems to have been no radical breakthrough in steel technology equivalent to the Siemens or Bessemer processes earlier or the basic oxygen processes later. In two respects, however, British firms were handicapped. The first was that their blast furnaces were smaller than those in the United States – and this relative smallness related to other processes as well – so that British firms did not benefit from economies of scale as much as the American firms did. And the other handicap was that the general quality of management seemed to be lower than that in America. One symptom of this, which was to be revealed by postwar studies, was that British firms employed far more people than their American opposite numbers did for virtually identical processes.

Obviously those generalizations are subject to major qualifications and many firms were exceptionally lively in looking ahead to the postwar opportunities. In 1944, for instance, Stewarts & Lloyds and United Steel put up a joint scheme for an integrated steel works on the Northamptonshire ore fields to produce $\frac{1}{2}$ million tons of billets. In the event this and an alternative scheme were thought to be too costly and billets ought to be imported it was thought. Round Oak proposed entirely to reconstruct its works. By mid-1944 Consett had produced four major alternative schemes, which it discussed with its neighbour, Ellis Hunter of Dorman Long, who was chairman of the BISF development committee. Its existing output was 7,600 tons a week, and its schemes proposed a range of outputs of up to 10,000 tons, yielding between 14 and 19 per cent on expenditure ranging from £3·2 to £6·3 million. A modernization programme of £3 million was agreed immediately. English Steel, which had spent £7½ million by the middle of 1943 on new wartime plant, also proposed large schemes. Lancashire Steel was more modest and cautious but even so it envisaged spending £1½ million in two years to renew equipment, and a further substantial sum for development. At Stewarts & Lloyds the 'urgent postwar expenditure' was £4½ million, and its development programme was for £38 million, with a further £5 million for the Stanton iron works.

These few examples are indicative of a series of major and minor proposals for the refurbishing and expansion of the industry. Put together, they come to an impressive total, and there was a need to put them together to see whether they made complete industrial and economic sense. It must also be remembered that the prewar restructuring of the steel firms had not gone very far when the war broke out. Colvilles, for example, was still a collection of plants belonging to its constituent firms and their 'rationalization' had not been legally possible until late in the 1930s, when already the pressure for war production inhibited new and radical schemes.

According to the Minister of Supply, in 1944 there was 'a case for drastic overhaul – not planned with the idea of keeping the least efficient producers profitably in business, but aimed at creating an industry adapted to natural conditions which if we make use of them, are still exceptionally favourable, an industry able to produce at least as cheaply as anywhere in the world. Here is a situation which will need firm and courageous handling not with the idea of preserving the existing structure and interests of the steel industry, but with the idea of providing Britain with an almost universally needed raw material at the lowest possible price.' It will be seen that against the background of the past forty years this was a radical and courageous statement. It was made because the wartime experience of attempts to raise output by increasing efficiency had led directly to a view of postwar plans. What was done for wartime purposes inevitably carried with it postwar consequences.

The need for modernization and the acceptance of some form of central control was also seen by a senior official of the BISF, who said in 1943 in an internal memorandum:

We must not take it for granted that postwar industry will be run on the same lines as prewar. Free and open competition may have been of great benefit in the past; it may have been responsible to a large extent for our technical development; and we may come to the conclusion that it is the only way to carry on British industry. But it has certain disadvantages – for instance, it tends to create an embarrassingly large number of perhaps desirable, but certainly not essential, specifications; it may, from a national point of view, unbalance the incidence of employment, and produce 'distressed areas'. After the war there may conceivably be some measure of government control to prevent mal-distribution of work as between various districts, but all I want to say at the moment is that we must not take it for granted that the old conditions will necessarily obtain. All this means that we must at least consider the possibility of some form of permanent control. . . .

It seems to me it is up to the Federation to frame the structure of the industry in such a way that any reasonable-minded government will be satisfied that the iron and steel industry, under the control of the Federation is capable of handling its own affairs, both internally and internationally, in such a way as to serve the best interests of our work people, our shareholders, our principal consuming industries, and the country as a whole.

This was to be the beginning of postwar plans. It sprang from the experience of wartime control, and from the confidence that full employment had led to full-capacity working and reasonable profits.

In looking at the postwar plans for steel it must be remembered that most people in steel, as in other parts of the economy, were very busy keeping their particular show on the road, whether in the steel works themselves, in the offices of the firms, or in the Federation and the government. The number of well-informed people who could spare any time for a broad forward look based on sustained thought was exceptionally small. Most young and middle-aged men were in the forces or the civil service. Further, there was a dearth of men and women in their thirties and forties capable of taking a forward look. Many steel firms had virtually no middle-management, in the modern sense. The prewar civil service had certainly not trained people to take broad strategic views. Thus the people able to look ahead were first the largely elderly leaders in the firms, drawing on their own lengthy but selectively remembered experience, then a small group of people who took the 'Federation' view evolved by Duncan just before the war and centred on Duncan, Oliver Franks and his small team in the Ministry of Supply, and a few journalists and politicians who relied upon views formed from earlier study, sometimes deep, sometimes shallow, but usually rapid and part-time, of such facts as were publicly available, or were available to them in the civil service on a semi-confidential basis. During the war there was a great deal of coming and going between official, political, journalist and business life, and so a common body of 'knowledge' of the steel industry was built up among these groups. But they were separate groups and remained so.

For the reasons just given – namely the absence of any large group of well-informed middle management with a common body of experience – the basis for judgements about steel was a very slender one. Until Laszlo Rostas published his comparisons of productivity per man in Britain and the United States, for example, it was not known for certain whether there was any gap between the performance of the steel industry in the two countries; all that existed were travellers' tales. 'Ingot' drew up a formidable indictment of the steel firms in 1936 which was incorrect in its technical judgements and muddled up the notion of 'social cost', while the Franks Report, though accepting many of 'Ingot's' arguments, was not as radical as it seemed because, resting as it did upon the submissions of individual firms, it had no objective basis for assessing them, arising from a body of well-formulated managerial criteria.

In assessing the ideas that went into the Franks Report, then, and into BISF's first development plan, it is important not to underestimate the degree not only of uncertainty about the future, but uncertainty about the way to look at the past. There were, indeed, several kinds of uncertainty. There was political uncertainty, as the next chapter will show. The coalition government went on until May 1945 and it was known that some Labour cabinet members wished it to continue. Churchill's Caretaker government took over and it was generally assumed that Churchill's prestige would win an election for it as Lloyd George's had done a quarter century before. There had been a wild boom and then a slump after the Armistice in 1918 and it was supposed that the experience might be repeated. On the other hand, Keynes at the Treasury and influential opinion-formers like Geoffrey Crowther at the *Economist* argued that an era of full employment and international free trade was about to begin once the immediate postwar dislocations were overcome.

When the war in Europe ended in May 1945 it was thought that the war in the Far East might last for at least another two years. In the event it ended in August. In July the Labour party gained a very large parliamentary majority on a radical and detailed programme. Demobilization was slow and measured. It at once appeared that the world economic dislocation was far greater than had been presumed and that from Britain's point of view the chief problem was the balance of payments.

In looking ahead there were several areas of economic uncertainty. What would happen to the prices of coal, iron ore and shipping? If coal prices rose relatively, then home ores (which used a lot of coke in the smelting process) would be uneconomic. If foreign ores were expensive and shipping rates were high, then foreign ores would be uneconomic. Would major new plants cost a great deal more to build than patching up the works that already existed? The Corby example influenced outside critics, but the cautious – or realistic – boards of Consett and Cargo Fleet put up proposals which essentially were for a tidying up of their existing firms. While the macroeconomic calculations by Rostas and others suggested that major integrated plants had given America a high productivity steel industry, and thus confirmed Brassert's judgements, more detailed studies showed that productivity could often be raised just as dramatically by a series of small changes. The implication of this view, of course, was that most of the massive new investment programme was economically unnecessary, a case argued forcibly on other grounds by the economist J.R. Hicks.

One central fact must be remembered. The 1919 experience of wild boom and slump, followed by well over a decade's depression, was deeply embedded in the memory of virtually every man and woman in public life, and especially in those on the boards of directors of the steel companies. Careful, cautious planning was the order of the day in the individual firms.

Inevitably, too, they were bound to be proved right. It was true that in the event, because the pattern and pace of postwar developments were largely dictated by events outside the industry's control, the forecasts made in 1944 were wrong. The Second World War altered the pattern of demand fundamentally. There was a loss of traditional export markets. On top of this there was the unexpected election of a Labour government pledged to nationalization. There followed the Marshall Plan and vast international projects culminating in the European Coal and Steel Community, none of which could be foreseen in 1944.

Despite the caution, however, a need for a radical change in production and structure was recognized within the industry and, as a prelude to the development plan, there were a number of significant alterations in company relationships. One of the most important was the formation of Richard Thomas & Baldwins in 1944 and other mergers were proposed, notably those of the Midlands group, which did not take place, but which led to very close cooperation between the four firms involved.

The need for a radical start was not a new idea. In South Wales, for instance, between 1932 and the outbreak of war, a great deal was spent on a number of new schemes, including the modernization of the Ebbw Vale works purchased by Richard Thomas in 1935. Shortly before the outbreak of war in 1939 this works, following the construction of a continuous strip mill, was producing 60,000 basis boxes of tinplate per week, as compared with an average weekly output of 1,100 basis boxes in the more common antiquated pack mills. A number of other developments, notably Corby, were on a similar scale, and so was John Summers's strip mill at Shotton, built just before the war.

But the scale of the postwar plans was quite different; it was to be a bigger programme altogether. In the summer of 1943 a postwar reconstruction committee was established by B I S F to make recommendations concerning the future development of the industry and the constitution of the B I S F. Behind this lay the knowledge that the Ministry of Supply was preparing its own schemes and was to ask B I S F to submit plans from the individual firms.

These plans were a matter of some complexity because the environment in which they were drawn up continually changed. In the first place the industry was looking forward to the end of the war even before war broke out. Could they get new plants with public money? Who would control the postwar industry? Then, till May 1940, during the 'phoney war' period it was as though nothing had changed. After that, for eighteen months or so, the immediate impact of the European collapse, of the bombing, and the need to allocate raw materials and output, overwhelmed everybody from the Minister to the workers. But, by the winter of 1941–2, people were complaining that the war was being lost; that Britain was not pulling its weight, and it was alleged that the steel firms, in particular, were concerned more to look after their postwar future than their wartime duties.

This was not true, as the last chapter has shown. The records of the firms show how hard the management and men were working. Yet, it had this element of truth, that new developments in steel took a long time; the war could not last for ever, though it might be long; and plans had to be made on the assumption that the firms would survive the war and would have to cope with their own problems. Meanwhile the Ministry of Supply Iron and Steel Control had become separate from the B I S F, though the links were strong. And, furthermore, it is clear that some ministers felt that there should be an official, as opposed to an industry, view of steel. So the Reconstruction Committee of the war cabinet asked the Minister of Supply (in consultation with the President of the Board of Trade) to draft a report 'on the measures required to secure in the postwar period an efficient iron and steel industry which would play its full part within the national economy in expanding the export trade and contributing to the maintenance of full employment.' Professor Oliver Franks (later Lord Franks), head of the Raw Materials Division of the Ministry, drew up the report, known as the Franks Report, on the future of the steel industry, and in response to his request the B I S F drew up its own plans from submissions by the firms. The Franks Report was completed in February 1945 and eventually approved by the Caretaker government that followed Churchill's coalition and circulated to the firms on 17 August 1945.

Oliver Franks was an Oxford philosopher who had become Professor of Moral Philosophy at Glasgow University just before the war. He had joined the civil service and rose rapidly in the Ministry of Supply and became head of the Raw Materials Division dealing with the iron and steel industry. Under the Labour government he became Permanent Secretary of the Ministry of Supply for a brief period, till he returned to Oxford as Provost of the Queen's College, to go, two years later, to Washington as ambassador.

His report was important for two main reasons. First, it established that the government expected to lay down its own conditions for the future policies of the steel industry, and probably in circumstances in which international trade was free. Next, Franks was the first 'outsider' to look at steel authoritatively since Montagu Norman had accepted Brassert's report in 1930. In doing this he began, unlike Brassert, from economics and not from technology.

In all these various stages of planning, the central issue turned on 'efficiency' as opposed to 'profitability'. At a meeting held on 9 November 1944, between representatives of the industry and the Ministry of Supply, 'Professor Franks hoped that the industry would have in mind primarily the efficiency factor. He was aware that other factors such as the social responsibility for a particular region were important, and the government no doubt would pay regard to these social and humanitarian factors. . . . He called attention to two factors specifically mentioned in the remit. First the export trade, the expansion of which was bound to be an important element in government policy, if we are to maintain our present standard of living. Secondly full employment – the government had stated this was one of their postwar aims.'

'Efficiency' raised immediately the question of costs and prices – whether or not they were 'reasonable'. It has been seen that before 1930 prices fluctuated wildly. Moreover, costs fluctuated too, because at full capacity they were low and at low capacity they were high. But at full capacity, were British costs too high anyway? By early 1944 the industry was concerned with an examination of whether the prevailing level of iron and steel prices was one which could be maintained in the postwar period. It was the considered opinion of a senior BISF official that 'if the present return to the industry cannot be improved there is no strong reason to suppose that there would be a need for advancing prices in the postwar period. Should costs rise, however, during the course of the next six months this position would require to be reviewed again.' It was decided that the question of postwar prices could be considered under two main headings: first, what relaxations, if any, could be made in central fund arrangements and, second, what would be the effect of postwar conditions on price levels?

Postwar conditions – the second of these headings – was regarded as incomparably the more important. Looking ahead as carefully as they could, the steel-masters thought that some costs would tend to be lower after the war. For a start, wartime costs would go. The blackout arrangements, dilution of labour and other special wartime arrangements would be removed and costs immediately reduced. At the same time, however, it was hazarded that these economies would probably be offset by continued increases in wage costs and coal prices. It was further felt that there might be some reduction in the cost disparity between high-cost and low-cost firms. The firms whose costs were most affected by the war were, by and large, those which had relied before the war on imported ore. If foreign ore became once more readily available it was felt that their relative position would improve.

As a result of the decline in ore imports home ore consumption increased by 30 per cent over the immediate prewar average consumption. It seemed that prevailing prices for home ores were reasonable, and some of the better equipped mines were producing ironstone at a good profit. This was mainly because of the mechanization of the mines, which had occurred under government exhortation and financing. Another reason was the considerable increase in output. The net result was that home and foreign ore prices seemed likely to be comparable.

Looking ahead into the postwar years it was suggested by BISF that if imported ores became available in prewar quantities with a substantial reduction in pig iron costs, and assuming the prevailing prices of home and imported ores were retained and that an increased output was achieved due to the use of richer imported ores, steel ingot capacity would also increase. This was of tremendous importance because it was estimated that the saving in cost due to a return to 'normal' quality of ores would amount to some £6 million per annum.

At the same time it was accepted that freight charges were unlikely to fall immediately to the prewar level. For example, for at least two years after the First World War shipping rates had remained high, though they then declined substantially in later years. Would such a pattern re-establish itself? Cautiously, it was suggested that it might be wise, therefore, to allow for a 50 per cent increase over prewar charges.

As long as the price of obtaining home ore was below that for imported material, producers, even those who normally required imported ore, would opt for home ore. In order to assist producers to return to 'normal' practices it was suggested that those favouring foreign ores should be given the opportunity of choosing, as far as price was concerned, between home ore with its low price and low iron content and foreign ore with its high price and high iron content. In order to achieve this, while freight rates were at an artificially high level, it was proposed that the government or some central authority should bear the excess costs incurred. 'There is no very strong case for a substantial changeover to home ore. (That is, the removal of substantial parts of the industry from the main coastal districts to the Midlands . . .).'

So iron ore was the first problem. But the biggest single item in the total cost increase was for fuel. The pit head prices of coal in 1944 were 105 per cent higher than in 1939 and 125 per cent above the 1937 level. This cost burden was further aggravated by a disproportionately large rise in blast furnace coke prices. The price of coke increased 130 per cent over 1939 compared with the 105 per cent increase in coal prices. This disparity was attributed to the fact that the prices of the byproducts of coking did not increase at the same rate as coal prices.

The burden of rising coal prices had long been a bone of contention within the industry. As early as 1936 Sir William Firth, then chairman of Richard Thomas and one of the more outspoken leaders of the steel industry, had made an attack on the coal trade in which he argued that it was ridiculous that 150 separate companies should compete between themselves to dispose of 75 per cent of the country's output. World competition made the existence of small family interests competing with each other in major industries impracticable, it merely engendered 'senseless and futile price-cutting competition which can only result in high prices to consumers and low wages to miners'. By January 1945 Firth openly advocated the nationalization of the coal industry. In an address on 'Cooperation in Industry' delivered on 12 January 1945 he said: 'When the war is over, unless we are to say goodbye to efficiency in all our industries firm measures must be taken to bring coal-mining in this country to the same level of efficiency as exists in similar mines in other countries and this, I am afraid, will be impossible without some form of nationalization.' He emphasized that Britain was the only coal-producing country in the world that had made no progress, in terms of output per man employed, for thirty years. This state of affairs was attributed to the fact that cooperation in the coal industry had been based on the profit motive, protected by a quota system that stultified competitive efficiency. Moreover, when chairman of a number of coal companies he found it almost impossible to modernize his collieries because the 'owners' organization had great influence in financial quarters. Impediments would have been put in the way of raising the necessary capital, and obtaining the necessary increased quota. . . .'

Many of Firth's criticisms were voiced in other quarters. According to a *Times* leader of October 1944, the coal industry was 'impoverished by technical backwardness' due to the 'failure of owners and governments to promote a determined policy of modernization . . . the owners have sought quick profits at the expense of ultimate efficiency.'

The significance of this will be well appreciated. Many steel companies had big coal interests. They were blaming themselves, as colliery owners, for problems they faced as steel-makers. The widely accepted solution to coal's problems was nationalization. What, it might be asked, of steel? There the problems to be faced were substantial; the industry faced rising raw material costs, and while it was thought that a return to 'normal' conditions would result in some cost savings it was also emphasized that the increased efficiency of the industry could also help in reducing costs – hence the need for modernization.

Franks' final conclusion on fuel was that 'as coal has been an important factor in causing the increase in British iron and steel prices and as there are no indications that Continental coal prices have risen as much as, let alone more than British coal prices, there are strong reasons for believing that any gap which was existing between British and Continental costs before the war is likely to have become wider rather than narrower. It is clear that a reduction of at least £2 a ton from this level is likely to be necessary in order to put British prices in a favourable position.'

As a result of this the report did not take the view that the industry should radically alter its location. There was no strong evidence that the industry needed to be re-located on home ore sites. But within districts, the report argued, the plants were often ill-located, and it instanced Ebbw Vale, a modern plant finished in 1938, where 'import and handling facilities' made costs 10s (50p) higher than at GKB's Port Talbot works, Colvilles' various works in Scotland and Consett on the North-East coast.

In this discussion, what was at issue was whether or not 'efficient' costs were as low as they should have been. Franks distinguished between such things as the availability of cheap ore, coke, scrap, and proximity to markets over which the industry had little control, and internal factors such as the efficiency of management, and the scale of operation which the firms could control directly:

Great Britain, as the fourth largest steel consumer in the world, has a home demand sufficiently large and compact to allow most of the economies of scale to be achieved whereas countries with smaller home markets, whilst they may produce at reasonable prices some of the more common finished products, are at a considerable disadvantage in providing many of the wide range of steel products they need. Unless, therefore, their natural advantages in the form of cheap high-grade ore and low-price coal are substantial, such countries are likely to continue to import many of their finished products.

On the whole the trend of recent events has been against the British iron and steel industry and in favour of certain countries which have developed their industry in comparatively recent years. . . . It is all the more important, therefore, that the British industry should be as efficient as the country's natural advantages and disadvantages will allow. Given the highest level of plant efficiency the British industry could still be an important factor in world markets.

The importance of Corby in this conclusion must not be underestimated. It was a new modern integrated plant, situated on an ore field, with new workers and new management. It contrasted well, it seemed, with other plants.

As Franks said, it was the quality of management 'which may mean the difference between an efficient and a backward firm . . . there are real problems of technical and managerial staff. . . . The difficulties in the steel industry after the last war . . . left their mark. . . .' This factor was 'all-pervading yet difficult to measure or isolate'; on-the-job training programmes for university graduates were of recent origin but they might help. The exchange of technical information between companies was suggested, together with the international exchange of information by visits to other steel-producing countries. But clearly the central matter was the modernization of the industry's plant. The report emphasized the need for great care over investment appraisal. It also laid great stress on the advantages of the economies of scale. The first question was the case of pig iron. For home ore producers a plant of four furnaces each producing some 3,000 tons per week would probably realize most of the economies of large scale production, but for high grade imported ore this optimum size was estimated at 5,000 tons of pig iron per week. These sizes were much higher than those of many of the blast furnaces then operating: ' . . . a substantial amount of pig iron is still being made in furnaces considerably less than ideal, and many of which are very old.'

'The steelmaking side', according to the report, needed far bigger plants. At Gary (mistakenly placed in Illinois), it was pointed out, a single plant produced 10 million tons a year which was too big for Britain. It was desirable, however, to build big new plants in six or seven districts, and with other specialist plants it was suggested that there would be at most ten major plants when the reconstruction period was over.

At the light finishing end of the industry Franks argued that more large continuous mills should be built. This would require greater product standardization. Rail production was taken as an example. In 1944 there were eleven mills producing heavy rails. The total heavy rail production at this time was some 500,000 tons per annum, 50,000 tons for each mill; an output some 50 per cent below normal capacity. As a result each mill was only employed on rails for short periods and had to switch their output to other sectional material thereafter. The report argued that the concentration of rail production in fewer mills equipped with specialized equipment would reduce costs by as much as £1 per ton of output. The reductions in costs which, it seemed from cost studies, could be achieved throughout the industry were only obtainable by additional capital outlay. Postwar costs of plant construction were likely to be substantially higher than the prewar level. An increase over 1939 of about 70 per cent appears to have been taken as a basis for calculation. It seemed that on average a return of about £1 per ton could be earned by building a completely new plant and there seemed every reason to suppose that a thorough-going modernization programme would pay for itself.

But what would modernization mean in terms of actual projects and capital expenditure? The first issue was the size of the industry. The BISF had suggested that the industry 'should plan and create as a short-term programme, a national capacity for producing 15 million ingot tons per annum, with the possibility of ultimately increasing it to 20 million ingot tons per annum'. This proposal involved an increase of at least 1 million ingot tons or about 7 per cent over the normal peacetime output at prevailing capacity of 14 million ingot tons. Franks argued that the BISF proposals assumed a complete cessation of pig iron imports. This would involve some form of tariff protection for the industry. 'It would appear premature for the government to commit itself to tariff or other action designed to make the steel industry completely self-sufficient.' This was a dreadful warning shot. Unless the industry modernized itself, the IDAC system might be wound up, and the figure of 10 million tons of ingots was used till the third draft of the report.

It must be recalled that this was the time of Bretton Woods and a new international enthusiasm. The Franks Report's radical tone must be interpreted against this background. A major purpose of modernization was to help exports and save imports. Between 1913 and 1929 Britain's share of the world export trade fell from 24 to 17 per cent, whilst that of Belgium and Luxembourg rose from 12 to 23 per cent. Due to the 1929–33 slump, world exports by 1937 were only 14·6 million tons, some 4 million tons below 1929. In 1937 the British share had fallen to 14 per cent of this reduced total. Between 1913 and 1929 iron and steel imports rose from 2·2 million tons to 2·8 million tons. Though they fell away to less than half this figure during the slump they rose again to over 2 million tons by 1937. The prospects for the British industry were thought to depend upon the future

of the German industry and the nature of conditions attached to any international loans or credits for industrial development or rehabilitation. There
was a fear that the United States might use its large-scale lendings to secure
preferential treatment for its industry; accordingly Franks argued that 'the
British iron and steel industry has much to gain from a free, united system
of large-scale international lending'.

Whilst it was accepted that British industry must produce steel at competitive prices – hence the modernization plan – it was also pointed out that
no matter how efficient the home industry a healthy export trade depended
in large part upon the nature of world trade. British tariff policy 'in the
1930s was largely defensive, to deal with the unfair trading methods of
certain other countries, particularly Germany'. As a result of this government
action there was, by 1939, in each of the major European steel-producing
countries a national cartel or price-fixing trade association, each a member
of the international steel cartel (*Entente Internationale de l'Acier*). The main
purpose of this international trade body, it will be recalled, was to control
the export trade by fixing quotas and price controls for each of the main
classes of steel products. Under the 1935 agreement between the BISF and
the other members of the international cartel, United Kingdom export
quotas were fixed on their share of trade in 1934. The other cartel countries
accepted in return an import quota to the United Kingdom of 525,000 tons
per year, although in actual practice expanding British consumption made
it necessary to import more than the agreed quota in most years. Then by
1935 the imports of most iron and steel products into the United Kingdom
were subject to import duties. With the outbreak of war these arrangements
were suspended and the cartel ended, all United Kingdom imports and
exports being subjected to licensing arrangements.

The report argued that 'at the end of that period [of modernization], the
industry should be well equipped to meet fair competition in the home
market, assuming, that is, that coal prices have also been tackled'. The
report added that 'it is possible that, for a year or so after the end of the war,
we will be able to sell most, if not all, our surplus steel production. But if
the German steel industry is left intact, and large German steel exports are
available as reparations, and if US lending has conditions attached to it
which favour the American industry the British export position will be
seriously weakened. Government action in the first instance should, therefore, be directed to reducing or avoiding these two dangers.' At the same
time Franks rejected BISF proposals that in order to protect the home
market and boost export sales a return to the international cartel combined
with a levy on home prices to subsidize exports would be necessary. Instead
the report advocated government action to secure that other steel-producing

countries did not subsidize their exports by charging correspondingly higher prices in their home markets. Failing this, the government would prevent organized dumping by foreign countries in the British market.

It will be seen, then, that Franks assumed a radically changed international position for the British steel industry; in a letter from Franks in May 1945 to the BISF the basis for the development plans was frankly put 'that the government regard the present unfavourable competitive position of the British iron and steel industry as a matter of urgent national concern and intend to give a high place in their plans to a speedy improvement of this position, and are prepared to take special measures to this end. The first aim of government policy will be to secure the rapid completion of a substantial volume of modernization and new construction.'

Individual firms should not be allowed to build as and how they liked. 'Considerable experience in the war period of planning production shows what can be achieved . . . rapid and important increases in production and correspondingly lower costs.' The emphasis should be on 'integration' in works on the same site – not 'purely financial integration'. Low production costs were associated with modern integrated works – Corby, Clydebridge, Ebbw Vale. In the long run, therefore, the aim should be to eliminate old capacity and to restructure the industry round a small number of integrated works.

It was for this reason that the report proposed so large a programme, suggesting that 'two-thirds of the existing blast furnaces should be replaced as soon as possible. At the end of this part of the programme the industry might be capable of producing a third more pig iron with about half the present number of blast furnaces in operation.' In semi-finished steel, 'at least three new units of around 450,000–500,000 tons are required. . . . One of the completely new units, which might ultimately produce 500,000 to 750,000 tons of billets per annum, should be based on the Midland ore field.' In flat-rolled products, 'two new modern continuous mills are required capable of producing 500,000 to 750,000 tons each. At the moment there is no continuous strip mill in this country capable of rolling sheets or plates wider than 50 inches. The motor car industry needs a limited production of wide sheets, up to 72 inches. It would appear therefore that one of the new continuous mills should be installed with a roll length of 80 inches capable of rolling sheets and plate up to a maximum width of 72 inches. For heavy sections, 'one of the most urgent needs is a mill for producing broad flanged beams, used in steel constructional work. No mill of the type required for this production exists in this country and a new plant with an annual output of about 300–350,000 tons is suggested.' Equally dramatic was the proposal for the light bar and strip trade, where 'much of the plant in the light rolling or re-rolling section of the industry is out-of-date according to modern standards. It is probable that two or three new re-rolling mills each with an annual capacity of about 150,000 tons will prove a necessary part of future development.'

This was a huge programme. What would it cost and who would pay for it? According to Franks: 'At current prices it is estimated that the modernization of the iron and steel industry covering complete new projects, replacements and rebuilding of obsolete plants would cost in the region of £120 million.' The money for the programme could be found; between 1932 and 1939 the industry had spent over £50 million on a number of new schemes. In the report any hesitation to continue to invest was discounted; and it turned out that FCI loans, profits under the wartime pricing scheme, and compensation for coal and railway wagon nationalization adequately financed the programme.

Much of the specialized equipment would obviously have to be purchased from abroad, particularly the United States, although the foreign exchange problem could be alleviated in part by taking some plant from Germany as reparations. Even allowing for an estimated expenditure on American contracts between £6–8 million in dollars, it was thought that at least five years would be required before the major schemes could be completed, because of the need to 'expand and improve the British plant manufacturing industry'.

These major schemes were designed for industrial efficiency, but full employment had to be achieved. As for employment, however, 'the picture was not entirely rosy. There would be no extra employment in steel in the development areas. If, however, the government persuade or otherwise cause a firm to locate its plant or disperse its plant in a way that adds significantly to the cost of the steel produced it should be quite clear that the responsibility is that of the government. This would inevitably carry with it the responsibility to see that the particular firm was enabled by the government to earn as high a profit as it would have done had it not been deflected from its decision.' On a more ominous note, however, it was also emphasized that 'such a commitment is however hardly compatible with securing maximum efficiency in industry and a price for British steel which will stand up to the fair competition of other countries.'

7

The Early Days of Peace

The war did not so much end as peter out; the fall of Germany took some months, between February and May 1945, and the war with Japan was then expected to last for several more years. The end of the Japanese war in August was unexpected. It did not catch the steel industry unprepared however. In this chapter we look back to the period of the preparation of the plans with which the industry faced the peace and to their implementation. It is necessarily political, because the industry's plan became the subject of intense political debate, ending in complex legislation. After the politics has been sorted out, a return will be made to steel properly considered.

The postwar plans of the industry were drawn up and took effect under difficult circumstances. There was first the switch from war to peace, and the unsettled conditions of the postwar world, economically and politically. In addition there was the fact that the Ministry of Supply had a policy for the steel industry, mainly drawn up by Sir Oliver Franks, now its Permanent Secretary, which ran counter to what had been received doctrine in the industry at large until the middle of the war, and which was still probably unacceptable as a whole to many steel firms. And, above all, a Labour government, pledged to the nationalization of the steel industry, had been unexpectedly returned to office, and the steel industry's chief official, Sir Andrew Duncan, who had been a leading minister in Churchill's wartime government, was now in the somewhat anomalous position of an independent Conservative-sympathizing Member of Parliament for the City of London.

As has been shown in previous chapters the price exacted by the government for the protection afforded by the Import Duties Act of 1932 was the reorganization of the industry and increasing governmental intervention in its affairs, including the fixing of prices under the auspices of the BISF and the cartel. There had also been acceptance of a doctrine developed by the Bank of England of industrial self-regulation which had a long history in Conservative philosophy, and which was accepted widely abroad by regimes of many kinds, from Nazi Germany to Roosevelt's United States. The main thrust of the plan, then, was to be the firms, acting together through the BISF, with government backing as appropriate.

One main theme of the Franks Report was the necessity of reducing British iron and steel prices. Action along two major lines was advocated.

During and after the war, iron ore and scrap were in short supply. Lincolnshire ore (above) *was extensively quarried and scrap was urgently collected* (below).

First Phase   Second Phase

Chase that SCRAP!

Iron and steel scrap is needed—*urgently*. Get it into the scrap merchants' hands! For the sake of the whole national effort—send in your scrap.

This appeal is made to works only. Transport and other facilities may make it possible to widen this later to cover household and other light iron and steel scrap.

BRITISH IRON & STEEL

The modernization of the steel industry began in 1945. Above is Stewart & Lloyd's remodelled Clydesdale works, and below a new welding machine at Corby.

Consett (above and below), *inland in Durham, was also remodelled in the postwar period. But still, as at* Shotton (overleaf), *the open-hearth furnaces were of a traditional design.*

STEEL
IS POWER:
THE CASE FOR NATIONALISATION

BY WILFRED FIENBURGH & RICHARD EVELY
of the Labour Party Research Department

"A most valuable contribution
to the current controversy
on the socialisation of.
Britain's iron & steel industry"

—*from the foreword by Morgan Phillips,
Secretary to the Labour Party*

net **3/6** net

"*Evening News*" (London)

"I suppose we'll 'ave a lot of those chaps in black coats and striped trousers 'anging around 'ere if they nationalises steel."

Nationalization – for and against (above). Was bureaucratization inevitable (the people in the below left cartoon are Labour cabinet ministers), and were the steel companies robbing the nation (below right)?

THE ARMING OF THE KNIGHT

THE GREEDY FINGERS OF THE STEEL MOGULS

Hugh Dalton (above left), *Chancellor of the Exchequer, firmly supported nationalization. John Wilmot, Minister of Supply* (above right), *tried for a compromise, supported by Herbert Morrison* (below right), *the Lord President. In the brief nationalization, Steven Hardie* (below left) *became chairman of the Iron and Steel Corporation of Great Britain.*

One of them, the first, was clearly impractical. It was for a reduction in the price of coal by at least 50p per ton. This would still leave coal prices some 75 per cent above 1939 levels while at the same time allowing a reduction of approximately £1 a ton in the average costs of producing steel. In the event this proposal was soon to be seen to be pure fantasy.

The second was a major modernization programme at a cost of at least £100 million. Hopefully this would reduce the overall price of steel by a further £1 per ton. This policy was adopted. In the event, it expanded capacity and at the same time helped to raise rather than reduce prices. Responsibility for seeing that the firms took the necessary action was placed on the BISF, although the necessity for government aid was recognized. There were many indications that the BISF accepted this responsibility. In 1944 it appointed an Economic Efficiency Committee, representative of all sections of the industry and having the assistance of consulting engineers and metallurgists. This committee was set up to advise firms on proposals involving substantial extensions of capacity and major schemes of reconstruction.

Its report appears in part as appendix 2 of the Franks Report. Government action was foreseen in such things as the control of coal prices, the control of imports, the control of iron and steel prices, the control of investments, the control of pooling arrangements, the location of new plants and obtaining American and German capital equipment through the release of American dollars and reparations agreements. Also, and above all, there was the argument that 'a five-year capital programme of this type should form an important part of postwar employment policy. Not merely would it enable the government to estimate more accurately the volume of private investment, but also it should make it easier, by arrangement with the industry, to accelerate or retard the rate at which the programme is undertaken according to the current needs of the employment situation.'

If the proposals for a five-year programme were to be accepted by the firms, the BISF and the government – as they were – there remained the question of the necessary government powers and machinery. Before the war the government's powers were largely a byproduct of the Import Duties Act 1932. The IDAC had been established in 1932 to consider applications for tariffs and to submit recommendations to the Board of Trade. The committee consisted of three members appointed by the Board of Trade and it had a small staff of its own. Franks looked ahead to free trade and in the immediate postwar years tariffs were not thought to be an appropriate way of controlling imports. Such limitation as was necessary could be best achieved by a system of import licences. Consequently, much of the IDAC machinery was redundant and in its place Franks advocated

Opposite The main architect of steel's postwar plan was Oliver Franks whose unpublished report was the foundation of official policy for the coalition, Labour and Conservative governments.

some form of quasi-independent commission dealing directly with a wide range of industries and advising the government on such matters as efficiency and prices. 'The merit claimed for the commission form is that it provides a buffer between the minister and the interests concerned. Any government body dealing with the iron and steel industry ... should ... satisfy three criteria: it should be in touch with the mainstream of government economic policy (e.g. the employment, commercial and location policies); it should provide for the clear location of responsibility on the government side; and it should have available the technical and specialist advice necessary to enable it to reach an independent decision.'

The exact means by which the government was to exercise its influence over the industry was an important issue. There was no necessary reason to suppose that the interests of the industry would always coincide with the national interest. It was for this reason that existing B I S F machinery had to be supplemented at official level. In the event a commission – the Iron and Steel Board – was set up in 1946. But by that time nationalization, a word studiously avoided by Franks, was a matter which was causing deep dissension. The dissension, it must be emphasized, was not over government control but over public ownership.

It was the almost universal acceptance of regular and coordinated development plans under central coordination, with official government approval, which marked the period 1939 to 1945 as something of a watershed in the industry's history, and profoundly affected the attitude of official, industrial and public opinion to nationalization.

It was certainly true, in one sense, that nationalization would make little difference to the industry, since many of its major decisions – on development, on pricing and on foreign trade – were subject to government assent, if not to public initiative. In another sense, however, the matter had symbolic significance, since most manufacturing industry was not in public ownership and even the nationalization of public utilities and fuel was controversial. A major shift of the frontiers of public ownership was widely accepted, but a shift into manufacturing seemed to raise issues of principle that deeply divided the country. Nationalization had practical significance, too, because if nationalization were to amount to a merger of the assets as coal nationalization did, decisions would be taken without too much overt acknowledgement of the separate firms' interests. It was, as we shall see, the firms that were of great significance since it was they that remained virtually unchanged by merger or winding-up for thirty years, and it was their boards which drew up the plans for the development of the plants.

Already, in the 1930s, the Bank of England and its ally, Sir Andrew Duncan, had been thwarted by the individual firms in their desire for regional and product 'rationalization'. In some instances the firms had acted directly contrary to the wishes of the Federation. During the war, the Federation became more important, chiefly because its own personnel became the personnel of the Ministry of Supply, which controlled steel. Even when non-steel men came in, like Franks, though home truths were uttered, they were not all that unpalatable to the Federation and at the end of the war, when the wartime control was adapted to become the Steel Board, in essence the wartime system was continued – firms, Federation, board, Ministry of Supply – in which the firms acted far more closely with the Federation than would have seemed likely ten years earlier.

Nationalization, therefore, stands out as a central point around which further discussion on the industry was bound to centre because it had the special character of seeming gratuitously to intervene in a system of public control that was widely accepted as a model which other industries might well follow. This view probably encouraged, more than anything else, the deep feelings of anger that nationalization aroused in the firms.

The roots of nationalization went back a long way. The trades unions had proposed it in a mild form in 1931. 'Ingot' had discussed it seriously in 1936; during the war Professor G.D.H. Cole and many other people argued for the nationalization of iron and steel. The model for a state-owned commercial board existed in London Transport and other industries were gradually being taken over by boards similarly composed. The experience of public control of the industry since the early 1930s was considerably developed by the wartime experience when government controlled supplies, determined prices, attempted to re-jig management in some firms and bought much of the output. Could this system of control be extended to formal public ownership of the firms?

The Labour party put steel nationalization into the programme called *Let Us Face the Future* on which it fought the 1945 election, held on 5 July and in which, as the votes were counted on 26 July, it won an overwhelming parliamentary victory. It was widely thought that Herbert Morrison, who was principally in charge of domestic policy, was not an enthusiast for this particular policy. Hugh Dalton, the Chancellor of the Exchequer, was, and so too was Ernest Bevin, the Foreign Secretary (and, after the Prime Minister, the most powerful member of the cabinet), and Sir Stafford Cripps.

The Bank of England, the railways, the hospitals and coal were to be nationalized, beyond question. In coal nationalization most of the big steel companies and some of the small ones lost large parts of their activities, eventually receiving exceptionally generous compensation for them. But to nationalize steel itself was a more complex task because of the great heterogeneity of the industry. It also had powerful friends at Westminster, in the

City, and in Whitehall. Nobody could pretend that coal was an industry that shone like a diamond in the imperial crown. The coal-owners were said to be detested by the miners and had little sympathy among the public at large. But steel? True, nobody could love a steel-master, but nobody knew who they were anyway. The workers in steel seemed happy and prosperous. Above all, the industry through the B I S F and the statesmanlike Sir Andrew Duncan seemed to be cooperating with the government in its development programme. The Iron and Steel Control was staffed mainly by ex-B I S F members to whom a few other people had been added. What the nation wanted was, it seemed, done by the industry, if it were possible and reasonable, without any fuss and bother. Certainly it seemed that steel was not making excessive profits. And, too, there was a development plan which was soon accepted by the government. So steel nationalization seemed less necessary to fair-minded people than other extensions of public ownership and it became more controversial as a result.

A key person in this matter was Sir Oliver Franks. His economic advice was listened to by the cabinet with great attention, and he was an expert on steel. Unusually for steel, he was neither a Scotsman nor an accountant, though he did come proximately from Glasgow. His judgement was thought to be mature beyond his years; aged forty he was over thirty years younger than many of the steel leaders. His report underlay the view of the civil service machine and of opinion-formers on the future of the iron and steel industry. Nationalization was not among these plans; on the other hand, what he proposed was not incompatible with it, though his joining the Iron and Steel Realization and Holding Agency in 1953 which denationalized the firms suggested that he was not an ardent nationalizer.

The Franks Report was presented to the coalition government in April 1945, but the response came from the Caretaker government which followed it. The report was circulated, as government policy, in August 1945. It is essential to make this clear because the exact sequence is important. The coalition government included several senior Labour members of whom two – Bevin and Dalton – were keen to nationalize steel. The Caretaker government excluded them but still included Duncan, the B I S F independent chairman, and it accepted the Franks Report, including the idea of an independent government commission to regulate steel. But two months later there was a Labour government which was committed to nationalizing steel and included Bevin, Cripps and Dalton, while Duncan, to his surprise, was on the opposition front bench.

These political changes led immediately to a discussion of the exact manner in which steel was to be controlled before it was possible to nationalize it. It was agreed that the public interest was to be safeguarded by an Iron and Steel Board. The terms and character of this board were agreed by the Ministry of Supply officials and the BISF, before the July election, and plans for its formation went ahead but thereafter the notion of having a board was distrusted by some socialists lest it was a device to stave off nationalization and by many steel firms because it was a possible vehicle for nationalization.

The longer-term uncertainties were obscured by the continuity of personnel and policies at the official level in the Iron and Steel Control of the Ministry of Supply and their close links with the BISF officials, who had worked together, and who were either in or out of the civil service by the pure accident of whether a post was categorized as an official or industrial one.

Steel was relatively low down on the list of industries to be nationalized; the Bank of England and coal were first, steel and sugar towards the end. The minister in charge of home policy, including nationalization, Herbert Morrison, the Lord President, was not himself an enthusiastic supporter of steel nationalization. In April 1946, Benton Jones of United Steel concurred with W. S. Morrison, the Conservative MP, that Wilmot, the Minister of Supply, did not want to nationalize the industry. The chief advocates of steel nationalization were Ernest Bevin, soon unwell and struggling with the Cold War, Hugh Dalton, who resigned as Chancellor of the Exchequer in 1947, Sir Stafford Cripps, and Aneurin Bevan, the Minister of Health, who became increasingly disenchanted with the government's performance. The 'new men', like Hugh Gaitskell, were at that time largely technocrats, with no desire to pass great cumbrous Acts of Parliament to show that they were true socialists if their aims could be achieved by other and less controversial means. At that time there seemed little reason to suppose that the industry was not 'playing ball'; it was doing largely what Franks had said it should, and Franks was soon once more in the public service as ambassador to Washington and one of the leading economic advisers of the government who had principally negotiated the Marshall Plan. The case for nationalization was largely an *a priori* one.

But that case was not wholeheartedly accepted, as has been seen, by Morrison and Wilmot, despite the government's announced intention in May 1946 to nationalize the industry. As a prelude to nationalization the government established the Iron and Steel Board in September 1946 under the chairmanship of Sir Archibald Forbes (a typical figure in the steel industry since he was a Scots accountant), 'to undertake the review and supervision of schemes for the modernization and development of the steel industry'. As early as June 1946 the government had approached the BISF inviting them to nominate four members to serve on the Control Board, two of whom the government would appoint. The board was 'expected to consist of six members, including a member of the general public, an accountant, a labour man and the chairman – one of the "steel" men was to be deputy chairman'.

The response to this approach was markedly cool. In a private meeting with Ellis Hunter the president of BISF and Sir Andrew Duncan the chairman of BISF in June 1946, the Minister of Supply, John Wilmot, said that the ultimate form of nationalization had still to be determined although he believed it unlikely that a board on the lines of the National Coal Board would prove desirable for steel. The Minister therefore suggested that it might be a help to the industry in ensuring a practical solution if they had representation on the board. In reply to this suggestion Ellis Hunter said pointedly that advice on any practical point could be secured from the Federation without representation on the board. No doubt this reluctance to be associated with the Control Board mirrors the Federation's opposition to nationalization. The lack of enthusiasm for the Control Board was most marked in the early months of its existence. In a letter from Sir Archibald Forbes to Ellis Hunter in November 1946, we find Sir Archibald writing: 'Now that this board has entered into the second month of its existence it is anxious to make some progress with its main function – the review and supervision of schemes for the modernization and development of the steel industry – and the board is somewhat perturbed that no major scheme has yet been submitted for its consideration by the Federation.' In a discussion with BISF in November 1946, Forbes, in an attempt to overcome these differences, took the view that any bureaucratic control of the industry was quite wrong and made it clear that the board did not intend to interfere with the administrative side of the industry but purely supervise broad policy.

The steel firms were passionately opposed to nationalization. Opposition from within the industry to the government's intentions may best be illustrated by reference to the minutes of a meeting held at Steel House in May 1946. Dr A.M. McCance, of Colvilles, a fierce Scot, said flatly that 'it was difficult to proceed with the Dalzell scheme until details of the government's plans were announced. . . . He felt the issues with the government should not just be confined to an undertaking regarding financial expenditure as there were wider issues involved.' This threat was spelled out even more directly by G. Baker of John Baker & Bessemers who said that 'progress would have to be held up until either nationalization was out of the way or the government undertook to find the money'.

Others were more cautious, but still implacable. Ashley Ward of Park Gate held that 'the threat to the financial position of the company was still an obstacle', while W. Killingbeck of Barrow Hematite Steel thought that 'the company had no right to go ahead with the scheme owing to the present uncertainty as to compensation'. His firm's financial record was not exactly brilliant but he made his point nevertheless, while H. G. W. Debenham of Skinningrove said tactfully that 'the company were anxious to go ahead but would require an undertaking regarding financial compensation before doing so'. Sir Charles Wright of G K B said, statesmanlike, that the company 'could not proceed with their major expenditure until the position was clearer'.

After discussion it was agreed that the B I S F should inform the government of 'the grave difficulties which made it impossible to proceed at the present time until discussions had taken place with the government which would remove some of the uncertainties and difficulties surrounding the present position'.

The industry, led by Duncan, Ellis Hunter and Benton Jones, cooperated shrewdly with Franks and his officials, and played a canny game. By 1945 the B I S F, under the presidency of Ellis Hunter, as Allan Macdiarmid had died suddenly, adopted a new constitution to coordinate the activities of the producers of each of the industry's main group of products. This was an attempt to incorporate the subsidiary price-fixing groups. Once more the B I S F's role was seen as being mainly advisory and every effort was made to ensure the greatest autonomy of individual producers. It was felt, however, that the magnitude and nature of the problems facing the industry necessitated a greater degree of 'central guidance' than was originally envisaged.

When Labour took office, there were in fact no detailed plans for nationalization; only a pledge to do it. In May 1946 a White Paper proposing to nationalize steel was issued. According to Herbert Morrison, then Lord President and chairman of the cabinet committee dealing with nationalization, Attlee raised with him a letter from Sir Andrew Duncan, proposing an Iron and Steel Board (not a statutory one such as was established in 1953 but in most other respects identical) to regulate the industry. Morrison negotiated with Duncan, and reached agreement on Duncan's scheme, together with John Wilmot, the Minister of Supply, and Ellis Hunter, the president of B I S F, after a series of meetings in the summer of 1947. In late July 1947 this agreement was then repudiated by a cabinet committee, chiefly on Aneurin Bevan's and Hugh Dalton's initiative, according to Dalton, who believed the 'compromise' was due to a lack of enthusiasm on Morrison's part for nationalization. Talks were broken off on 11 August 1947. As a result, Duncan and the steel barons felt they had been diddled; Morrison, in charge of the legislative programme, was less than enthusiastic for the bill that came forward; and the Labour cabinet showed signs of strain over nationalization. When the Iron and Steel Bill was debated on second reading (17–18 November 1948), it was clear that though G. R. Strauss, the new Minister of Supply, was speaking from conviction, the high tide of the socialist flood was over, as Hugh Dalton was later to note.

Apart from the general argument for nationalization which applied to all concerns, and the argument for the control of 'basic' industries, like fuel, transport and steel, there were particular arguments for steel. One, which was rarely put directly, was that the TUC and the Labour party had been specifically committed to nationalize steel since the early 1930s and to retract now would seem to be a serious defeat for the middle and left wing of the party. But, more specifically, the steel industry was a 'monopolistic' industry (the word more correctly but less frequently used was 'oligopolistic'). A monopoly, or oligopoly, economists from Joan Robinson to Allyn Young agreed, restricted output, raised prices and slowed down the rate of technical progress. Evely, one of the authors of the most persuasive book advocating nationalization, was secretary of the International Co-operative Association and editor of *Cartel*, devoted to the analysis of monopoly.

The case was that prices were too high, because the rate of profit was fixed on over-valued and out-of-date capital assets. The Central Stabilization Fund meant that 'a price is fixed in relation to the costs of production of a representative firm. But some firms are so bad that they cannot make a profit at this price. So they are paid money which has been contributed by the consumer. This means that they can keep on paying dividends.' The basis for this statement was the annual reports in wartime of the House of Commons Select Committee on Expenditure.

On investment, the examples of Jarrow and of the near-failure of Ebbw Vale were used to show that the existing firms were not interested in social and regional policy, while the investment that had been undertaken had not led to greater efficiency because it had been frittered away on bolstering up individual firms. This was in conflict, of course, with the social and regional argument just presented, but the conflict was partially resolved by indicating that with lower prices and greater efficiency, total output would be higher. In particular, importance was attached to home-ore sites – Corby once more loomed large – and to the need for integrated steel plants.

The arguments for nationalization were partly socialist – that is to say, that property should not be privately owned – and partly what might be called generally 'economic', in that unemployment could only be averted if major investment goods industries were directly publicly owned and enabled to run at a loss if necessary to gain wider public benefits. In steel, however, there were more particular arguments. These were that the division of control between four levels had led to unadventurous investment decisions, that in consequence the industry was unnecessarily inefficient, and that

Opposite *Teeming steel into ingot moulds at Port Talbot.*

public ownership would enable the bureaucratic system necessary to control a private monopoly, to be dismantled.

The compromise of the Iron and Steel Board exercising control while the firms stayed in 'private' ownership was rejected on the grounds that it would be bureaucratic, that it gave insufficient powers to the centre to drive for modernization, and that it left the monopolists – or oligopolists as they should surely have been properly called – in effective control of the industry and 'they want to play the old game of big demand, plus small supply, equals high price . . . there is no guarantee that firms will be willing, should circumstances alter, to undertake the developments to which they are committed.' Since monopoly was inevitable for technical reasons, the conclusion was that only a publicly owned industry would be fully responsible to the public. 'Greater efficiency depends, in the long run, upon a gradual remoulding of the geographical pattern of the industry. . . . It means building new towns in the right places . . . and providing other work for the people who are left behind.'

As the debate proceeded, industrialists and managers had moved from the spirit of 'pulling together' to a deep anti-socialism and anti-nationalization that welled up especially strongly over steel nationalization. The spirit was conjured up by the steel industry. The various Nationalization Acts created boards to run industries and the appointments to them varied from the dull to the bizarre, ex-generals and ex-civil servants looming as large as they not very adequately could. The nationalization of coal was followed by (but did not cause) a fuel crisis; the railways needed vast capital investment to become efficient as their rolling stock was obsolete and worn out; it followed that nationalization was not regarded as a panacea for industrial ills, and the concept of a board owning and controlling the assets was not as acceptable as it had been.

The matter of the form of steel nationalization came to cabinet several times. Finally, a bill was prepared. It followed the now usual pattern of acquiring the companies, rather than the assets, as had been the case of the coalmines; but it left the companies as the major operating units, with the Iron and Steel Corporation of Great Britain as a holding company.

The structure of nationalization perpetuated much of the system that had been set up during the war. First there was the Ministry of Supply. Then there was the corporation, replacing the Iron and Steel Board, which in turn had replaced the Iron and Steel Control. The B I S F was to continue as an independent entity. The firms, owned by the corporation, and their boards appointed by it, were to continue. In the circumstances the maximum amount of confusion resulted over any major investment decision, since effective initiative rested with the firms, and the corporation (which was

Opposite *Soaking pits at Anchor.*

keen to build a steel plant at Rosyth for example) was not easily able to exercise an independent initiative. The structure was completely different from the coal industry, where the coal-mining assets – not the firms – had been nationalized, and grouped into regional bodies. This grouping appeared in the three or four years after nationalization to be conspicuously unsuccessful, both from the point of view of financial losses, of managerial ability and of coal output. But, ultimately, it was to be the pattern that was to prove durable because it enabled assets to be rationalized. What coal nationalization did show, of course, was the acute shortage of managerial skills for larger bodies, and the need for major physical investment programmes to close old pits and develop new ones. Similar problems arose with the railways, and also arose in the private sector as larger groupings came about in many industries.

As a result of all these comings and goings the steel nationalization bill was delayed till late on in the Parliament and since it was long and complex it took a long time to pass through all its stages. It was also said to make steel 'a political football', although the steel firms had never been politically neutral and nor had the unions. In 1936, for example, Lysaghts, Richard Thomas and United Steel were paying £100 a year each to the Conservative association in Brigg, the division where Scunthorpe was. When the bill was finally law, in 1949, the Parliament was so near its end that the Act's full implementation was delayed until after the election, which took place in February 1950, leaving Labour with a small majority and the possibility, perhaps the probability, that the Conservatives, pledged to denationalization, would return to office relatively soon. The Iron and Steel Corporation of Great Britain was appointed, in which was vested the securities of all the major steel companies. No 'steel-man' except Sir John Green would serve on the corporation, and S.J.L. Hardie, the chairman of British Oxygen, and inevitably a Scot, was appointed chairman.

It would be stretching the truth, however, to say that the personnel of the Corporation was impressive, though it would also be stretching the truth to imply that they fell far below the level of most persons serving on the boards of the steel companies.

When Hardie was appointed, Ellis Hunter effectively refused him all collaboration with the BISF. Meetings never took place between the two, although minutes suggest that they did, since Hunter was convinced that he had been diddled once by Herbert Morrison and any creature of the government was capable of infinitely bad behaviour. In January 1951 many firms, including United Steel, refused to cooperate with Hardie about anything until legally obliged to do so. This will give an idea of the zeal with which nationalization was opposed.

8

The Reconstruction of Steel

That then was the political background to the first development plan (as for convenience' sake we shall call it). In this chapter we describe the drawing up of the plan and its implementation. It must be remembered that there were three major matters in the background. The directors of the firms were deeply involved in discussions about the future of the industry, in which their own careers and position were at stake. The next was that the initial programme of projects was hastily assembled and as experience was gained its character inevitably changed for technical, financial and idiosyncratic reasons. Thirdly, as the plan progressed, increasingly memories of the 1920s and 1930s were forgotten, and the prospects for the 1950s and 1960s became more and more important. A future of permanent, though not necessarily steady, economic growth was a likely possibility and, for the first time since the First World War, significant technical and managerial development came to the forefront of the discussion in almost every firm and plant.

The Plan and Productivity

Ellis Hunter, as president of BISF, was largely responsible with his officers for drawing up the December 1945 plan, issued in May 1946 as a White Paper. Sir Andrew Duncan – an 'independent' Member of Parliament – was back as chairman of BISF, while Sir Archibald Forbes became chairman of the Iron and Steel Board. It was upon those three men, and their staffs, that the planning of the industry largely fell, though the projects that they discussed and circulated originated with the firms as we shall see.

The one thing agreed by all parties to the dispute on the future ownership and control of the industry was that the first plan was broadly acceptable. At the end of the war the industry was in a strange state. That is to say, its output was high, profits were satisfactory and it had done a good job in the war. But much of the plant was old and out of date and to face the modern world the modernization plan had to be substantial. Would it be like 1919 to 1921, a boom and then a slump? Would foreign countries and especially

Germany reconstruct their industries and engage the British firms in inter-national competition? It was this sort of possibility that the first plan was designed to meet. It was a compromise between caution and hope. The general objective of the first plan was to modernize and increase steel capacity to 16 million tons per annum – an output reached in the war but greatly above that of before the war. That is to say, moderate economic growth was allowed for. More important, it was assumed that output would average 94 per cent of capacity, or 15 million tons. In other words, full employment was expected. In addition, half a million tons of imported steel was assumed, this figure having been agreed following discussions with the government. This suggested that foreign competition would not greatly intensify. The total supply of steel was therefore to be $15\frac{1}{2}$–16 million tons. During the interwar years, the demand for steel rose. Home deliveries in the five years 1920–4 were about the same as in the period 1910–14 – just over 5 million ingot tons. By the end of the 1930s deliveries had doubled, to over 10 million ingot tons in 1935 to 1939. What had happened was that consumption per head had risen. According to the steel industry this was attributed to the use of improved methods and equipment in the manufacturing industries. This led to the increased use of material per worker per unit of time. Partly, too, however, the rising standard of living in the interwar period showed itself in an increase in the use of domestic equipment in houses and a greater use of steel for consumers' goods – cookers, refrigerators and cars were obvious examples.

The BISF looked ahead to 'a slower increase in consumption per head than was experienced in prewar years' in the early 1950s. They also pre-dicted intensified international competition. This led them to regard the 1950 output target as one that would represent a sort of plateau. But the use of steel would change, as the prewar experience had shown, with its decline in the demand for steel for shipbuilding and the rise in the demand for steel for building.

The maintenance of full employment was a crucial assumption. It was partly because of this that in the BISF report a great deal of consideration was given to the location of proposed iron and steel developments. Regional unemployment had been serious and steel had played its part in adding to the number of unemployed in Scotland, Wales and the North of England. But chief among the factors influencing location decisions was a new fact – the wartime rise in the price of coal. This rise in coal prices tended to make production on home ore sites, where ores were of lower grade and required additional fuel for smelting, relatively less advantageous than it had been before the war. Development on cheaper foreign ores was likely to be cheaper.

In December 1945 the total cost of the iron and steel programme for the first development plan was estimated at some £168 million. The annual expenditure envisaged rose to a peak in 1949, and fell to very little by the early 1950s. Most of the planned investment was in small units. It was on this basis, of supporting projects in the pipeline, that the development plan was undertaken. Investment had to be approved by the government. The development plan was issued in May 1946 as a government White Paper. The five-year plan was designed originally to be a series of proposals for investment to be completed by the end of 1950. Its central feature was a target. That target was for 16 million tons a year for the five years 1950–4. The largest of the schemes was the construction of a completely new plant, including a continuous hot strip mill, at Margam, South Wales. The remaining £104·5 million out of the total of £168 million was to be allocated between thirty-eight other schemes not considered urgent enough to warrant immediate ratification, including schemes at Corby (£16·5 million), Scotland (£20 million – including a continuous hot strip mill), and at Consett in the North-East (£10 million – also including a new continuous hot strip mill). The plan therefore involved the construction of four new steel plants, including three new strip mills at a total cost of some £60 million, as well as a whole series of smaller developments.

One of the major difficulties was that much of the new equipment needed would have to come from America. Europe lay in ruins. The problem was to get the dollars in order to avoid unnecessary delays in the execution of the plan. It was recognized, though grudgingly by the government, that some plant would have to be imported from the United States. R. M. Shone, secretary of the BISF, wrote in February 1947 that 'the main effect of importing certain items of steel works plant from America for the modernization and development plant is to speed up its completion'.

Not only dollars were short; there was also a severe shortage of coal. The earlier the modernization of British steel production could be achieved the greater the possibilities of economies in fuel consumption; these were estimated at some 25 per cent per ton of pig iron and steel. Speed was thought to be essential to achieve these fuel economies. Once more, however, fuel shortages were not destined to last for ever. The more general case for speed lay not only in the saving of dollars, and of coal, but in greater all-round efficiency. In the first place there was likely to be a dramatic reduction in capital costs. 'Another consideration bearing on the import of plant from America is the greatly increased cost of the schemes if the building period is spread over ten years. This means not only greater aggregate expenditure on plant and buildings but loss through locking up productive capital over an extended period.' The other side of this coin was, of course, a rapidly increased productivity of labour. It was argued that with new plant and adequate fulfilment of the plan an increased output of steel would be secured with an important reduction in the amount of labour required per ton of output, 'thus making possible a much more efficient utilization of the labour force in the country'.

Assuming a high level of capacity working and no change in the 1946 pattern of working hours it was estimated that at most two thousand men could be saved on the production of pig iron; largely due to the fact that on completion of the plan there would be additional blast furnace capacity for 1·75 million tons of pig iron with twenty-nine fewer furnaces.

Similarly the plan also provided for new steel ingot capacity of some 5·8 million tons, replacing 4 million tons of old furnace capacity and giving a net increase of 1·8 million tons. The fact that this new furnace capacity was to consist of large modern furnaces, mainly at integrated works meant a greatly reduced labour requirement per ton of steel ingot produced. The extent of this potential labour economy can be appreciated from the figures of steel ingot output per head at Richard Thomas's works in the first half of 1946; at Ebbw Vale 686 ingot tons were produced by each worker; at Panteg it was 229 ingot tons, though admittedly Ebbw Vale was a bulk steel-maker and Panteg specialized in stainless steel.

In the light of hindsight, the plan seems somewhat cautious; it was below the productivity levels that a few years later the defeated Germans and Japanese were to achieve and it was below the American levels already achieved. But, in fact, criticism at the time tended in the opposite direction. Although generally accepted by the government and those in the industry, the development plan was not without its detractors. Thus a London automobile engineer raised the following questions in a letter to Sir Andrew Duncan: 'Whether you really considered that the iron and steel industry would propose, in more normal times to spend as much as £168 million on extending its production from 13½ million tons per annum to 15½ million tons per annum ... should the government's proposals go awry, the industry might find it is saddled with a promise which economically it ought not to keep.'

The Plan and Prices

One major question that has to be explored, therefore, is productivity and efficiency. This was related, as the automobile engineer's letter showed, to prices. If the right price policy were adopted for the industry, the incentives to achieve efficiency would be very strong. It has already been shown that for many years competition between firms was limited by agreements fixing prices and allocating orders and the exchange of directors. After the establishment of IDAC, and joining the cartel in 1935, the industry officially regulated some matters. At the end of the war, as has been seen, free trade was envisaged as the probable international environment, but it was agreed that 'a common system of prices should be established by agreement within the industry, subject to government approval', and what Franks referred to as 'an appropriate price policy [which] may assist the general plan for raising the efficiency of the industry'.

The BISF report of December 1944 held that such a policy should seek to determine maximum prices – not minimum prices – so that price levels were related to the costs of efficient plants and a reasonable return must not only be allowed upon the capital invested, but the return must be adequate to enable the industry to set aside a sufficient amount towards replacement of plant, research and development. Above all, a small rate of profit on a large turnover should be aimed at rather than vice versa and price levels should, if possible, remain constant for a period of at least six months.

Steel is not one thing. It is a huge variety of different products. So there had to be a wide-ranging price policy to cover all those products. But on what basis? The wartime price control raised the issue directly. Up to 1941 only primary steel products had their prices controlled. This control was undertaken on the basis of ascertaining production costs in representative firms, deriving a weighted average which allowed for tonnages produced and then allowing for a mark-up for profit and depreciation.

Under the 'Shone'-type system a number of 'prices funds' were established to subsidize high-cost producers and imports. Sir Allan Macdiarmid argued that this led to distortions so that firms did not feel the true impact of costs. As a result, inefficient firms were kept in production. According to Macdiarmid, both Shone and the industry 'were caught up like Laocoon in coils of such complexity that they could never be untangled'. In this context Shone himself later argued that the artificially low steel prices of the postwar years were at the expense of profits and hence internal funds for investment.

Elizabeth Ackroyd of the Ministry of Supply who had helped to draw up the Franks Report later explained the price control system. It was of average cost for each of a hundred or so groups, plus a standard margin for profits and depreciation. These were maximum prices and were imposed under the Defence Regulations. At the same time the Industry Fund imposed a levy on all producers that was used to reimburse high cost producers. Export prices were controlled by the various manufacturers' associations. In practice, of course, the maximum prices were regarded as standard prices.

Indeed, some of the firms found that they were in real difficulties. Prices were controlled. Profits, though good, could hardly finance so relatively large a programme. Now there was the threat of inflation which raised the cost of the investment to be undertaken. The firms were all different from each other. They were autonomous. They could be cajoled, exhorted, persuaded, but in the last resort they were independent of the government and the B I S F. In writing about the industry, therefore, it is important to realize that the story is the story of the firms and the plants that they owned. Some firms were big and diverse. Some were small and specialized. In this book it is possible to pick out instances of firms that were of special interest, either because of special problems, remarkable achievements or an outstanding man, in order to build up the picture. Inevitably the picture was more complex than can be presented in the confines of one (or many) books, but what is put here is, it is hoped, a tolerably fair picture.

The Plan and Its Implementation

The postwar plans for the steel industry envisaged a series of new plants on new sites and, above all, a series of developments of existing sites. Several things had to be considered. Were old works to be closed? And, if so, were the new works to be located at or near the old works? What new technical and economic considerations arose, and what was the balance of these considerations as compared with social considerations, such as unemployment and regional development?

The capital equipment of the industry varied from the fairly new to the very old. It will be recalled that there were two relatively new strip mills at Shotton in North Wales and at Ebbw Vale in South Wales. There was a new integrated steel and tube works at Corby. Lancashire Steel and Sheffield specialized in wire, and Sheffield in high-quality alloys and other special steels, all produced in relatively modern plants. The North-East coast concentrated on plates. Scotland specialized in plates, too, but produced something of most things. Each area had its own special character. Thus Colvilles dominated Scotland, R T B dominated South Wales, while Sheffield was the domain of United Steel and Corby of Stewarts & Lloyds. In the plan the development of products was not to be exactly proportional – sheet steel for example was to develop more than plates – and, above all, the shortage of pig iron was to be tackled. It followed that different areas had different rates of development and therefore, and above all, that the firms had different policies about expansion.

Putting all this together a pattern of future development emerged, especially in the proposed regional schemes of the development plan. In what follows we look at the plan and its implementation, in the light of the circumstances in the latter part of the 1940s.

In *South Wales*, a crucial area with severe prewar unemployment, the plan said that 'the strip mill has been located in South Wales because it is necessary to choose a site well placed for imported ores and making use of existing labour and experience'. In other words, South Wales had to be developed on several criteria, and indeed South Wales best illustrated all the problems of the industry. Many old works were virtually derelict. Ebbw Vale was a great new works in what many people thought of as a geographically highly unsuitable site. But South Wales had suffered from chronic mass unemployment and both the coalition and the Labour governments were determined to create full employment by every means in their power, including a full-scale regional policy. Hugh Dalton, President of the Board of Trade in Churchill's government, and Chancellor of the Exchequer in Attlee's, was especially determined to see the regional policy fully implemented and steel nationalization was proposed as one means among many for doing so. Against this background, therefore, the decision was taken to urge the building of new works in South Wales. Another problem then arose – how was it to be financed and organized, either through a new company, or existing companies, pending possible nationalization? The answer to this was by a series of mergers and joint holding companies and, in particular, the Steel Company of Wales (SCOW), formed largely by RTB, the new amalgamated South Wales firm.

Richard Thomas, under E.H. Lever's calm direction, did a good job during the war. Ebbw Vale proved invaluable. In 1942 the firm began a reassessment of its colliery interests. The firm was thoroughly profitable, paying $6\frac{1}{2}$ per cent on its preferred shares, and an ordinary dividend of 5 per cent. By 1944 this had increased to 10 per cent and $12\frac{1}{2}$ per cent respectively. When these rates were voted, Sir James Lithgow resigned from the board in protest. The troubled days of the 1920s and 1930s were well behind it. Electrolytic tinning was to be introduced, using American methods, after careful study, and links began to be forged with Baldwins.

The board was a competent though conservative one. It decided to reorganize but to retain its colliery interests; it sought to influence government policy in the tinning industry but not to pre-empt it, though agreement was obtained from the Ministry of Supply that it would have priority after the war in introducing electrolytic tinning, and in fact agreement was ultimately given by Professor Franks to start installing the new process during the war. The problems of modernization in the tinplate industry were under continuous review in South Wales, and a 'syndicate' was proposed to instal a new strip mill. This led Lord Dudley to propose 'active cooperation' with Baldwins. This was in the context of a redundancy scheme, agreed by 94 per cent of the trade, that led to the closure of a great many small mills which raised acute problems for the Board of Trade, that Hugh Dalton eventually cut through and solved. In November 1944, Richard Thomas bought Baldwins for £5⅔ million despite Sir William Firth's passionate protests.

The first board meeting of RTB was held on 25 January 1945. It was a new-style firm dealing with new problems, and the board discussed letters from Professor Franks of the Ministry of Supply and talks with Hugh Dalton, the Labour President of the Board of Trade. Having Lever of the Prudential in the chair, and Colonel Neilson, a chartered accountant on the board as joint managing director with Lever, showed how dramatically different things were since 1938; the government was infiltrated by socialists and academics who exercised real power, and the firm was run by businessmen. The death of Sir Edward Boyle on 31 March 1945 symbolized the end of 'the shareholders' as a powerful force, and the drowning in a torpedoed ship of Beaumont Thomas, and the death of his son Nigel in Normandy, tragically signified the end of the Thomas steel dynasty.

In August 1945 E.H. Lever outlined proposals for the modernization of the South Wales steel and tinplate industries: 'The South Wales Scheme'. According to Lever, 'the need for further modernization of plant in the tinplate and sheet industries has long been recognized, but progress has been difficult on account of the large number of small independent companies, especially in the tinplate industry, owning small units of plant, and by reason of the fact that modern methods demand large individual units which can only be erected at a very high capital cost.'

This puts one major problem of the steel industry in a nutshell. With the exception of RTB's modern plant at Ebbw Vale the output of tinplates was produced mainly in hand or 'pack' mills. This method had been superseded by a new process of high speed continuous-rolling which was much less arduous for the workers than the old hand-mill method. The first step towards the modernization of tinplate manufacture in South Wales was a redundancy scheme evolved by the trade itself and put into effect by the Board of Trade in 1945. Having cleared the way by the redundancy scheme the next step was to formulate a coherent plan for the South Wales Scheme. This involved close collaboration between two big firms. The dominant figure in the industry was Lever. His proposals included a scheme for the erection at Port Talbot of an 80-inch hot strip mill capable of producing 18,000 to 19,000 tons of output per week. This would be the major scheme for South Wales. Alongside it would be two other schemes. The first of these was the conversion of the old-type sheet mills owned by Lysaghts (a subsidiary of GKN) at Newport into a modern cold reduction plant. The second was a proposal for the erection of two large cold reduction plants for tinplate. In October 1945 RTB and Guest Keen & Nettlefolds agreed to build a hot strip mill at Port Talbot, and two cold reduction plants in West Wales. Technologically and economically the whole proposal had been one scheme. Why was it proposed as three parts? E. H. Lever told the Treasury on 14 November 1945 that 'the most economical arrangement both from the point of view of capital and working costs would have been for the two new cold reduction plants which it is proposed to erect in West Wales to be located on sites adjoining the proposed new Hot Strip Mill' – that is at Port Talbot – but for 'sociological reasons' this arrangement did not accord with the ideas of the government departments concerned. They were seriously concerned with unemployment. Tremendous pressure was put on them by Members of Parliament, some of whom held high office in Attlee's government. Their wishes were for the hot strip mill to be located at Port Talbot, which was what RTB wanted as well. But they also wanted one of the cold reduction mills to be in the Swansea district and the second cold reduction mill to be in the Llanelli district. This was what the Board of Trade, especially concerned with regional policy, proposed to the companies. In reply to these 'suggestions' – suggestions backed by strong authority – Lever pointed out that 'from the point of view of capital costs, it is obvious that the arrangement will increase the cost of providing various services and other items in addition to increasing our machinery spares'. Moreover, 'the interposition of handling and freight charges between the processes owing to hot strip having to be conveyed from Port Talbot to Swansea and Llanelli for further processing will naturally increase the costs of manufacture'.

He therefore thought that 'the government should compensate the parties both for the increased capital costs and for the higher working costs which will result owing to the proposals having to be brought into line with government policy.' Particular abhorrence was expressed at the use of the steel industry as a political football, a development which had delayed much needed structural reforms. The main case for nationalization was that the steel industry was in a confused state; in South Wales that fact could hardly be denied since it was evident to the most casual observer. Thus, in the belief that 'the best hope of heading off nationalization lies in keeping the matter out of the political field', Lever forwarded a number of 'revised' proposals, arguing that it was necessary for the industry to prove the economic validity of its argument by deeds and not by words. This could be done by ensuring the efficient operation of the new scheme. To achieve this end the new proposals involved the formation of a separate company to acquire the assets of GKB at Port Talbot, Lysaghts at Newport (a subsidiary of GKN) and other such works 'as is necessary to complete the integration of the new developments'. It was out of this proposal that the Steel Company of Wales was developed. This company was to revivify large parts of South Wales. Its formation is therefore of special interest. The arguments in favour of the proposal to form a new company centred around the technical and economic advantages of establishing an integrated plant with an identity of financial and economic interest. But 'integrated' did not mean quite what it seemed, since the works were geographically scattered and it seems that 'integration' was used to refer to 'the identity of interest between the ownership of the hot mill and the cold reduction mills. . . .'

In order to avoid the problems of divided responsibility under a system of joint control it was suggested that one of the major companies interested in the Port Talbot and Margam works of GKB, that is GKN or RTB, should buy the other out. After a series of complex negotiations a conclusion emerged, best expressed simply, that because GKN lacked appropriate experience of the tinplate trade it was felt that the works should be under the auspices of RTB. Lever was a powerful, magnetic man. RTB was his firm. A major stumbling block to the Lever proposals, however, concerned the position of the Lysaght cold mill under the new scheme. A suggestion that the Newport mill should be transferred to Margam was resisted by Sir Samuel Beale, representing GKN, on the grounds that it would be detrimental to the interests of both the management and shareholders of GKN. Lever had little faith in the compromise proposal that some co-operative arrangement between the new company and Lysaghts could be devised. Lever said, 'speaking only for myself, I take the view that much as I dislike nationalization in its application to the whole industry, it would, in this case, be the lesser of two evils for the undertakings to be under one control and owned by the state than to have divided control under private ownership.'

By the end of 1946 members of the BISF development committee not directly concerned with the South Wales Scheme reviewed the disagreement between RTB and GKN. After much deliberation it was decided that the 'overall efficiency of the plant was of paramount importance and that this could be best achieved by physical integration of the cold sheet mill with the hot mill'.

This was a major development. It had its origins in the weak state of the Welsh tinplate industry and the desire to rationalize it. The government, especially, wanted to bring prosperity to Wales. And, with nationalization now proposed, the firms sought to make a pre-emptive strike. The works to be taken over by the new company included fourteen tinplate works belonging to RTB, but excluding its Ebbw Vale works; the Port Talbot and Margam steel-making complex of GKB; four tinplate works of Llanelli Associated; and the Briton Ferry Steel Company. It was also proposed that a new company, a subsidiary to SCOW, should be established to purchase the two Newport steel works of Lysaghts.

In a 'last minute decision' the Briton Ferry Steel Company decided to opt out of the scheme because of prior demands upon their liquid resources – viz: the construction of a strip mill producing 5,000 tons of steel per week and costing £1¼ million. This decision, however, although (to put it mildly) inconvenient did not radically affect the proposals.

At RTB a vigorous policy of closure, such as of the Grovesend and Gilbertson works, was adopted, and a final winding up of those firms and their managements were put in charge of the West Wales sections, scheduled for closure, while T.O. Lewis and H. Leighton Davies were put in charge of the new cold reduction plants. Loan stock was issued at 3½ per cent for £2½ million, and coal nationalization, accepted as inevitable, increased the liquid capital available by £800,000 as well as £141,000 for railway wagons following the nationalization of the railways, and so reduced the advance required from the Finance Corporation for Industry. Thus it was that SCOW came to build Margam, and that eventually other works went ahead as planned. That, then, was how the South Welsh firms reacted to the plan. They had serious problems to face.

The *North-East coast* was another area with severe unemployment. Discussions were held in early 1945 between the steel-makers, including Chetwynd Talbot, and Sir Andrew McCance and Sir John Duncanson, the iron and steel controller, about a merger and rationalization of the local companies, a recurrence of discussions that had taken place on and off for twenty years. A holding company was suggested. Similar negotiations took place elsewhere, especially between United Steel and Stewarts & Lloyds – with a view to setting up new firms to deal with the major reconstruction the industry would require after the war. None of these negotiations were successful, though they continued till well into 1947.

It is interesting to speculate why these mergers never took place. Partly it was because the legal negotiations were tedious and complex. Partly it was because the senior men were indeed very old, and did not wish to seem to pre-empt choices. But, above all, there is the sense that life just went on, immensely busy. On 25 July 1945, for example, Cargo Fleet approved a plan to spend £5 million over the next five years, and till 1950 the spending of that sum – which steadily increased – preoccupied the management. At Consett, the neighbouring firm, a series of major plans was drawn up, and by the autumn of 1944 a scheme of £4½ million was approved. By the summer of 1945 the firm was going ahead with a modernized melting shop and a new plate mill. Its discussions with Dorman Long on a 'ten-year plan' for the two companies were essentially a side issue to the major concern of the firm which was its own redevelopment programme. By an irony, in February 1946 Sir Charles Bruce-Gardner became a director and he who had been the arch-rationalizer became a shrewd counsellor to the well-run Quaker firm that every rationalization plan had closed down or moved. In November 1946 the problem that BISF faced in fitting together the plans of the different firms was well illustrated by Consett. The firm's plan, now well under way, had risen to £5·2 million but South Durham was also building a plate mill, and the country urgently needed more billet capacity. Since Stewarts & Lloyds were building up their billet capacity, Consett fell back in the queue for approval, and the South Wales strip mill project was also given priority. So Consett had to await approval – with consequent delays in supplies, building permits and labour. In the delay BISF raised once more the question as to whether Consett was the right location for iron and steel and the firm considered moving, not to the Tyne as originally proposed, but to the Wear. But in the event they got an allocation of £9¼ million to buy plant, and they stayed where they were, observing the 'North-East coast scheme' with some cynicism. They manfully played their part in discussions with Ellis Hunter and Forbes, but drew attention to the uncertainty of the times, that to close down Cargo Fleet's Hartlepool works would cause unemployment, and that the previous three approaches for a merger with South Durham and Cargo Fleet had been a failure. The most that could be hoped for was some financial link-up between the firms to finance development, and in 1949 Consett agreed to concentrate on heavy plates, leaving light plates to South Durham. The net effect of all this discussion was the preparation of a plan to spend a further £7 million on new billet plant and to leave Consett where it was. By the early 1950s, then, the North-East coast had a series of reconstructed plants but no merger had taken place.

In *Scotland* the position was different. The development plan proposed concentration of new schemes on the Clyde. According to the memorandum of January 1946, 'the advantage of location on the Clyde as compared with the existing Scottish locations is not very large . . . viewed over a fairly short period of time, therefore, it hardly appears economic to make the change. Unless, however, a change is made at some stage, Scotland will be permanently saddled with production at an unnecessarily high cost level. Also, the long-term planning of the industry would be prejudiced. To attempt to make the necessary replacements of obsolete plant by expanding at the existing works would stretch to the uppermost limit the present plants and would prevent the full economies of modern layout ever being fully realized.' The proposal was for an integrated works on a deep water site. Scotland, however, as has already been seen, largely meant Colvilles, since the other firms were small, except for Stewarts & Lloyds which had an agreement with Colvilles and whose main works was now in Northamptonshire. Colvilles was a federation of several plants, scattered over a wide area, from Glengarnock near the Ayrshire coast, to Clydebridge, Dalzell and elsewhere round Glasgow. It was run by Sir John Craig, with the technical expertise of Andrew McCance, the managing director, dominant in the formulation of policy.

During the war the firm was fully extended, and nearly £1 million was spent on new plant. In the autumn of 1943 Sir Alexander Dunbar of BISF wrote on behalf of Professor Franks to enquire about proposed capital expenditure in the five years after the war. By the autumn of 1944 Colvilles replied, proposing to spend £5–6 million on a new melting shop at Dalzell, a continuous billet mill, a light section mill, a wheel and axle plant, and improvements to the plate and sheet mills. Their priorities were to do deferred repairs first, then to replace obsolete plant but not to expand capacity, then to replace some obsolete plant with a potentiality for higher output, and only then to allow for expansion. The firm was run still as a collection of subsidiaries with group finance and group sales (though some individual agencies were retained) and it is clear that the delay in reorganization before the war had created a firm with a number of powerfully rooted local concerns that could not easily radically change.

In December 1945 the BISF proposed schemes costing £31 million for Scotland, including a £22 million integrated works on the Clyde like that originally proposed by Brassert to Lord Weir; Colvilles were fundamentally opposed to the scheme, and suggested instead that the Clyde iron works should be developed to remedy a local shortage of pig iron. Discussions dragged on, and in early 1947 Colvilles said that 'some investigation of the position at the present time had shown that economically, neither Gartsherrie nor the Clyde site recommended by Brassert was as suitable as the Clyde iron works site.' By the summer of 1947 Colvilles told BISF that for £15 million they could develop the Clyde iron works, together with other developments (such as those originally suggested in 1944) at Clydebridge, Glengarnock and Motherwell for £15 million, which compared favourably with the £28 million an integrated works would cost on a deep water site. The Minister of Supply was 'being pressed politically' about Scotland, and Craig suggested that Colvilles' and Scottish policy should 'be based on our own capacity to sell and not on any arbitrary percentage of the United

Kingdom production'. By Christmas Eve the Iron and Steel Board was regretting the omission of a deep water scheme from the development plan, and Colvilles and BISF were to submit alternative proposals. Bairds and Scottish Steel, the other major firm in Scotland, were keen to build new blast furnaces at Gartsherrie, and Stewarts & Lloyds, irritated by Colvilles' restrictive attitude, decided to build additional blast furnace capacity at Clydesdale for the tube works. Colvilles ploughed steadily on, however, and finally agreed to seek to proceed with a scheme for a section mill at Glengarnock, a four-high mill at Clydebridge, a continuous billet mill in Lanarkshire, blast furnaces at the Clyde iron works, an ore handling plant and extra coke ovens, estimated to cost £20 million.

This plan, though big, was a conservative one. In 1948 Sir John Craig at seventy-four years of age had completed sixty years service with Colvilles. Sir Andrew McCance, his successor, was already sixty years old. The younger management was correspondingly kept down. Sir Archibald Forbes was concerned that Motherwell was far more expensive than a deep water site would be; McLintock's, the accountants, investigated the costs of the two proposals. But Colvilles won. Gartsherrie, the blast furnace plant proposed by Bairds and Scottish, was withdrawn and the deep water site sank into oblivion. Throughout this period there were continual worries about the shortage of pig iron, and the demand for steel – especially steel plates – was extremely high. Colvilles reached record output levels. It is interesting that the firm should have been so resistant to major schemes at any new site and that its own plants were only extended with seeming reluctance. The financial position was reasonably secure and the firm had a substantial body of highly competent staff and workers. It had, however, an inherent caution, perhaps born of the unhappy 1920s and 1930s, and even when it was nationalized it did not change its tune about the outlook for investment in steel in Scotland. Before the Colvilles scheme could be approved the Iron and Steel Board was dissolved, and because of financial uncertainty, and the view of the National Coal Board that Scottish coking coal would not be fully developed until 1964, only relatively minor parts of the schemes were proceeded with – notably the blast furnaces – as immediate needs manifested themselves. Colvilles therefore did not in any sense meet the terms laid down by BISF and the Iron and Steel Board for a national plan.

It may be seen that the plan was based in practice upon individual firms, and emerged from their own proposals. A national plan was not laid down and the regional consequences worked out. The plan was the sum of the firms' plans. Proof of this, if any is needed, is shown in the case of the *Midlands*, which included the North-West coast, the Lancashire and

Opposite *Temper mill at Gartcosh.*

Cheshire coalfield, the Birmingham area and Lincolnshire, Yorkshire and Northamptonshire.

In Lancashire and Cheshire, in order to build a fully integrated steel works, and because there was no suitable site on the Mersey, the major development was to be at John Summers, at Shotton in North Wales. The Lancashire Steel Corporation was an important part of the industry, but its plans were exceptionally cautious.

In 1944 Lancashire Steel's cash surplus was embarrassingly large and its profits were sufficiently great to enable it to float ordinary and preference shares. John E. James reached the age of seventy in that year, and he kept a strong control of the firm, agreeing with some apparent reluctance to a plan to spend £1½ million in two years for the renewal of plant and equipment. The development scheme for the first plan was to cost a mere £600,000. Indeed, no major programme was prepared until the second plan – when in 1951 it was proposed to spend £6·7 million out of the firm's own resources.

John Summers also made good profits in the war, though it was still closely supervised by the Bank of England, which prevented an amalgamation with United Steel, Lancashire Steel and Stewarts & Lloyds in 1943. But in August 1945 the Bank of England debenture was repaid, and a major postwar plan was agreed, to finish the strip mill, to build a new steel works, to put in a new slab mill, and to raise output. This scheme eventually cost £13¾ million – considerably above its estimate – but it left Shotton as a major steel producer.

The outlook was less bright on the *North-West coast*. In the January 1946 memorandum it was said that 'steel production on the North-West coast is not likely to continue to be economic for a long period. Barrow steel works is already highly uneconomic and it would appear undesirable to spend money in an attempt to increase its efficiency. With the decline in demand for acid steel, the economic basis for a substantial industry on the North-West coast is disappearing.' The United Steel works there were chiefly concerned with rails, whose production had been concentrated at Workington with transferred production from Steel, Peech & Tozer and Samuel Fox, and acid steel was produced from local ore, together with ore imported from Sierra Leone and Norway. The source of profits in the group was the collieries, which were nationalized in 1947. In the event, it was decided to concentrate on producing iron ore and limestone, to feed two blast furnaces producing hematite iron – 300,000 tons a year – and a Bessemer steel plant, which fed rail and cogging mills. Total expenditure in the first plan was £2 million; output was raised slightly, and the plant modernized; but Cumberland was no longer a major part of the industry.

About the *Birmingham* area there was no doubt. According to the BISF

Opposite *Making tubes is a major steel activity.*

memorandum of January 1946, 'the availability of scrap and local markets makes it desirable to have a scrap-using works in the Birmingham district.' It was on this basis that Round Oak was developed.

The crucial decisions concerned *Lincolnshire, Yorkshire and North-amptonshire*. As far as the BISF was concerned, 'the main developments in the Lincolnshire area, the new billet mill at Lysaghts and the modernization of section production at Frodingham, are as much development in the Lincolnshire area as should be envisaged in the five-year plan. . . . It may be undesirable to envisage further building in Lincolnshire in view of the ore limitations.'

The question at issue was the whole future of major new green field sites. The existing programme was a patch and mend affair. Here was a possible new breakthrough. The planners were undecided as to whether there should be an amalgamation of the Lincolnshire works, concentrating on Appleby-Frodingham, or the development of production on a new site – possibly on the Humber. It was pointed out that 'a Humber site, to which both ore and coal would be transported, would not represent low-cost production of billets as could be achieved on a home ore site to which coal alone was transported.' Eventually it was decided that the new integrated plant should go to the better situated Consett-owned site on the North-East coast. The proved pattern was to be kept.

In November 1944 the Midland group of firms prepared two alternative proposals for an integrated steel works producing half a million tons of billets. They also approved the rebuilding of Lord Dudley's Round Oak works. But by March 1945 it was thought such a plant would be uneconomic as imports would be cheaper.

The board of United Steel was deeply involved with national plans and knew the priorities agreed with the Ministry of Supply. Hilton and Macdiarmid had been presidents of BISF. So by September 1945 a new integrated works was proposed by United Steel and Stewarts & Lloyds jointly, though with reluctance. There was a possibility of a new works at Corby; another possibility was a site near Grantham. One of the problems in running the firm was that the people running divisions were often extremely elderly; in 1945 when James Henderson, who had been commercial director of Appleby-Frodingham died, he had joined Frodingham fifty-six years before. In 1949 when Gerald Steel became managing director, Benton Jones who had joined Rother Vale in 1902, remained executive chairman. The effective head of the firm was Gerald Steel who had been sent a series of fatherly letters by Hilton in the years 1929 to 1931, while he was running the Indian end of United Steel, indicating that he was being groomed for the top. His apprenticeship had lasted a long time. It was a big firm, with wide interests, and it thought of itself as a nucleus of the Midlands grouping that was to amalgamate with Stewarts & Lloyds, Lancashire Steel, and John Summers, with all of which it had close connections. It sought to buy Redbourn from R T B in 1946 and it financed its own reconstruction as the other firms did. Above all, it faced the prospect of a major development at Scunthorpe.

Its major new concern was Appleby-Frodingham. It had started out as a number of separate plants; 'in the middle thirties vast extensive programmes were planned and in part executed. A modern blast furnace plant went into operation in 1939. . . .' In January 1944 it was proposed to add major new coke ovens, to add two blast furnaces, and to replace the section mills. As the plan developed, those mills were altered to include a cogging mill, and extended, at a cost of £3 million. It will be seen, therefore, that in the first plan, the emphasis was on consolidating Appleby-Frodingham, which was also a major source of iron ore. The major project planned was the Seraphim blast furnaces, on which the preliminary work was done in the first plan.

The firm as a whole spent £20 million under the first plan. The major outlay was at Steel, Peech & Tozer where trade in rolled steel was expanded by the expenditure of £3 million, while at Samuel Fox there was an expansion of the alloy steel production by the expenditure of £2 million. The effect of this expenditure was largely in cost reduction. As a result the United Steel group had rationalized its output; it had organized its managerial structure; and it was ready to undertake further major development of over £33 million in the second plan.

Meanwhile Stewarts & Lloyds decided to spend £4½ million on urgent postwar expenditure, and when Sir Allan Macdiarmid died suddenly just after the end of the war his successor, A. G. Stewart (who joined the boards of United Steel and Tube Investments) presided over a board that decided to spend £38 million on reconstructing and extending the Corby works, and a further £5 million on the Stanton iron works. Clydesdale, too, required £2 million to be spent on it. In fact the work proceeded more slowly than was foreseen, largely because of shortage of plant and shortage of housing. A great deal of effort was spent on preparing a major 'greenfields' scheme at Corby, to raise output to 1¼ million tons, which in the event was not proceeded with, and the extension of Corby works was continued.

It will be seen, therefore, that the Midlands plan, which rested upon a series of major new developments, was somewhat abortive. It led to a big expansion of output at Corby, to major plans at Scunthorpe, and to cost-reducing expenditure at Sheffield. But, in essence, the big growth occurred in the second and third plans, not in the first, at least as far as United Steel was concerned.

The Plan and Its Achievement

How much did the first development plan succeed in achieving its objectives? To answer that question, the objectives have to be looked at carefully and set against the actual achievements. Certainly by mid-1946, 'there was an impression in the City that steel firms were not proceeding with modernization owing to the proposals for public ownership. It was agreed [by the United Steel Board] that this view applied only to certain Scottish firms and not to the bulk of the industry.' Nevertheless, after September 1946, some steel firms were not undertaking capital investment in their coal mines for fear that the expenditure would not be reimbursed under nationalization. Nationalization and its attendant hopes and fears certainly played its part in delaying the plan. 'First impressions of the operation of the Coal Board', reported one steel firm, 'present a gloomy picture. It appears that . . . the Civil Service model is being followed, little or no individual discretion being permitted.'

The first development plan drawn up in 1945 was in effect a five-year plan, due to be completed by the end of 1950. However, by December 1947 it was recognized that completion would not be achieved until 1952 or even later. Indeed, even as late as February 1952 it was found that expenditure was only 70 per cent complete, while by December 1952 the actual cost of the first development plan was given as £401 million in 1952 prices. The original 1945 estimate of total cost was (in 1952 prices) £340 million – or £168 million in 1945 prices. Partly the hold-up lay with raw materials. Fuel, especially coal, was extremely short. John James was worried about supplies of scrap in 1947, and felt that the low prices offered for it unduly reduced supplies, by making people keep machinery going far longer than was necessary. He was correct. The BISF policy was to discourage scrap exports but it reduced the supply of scrap by keeping scrap prices down. As a result it increased the need for pig iron production, and so increased the costs of the development plan. The shortage of raw materials and the acute shortage of labour made the whole matter of the increase of capacity and its modernization very difficult.

Steel itself was as a result in virtually permanent short supply. For instance Sir Robert Barlow of Metal Box put pressure on the government to increase supplies of tinplate. The Ministry of Supply also pointed out that new American mills were far more productive than those in Wales. The explicit accusation was that the Welsh tinplate firms were deliberately slowing up their expansion programme. Lever of RTB was furious at this accusation; and it had a direct effect in hastening the development of the Margam plant to a larger capacity than it could reasonably be expected to find a demand for. It also led to a conflict between RTB and SCOW for extra capacity that neither believed in, and which they thought would leave one or the other with a surplus of steel on its hands.

The major debate at first was about home and foreign ore. The industry, and especially the BISF and the Ministry of Supply, held that foreign ore would eventually be abundantly available. Traditionally, heavy industries were located near their sources of raw materials because the costs of transport were so high that it was cheaper to move the finished product to the market. Where coal and iron ore were close together, a steel works tended to be built. As British ore became less suited to several important processes, and as its costs of extraction rose, cheaper foreign supplies were used and these came chiefly from Europe, so that iron and steel was no longer necessarily located on or near the chief sources of raw material. Ports to unload the iron ore had become more important in the interwar years.

The possibility of building a steel plant in or near Corby or Scunthorpe, or even in North Oxfordshire seemed attractive when foreign ore, at the end of the war, was about a quarter or a third more costly than home ore, even after allowing for the costs of reducing it. When you added to this cost difference an absolute scarcity of shipping, reflected in high charter rates, it seemed that a serious error of judgement had been made in not concentrating expansion on home ore fields, but the major firms and the government disagreed with this view and they turned out to be right. After 1951, the terms of trade began to move in Britain's favour. New reserves of ore were discovered, and others were developed, in Mauretania and elsewhere. Freight rates fell and big new ships began to be built which were significantly more economical for bulk transport than earlier vessels. There were those in the government service who had argued for a site that would be suitable for 'cheap' home ores; this implied the use of a basic Bessemer process and a site near a berth suitable for large ships should the foreign ores turn out in fact to be cheaper; this suggested Immingham on the Humber.

Even so, a high output of home ore was maintained and serious attempts were made to survey the reserves, and to increase output. But Corby was not much expanded beyond its original possibilities and no new steel works were built in Oxfordshire on the orefield there which was big enough to allow a major development and on which Stewarts & Lloyds were negotiating a site.

Indeed, from 1946 to 1956 ore imports rose from 6·7 million tons to 14·8 million tons. In this great expansion BISC (Ore) Ltd. took a major part in the search for new ore fields – Conakry and Mauretania for example – in which it often took a financial share; it helped to push for the building of new ore carriers, of larger size, especially developed for iron ore, and it helped to prepare the redevelopment of ore terminals in the ports. In the process the picture of ore supplies was revolutionized. Home ore production, which had been a chief concern of those critical of the siting of new capital investment in steel, became less significant as a proportion of the whole than it had been; and cheap foreign ores became a central determinant of the future plans of the industry.

It followed, then, that the postwar plan envisaged sites chiefly away from the home ore fields, and the issue then became one of the appropriate location of new developments on existing sites. Here the pressures were for existing works to be developed. The major Scottish scheme was modified in favour of development on existing sites. The gain to be secured from transferring a major part of production from the centre of Scotland to the Clyde coast arose from pure location and raw material grounds. There would be greater proximity to markets and much easier importation of ore. But the likely gain was insufficient to compensate for the very substantial extra capital cost which would have been involved in transferring production from the Motherwell area to the Clyde estuary. Once this decision had been made the pace of development in Scotland was largely determined by the availability of coking coal supplies, which gradually expanded. Corby was a new plant built just before the war. The decision to develop the existing Corby site meant that the pace of expansion was set by the availability of labour. This in turn was determined by the rate at which new housing could be constructed.

In order to raise the capacity of the industry from the 1945 level of 14 million tons to 16 million tons by 1952 the development plan envisaged building twenty-four new blast furnaces, all over 20 ft hearth diameter, by 1952–3, that is a building rate of rather more than three furnaces per year. Up to 1949 only five furnaces had been completed, giving an effective building rate of only 1·25 furnaces per year. By December 1951 the building rate had risen to 1·5 furnaces per year and nine furnaces had been completed. Even as late as June 1954 only eleven new furnaces had been constructed. Thus, in spite of the fact that the new units, particularly basic pig iron furnaces, were larger than previously anticipated – in June 1954 27 per cent of all operational furnaces were over 24 ft hearth diameter – the average output per unit, due to the retention of older furnaces with a hearth diameter of less than 18 ft, was lower than envisaged by the 1945 plan. For example, the average weekly output per furnace for basic iron was 137,000 tons in 1954 compared with the 1945 estimates of 160,000 tons to be achieved by 1950. All told, the extent of these delays is indicated by the fact that after the war it took some four years to build a blast furnace, compared with two years before the war and two years in America.

Nevertheless, in spite of these delays the production of basic and hematite iron rose from 5·9 million tons in 1945 to 7·7 million tons by 1949. Similarly steel production rose from 11·8 million tons to 15·5 million tons. However, according to a 'Review of Present and Future Iron and Steel Making Capacity' produced by the BISF advisory committee on development in July 1950, 'the considerable increase in steel output achieved since 1945 has been mainly due to such factors as the use of oil firing, the continuous working week and high scrap charges. New construction and modernization completed up to the end of 1949 has only contributed approximately 30 per cent of the total increase.' Existing capacity was being used more fully and more effectively, and small but significant innovations, like oil firing, were being introduced. But this was not the great programme of cost-reducing modernization that might have been hoped for. As the memorandum said: 'The short fall in modernization and concentration mainly arises because the three new integrated plants in Scotland, North-East coast and the Midlands have not gone forward. This delay has been largely due to rising capital costs. [Indeed] . . . the high cost of new plant and other factors, including in the case of Northamptonshire, labour availability, have caused a postponement or extension in the timing of the larger projects.' It was this that set the scene for the second plan.

9

New Problems and Solutions

The Government and Industry

In the autumn of 1951 the Conservatives were returned to office pledged, among other things, to denationalize steel. The immediate effect on the industry was negligible since in its brief period of office the ISCGB had done little to change matters and it was soon given a standstill order by the Minister of Supply, Duncan Sandys. But in the next decade the effects of the form of denationalization were profound, since it 'preserved' the firms, and it subjected them to a negative rather than a positive supervision. By the time the industry was renationalized, according to a White Paper in 1973, 'investment in the British steel industry during the mid-1960s was low compared with that of its international competitors, and the companies from which the corporation was formed in 1967 were, in general, financially weak. Nationalization brought to BSC a large number of works with obsolete technology and low productivity.'

This chapter traces the path that led to that situation. First, it was not certain that steel would be denationalized but on 12 May 1952, in the evening, Mr Winston Churchill told Sir Ellis Hunter that the government would proceed, and in November 1952 the bill to denationalize was presented, together with a structure of public control as originally agreed by Andrew Duncan and Herbert Morrison in 1947. Morrison criticized the new bill, correctly as it turned out, because the Iron and Steel Board's powers would be essentially negative. The strip mill case illustrated this a brief five years later.

In the meantime the steel industry was working to capacity, exceeding its targets, and the firms made record profits. The conclusions reached in a report for OEEC that Europe was heading for a steel surplus of 8 million ingot tons in 1953 were rejected. At United Steel, for example, the commercial director, 'thought that the report was perhaps biased by the principal author's interest in the Belgian steel industry and that the excess had been overstated. . . . In the circumstances visualized, the British industry should be favourably situated. Its position as a low-cost producer had been enhanced by devaluation in 1949 and its connections with the sterling area

Dismantling the open-hearth shop at Templeborough (above) which was replaced in 1962 by electric arc furnaces. These and the Four Queens at Appleby-Frodingham (below) represented a big increase in capacity.

Sir Robert Shone (above left) *of the BISF* (*and later of the Iron and Steel Board*) *helped plan the major redevelopment of steel and Sir Archibald Forbes* (above right), *chairman of the Iron and Steel Board, supervised it. Colville's undertook a major expansion, planned by Sir Andrew McCance, second from right, and Sir John Craig, far right* (below).

Lackenby (above) *and Port Talbot* (below) *show the kind of steel development planned and built in the 1950s and early 1960s. The Port Talbot works* (overleaf) *overshadowed the town.*

A modern blast furnace (opposite) *being built at Llanwern in 1973. The hot mill* (above) *was controlled by computer processes.*

gave it preferential opportunities in the export market. Its development schemes had been planned with an eye to the world demand for individual products.'

It was in these circumstances that BISF and the Ministry of Supply had to make arrangements for the second development plan, due to begin in the early 1950s. In this plan the ISCGB was hardly involved at all. No nominee or representative of the Iron and Steel Corporation ever attended a meeting of any company board (the banks had acted very differently when they had taken over). The chairman of a committee of eight chairmen formed by Hardie was Sir Ellis Hunter, of Dorman Long, and it included Sir John Craig of Colvilles, Lord Dudley of Round Oak, Sir Walter Benton Jones of United Steel, E.H. Lever of RTB, Richard Mather of Skinningrove, A.G. Stewart of Stewarts & Lloyds, and R.F. Summers of John Summers. None of them had a strong view on the technical rationalization, on a regional or product basis, that might be desirable. As it was, most industry-wide negotiations were conducted through the BISF, and after the election in which the Conservatives were returned, most boards made immediate preparations for denationalization. In Wales, for instance, the chief plan was a merger of RTB and SCOW, which was agreed to by the government and the Iron and Steel Corporation in September 1952. Lever became the chief executive, with H.F. Spencer and Julian Pode as managing directors. Oddly enough, by the time this was done, relationships with the corporation were excellent. The merger never occurred and the firms were left to do almost exactly as they liked.

Because of the experience of full employment, the success of the export drive, and the rearmament programme, the estimates of long-term future demand had been raised by BISF from 16 million tons to 18 million tons a year. The reason for this, it was said, was that it was largely due to the greater dependence of exports on manufactured goods made from steel, like motor cars, and also because of a higher degree of substitution of steel for other materials such as timber and glass, especially in construction. This unforeseen increase in expected demand, which was far higher than any of the original estimates, further stimulated the need for expansion and modernization. In 1951 the rearmament programme was so large that 'the industry was in a state of chaos'. Indeed, the industry was only able to accept the higher target because of the increased production obtained from comparatively small innovations such as oil-firing and because of the retention of older plants. This retention was thought to be an economic proposition because the rapid rise in capital costs of new plant made steel produced by new methods seem less cheap than it would have been.

The unexpected retention of old plants meant that the saving in fuel

Opposite *The Anchor project was the major planning project of the late 1960s. The first billet was rolled in 1973.*

originally hoped for was never achieved. Instead of achieving by 1950 an expected average coke consumption of 18 cwts per ton pig iron, estimated consumption was in fact $19\frac{1}{2}$ cwts of coke/ton pig iron in 1953–4. Moreover, the postponement of the Northamptonshire development, along with the retention of old works, had the effect of altering the balance of production towards a greater dependency upon imported ores.

The original proposals were revised in the light of experience. In the first place the postponement of the proposed new integrated works in Scotland and Northamptonshire meant a curtailment of proposed output there. The retention of old plants on the other hand meant a significant increase in actual and proposed output on the North-West coast and in Sheffield. This goes a long way towards explaining the pattern of the steel industry in the 1950s. The coastal sites were more important than planned. Above all, the increase in pig iron production by 1950 was a third more than in 1945 instead of a sixth more. This increase was largely due to the retention of old plants on the North-East coast. In 1951 a new blast furnace was approved at Appleby-Frodingham though it was not in the plan and this was doubled two months later. Even in this instance, however, the furnace was postponed; as Gerald Steel explained: 'By the time the application came before the Finance Committee, however, the potential availability of ingots from the melting shops had increased by about 900 tons a week due to certain improvements and new techniques which had been introduced during the previous year or two. This effect was masked by the reduction in the overall output of the melting shops consequent upon the shortage of iron and it has only just been appreciated.' He added, new 'various small improvements' could be made, which would obviate the need to spend £615,000 to get a mere 250 tons of ingots a week.

The pattern of output increases from 1945 to the early 1950s found the biggest increases in the Midlands. But the switch to overseas ores which emerged from this pattern suggested severe strain on the long-term supply of foreign ore and scrap. Demand was rising and the new capacity was slowly coming into use, but there was a world shortage of raw materials. As a result, 'in view of the tight raw material position it seems desirable that, wherever practical, withdrawal of old antiquated plant should take place as soon as possible in order to save holding any stocks of pig iron at the works and to make available for scrap some of the equipment. The alternative of spreading limited raw materials over rapidly increasing steel capacity would only result in general inefficiency.'

Raw materials had been a perennial problem since the war. The fuel savings hoped for had not emerged. Iron ore raised similar difficulties.

The hallmark of the first development plan was the introduction of modern steel-making processes in large integrated plants. Though few such plants were built modernization did take place. The issue in the early 1950s was what was to happen next. The process of denationalization was not simple. The firms and their managements had remained virtually unchanged, but the shareholders had been compensated and had disappeared. Shareholders, after all, are a shifting population. A series of equity issues on so big a scale would utterly have disrupted the stock market, causing falls in share prices; and the weaker steel firms would have had to have been sold at knock-down prices. An alternative would have been to have dissolved the companies and to have sold the assets. The price at which the shares were sold, and their nature, showed the difficulty that faced a government trying to sell off a major industry while it was virtually certain that a future government – possibly the next government – could reverse the process. RTB never returned to private ownership. The rest were put on the stock market and a rise in share prices was essential if the issues were to be successful. The profits from such easy capital gains were hardly a non-contentious prospectus for a non-political settlement of the future of the industry.

The iron and steel industry, as then broadly defined, embraced 350 firms, of which seventeen or so were the major concerns, and it employed nearly 300,000 people. Its output was worth about £700 million. Though the major firms were nationalized they were all organized in the BISF, and in ten conferences, on a product basis, which fixed prices and output. The Ministry to which they were responsible was the Ministry of Supply. Under the 1953 Act it dealt with them through the new, statutory Iron and Steel Board, and also through the Iron and Steel Holding and Realization Agency which owned (and was to sell) the firms, as the successor to the Iron and Steel Corporation of Great Britain.

The Iron and Steel Holding and Realization Agency was set up on 13 July 1953. By the autumn of 1954 the agency, whose chairman was Sir John Morison, and which included Sir John Green, the chairman of the ISCGB, Sir Oliver Franks, who had devised the postwar plan for steel, and C.P.L. Whishaw, of Freshfields, the Bank of England's solicitors – representing as it were the forces of those who had from time to time sought to remould the industry – sold, through a consortium of merchant bankers, a number of leading companies, chiefly to the former shareholders or, rather, to interests representing them. Charles Clore's offer for South Durham was rejected on this ground, not only because of Chetwynd Talbot's horror at the idea. The major sales by public offer were of United Steel, in November 1953, Lancashire Steel in January 1954, Stewarts & Lloyds in June 1954, John Summers in October 1954, Dorman Long in November 1954, Colvilles

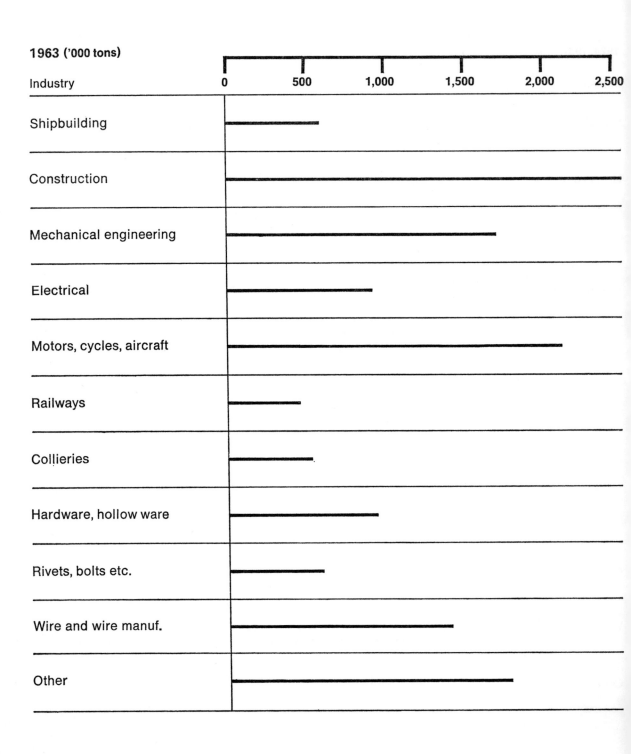

Steel consumption by industry groups

1963 ('000 tons)

Industry

	0	500	1,000	1,500	2,000	2,500

Shipbuilding

Construction

Mechanical engineering

Electrical

Motors, cycles, aircraft

Railways

Collieries

Hardware, hollow ware

Rivets, bolts etc.

Wire and wire manuf.

Other

Steel consumption by industry groups

1924, 1937, 1963

Industry %

Industry	Year	0%	5%	10%	15%	20%

Shipbuilding — 1924, 1937, 1963
Construction — 1924, 1937, 1963
Mechanical engineering — 1924, 1937, 1963
Electrical — 1924, 1937, 1963
Motors, cycles, aircraft — 1924, 1937, 1963
Railways — 1924, 1937, 1963
Collieries — 1924, 1937, 1963
Hardware, hollow ware — 1924, 1937, 1963
Rivets, bolts etc. — 1924, 1937, 1963
Wire and wire manuf. — 1924, 1937, 1963
Other — 1924, 1937, 1963

in January 1955, Firth Brown in March 1955 and Hadfields in July 1955. Round Oak was sold to Tube Investments in September 1953, GKB to GKN in May 1954, English Steel to Vickers & Cammell Laird in June 1954, and a number of smaller firms at the same time.

The 1955 general election caused a slowing-up of sales, but its result, a Conservative majority, led to an acceleration of sales, Consett in December 1955, South Durham in January 1956, Park Gate in 1956, the Steel Company of Wales in March 1957.

By the autumn of 1957, ISHRA held £125 million of debentures in denationalized companies, and £46 million of loans to SCOW and John Lysaght's. It had sold £154 million of securities to the public, or privately. One major point stands out. Little attempt was made to reorganize the industry by merging firms. For example, Scunthorpe was left divided between several interests; the North-East coast still fell into three separate groups; SCOW was divided from RTB. The next point is that part of the steel industry – a few major firms, a number of smaller ones, and a mass of debenture capital – remained in public ownership. After Sir John Morison's death in 1958, Sir Herbert Brittain became chairman till his death in 1961, but he was not able to sell RTB, and in March 1959 the Minister of Power lent the company £60 million to build a new integrated steel works at Newport, whose central feature would be a hot strip mill. The following year the proposed capacity of the scheme was extended and the loan raised to £70 million. The agency succeeded in disposing of a substantial part of its prior charge securities, after the 1959 election. Three firms – Bairds & Scottish Steel, John Baker & Bessemer, and Skinningrove – were sold to Iron and Steel Investments, a consortium of steel firms, in February 1963, but RTB remained obstinately unsold by the time the Labour government was elected in October 1964.

Over the whole period of 1953 to 1964, then, the industry's finances were dominated by the problem of selling the shares of the companies in the City. At the same time, however, the industry was controlled by another government agency that had essentially negative powers.

The Iron and Steel Board was the second agency established by the 1953 Act. It represented the legislative recognition of Duncan's ideas of a public body which would supervise but not dominate a privately owned industry. Its last report succinctly recorded the failure of this concept. It had no major power of initiative in investment and it could not reorganize and amalgamate the firms; it is also fair to say that it tended to support the steel 'establishment' and to dissuade 'adventurers' from pushing ahead. The ownership of the firms was initially in the hands of ISHRA, which was enjoined to sell the firms back to their 'previous owners', and which did not use its latent powers to reassemble the assets as viable business units. They were frozen in the posture that the City had left them in the late 1930s. The Iron and Steel Board, moreover, was sandwiched between the Ministry of Supply (and then Power) and the BISF and that circumscribed its powers of initiative and suggestion.

Its chairman was Sir Archibald Forbes, an accountant who had risen high in the Ministry of Aircraft Production, helped by Sir Lincoln Evans, of the unions, and Robert Shone of BISF, and a selection of part-time prominent businessmen and trades unionists, including McCance of Colvilles and Rollason of John Summers. Their first task was to approve the development plan for 1953 to 1958, which was that prepared by the industry in 1952.

Initially, the new blast furnaces at John Summers, and at Appleby-Frodingham and the Bilston branch of Stewarts & Lloyds came on blast, together with the rebuilt furnace at Consett, so that the last part of the first plan yielded larger supplies of pig iron. Other developments, by South Durham in pipes and Colvilles in pig iron, were essentially concerned with the extension of existing works. On price the board adopted the BISF policy in its entirety, particularly the Industry Fund. This was hardly surprising since Shone was a full-time executive member of the board. By 1955 expenditure on new plant, which had fallen from a peak in 1952, began to revive. This was because steel output was still rising, not having reached the expected plateau after the postwar reconstruction. The big need was for extra sheet and tinplate capacity, so John Summers' works at Shotton were extended, and proposals were invited for a 'fourth' plant. Demand for plate was greater than expected.

In 1956, Sir Andrew McCance became president of BISF and A. G. Stewart of Stewarts & Lloyds took his place on the Iron and Steel Board. By this time the third plan was being prepared. There seems to have been some realization that the second plan was not initially as ambitious as it perhaps ought to have been and there was a feeling that demand was shifting in a way that had not been anticipated. Two major new extensions were approved for SCOW and for Colvilles – the latter to produce an extra $2\frac{1}{2}$ million tons of ingots a year. By 1957 the Appleby-Frodingham expansion was beginning to bear fruit, and so did the tinplate mills at Velindre, and a massive total programme was initiated which came into operation around the year 1960, as the investment figures show.

The 1957 development plan was therefore ambitious – it envisaged an extra 8 million tons of capacity in 1962 over the 22 million or so that existed in 1956. Most of this extra capacity, however, was to come from on-going plans, not from major shifts in the balance of the industry. This arose from two circumstances – that the plans came from the firms, and from a 'hesitation' in the economy which made people doubt the basic premise of the plan, namely steady economic growth. It was thought urgently necessary that there should be a 'fourth' strip mill, and either a new integrated works on the Northamptonshire ore field north of the Welland or by extending Corby. The board first refused RTB's plans for Newport and, clearly, a major factor affecting this rejection was that RTB had as yet no private shareholders, which in turn reflected doubts about its total competence. In 1959 Sir Cyril Musgrave became chairman of the board, while Lincoln Evans and Robert Shone remained members. As the last major act of the Forbes chairmanship, the 1962 total steel target was reduced by 1 million tons, and the RTB plan for a strip mill at Newport was approved, together with one at Ravenscraig for Colvilles.

As this was widely regarded as an unwise decision it will be considered later in greater detail. Here it is considered in the context of the Iron and Steel Board's planning. The board told the government that public finance was necessary for so major a project. It looked at Grangemouth, Immingham, Kidwelly and Swansea. Ultimately, however, it had to be either Newport or Ravenscraig, both of which had greater 'net advantages' over the other sites. RTB's scheme for Newport was approved in January 1959; Colvilles' was approved in April. Colvilles' scheme was not the one originally chosen, and the board stated frankly that the decision was made by the minister. It is known that it was a cabinet decision taken for regional purposes, as the Prime Minister told the House of Commons in November 1958. In this respect, therefore, the Iron and Steel Board had failed in one of its main functions – to take steel out of politics.

It became increasingly doubtful, too, whether its other main function, which was to promote efficiency by vetting the development proposals and formulating them in industry-wide plans, could be effectively exercised without more positive powers. Apart from the strip mills, the early and mid-1960s were years of relatively low investment in steel. They were also years of low profitability, probably (as will be seen) because of the price policy agreed by the board and the BISF. The momentum gained in the late 1950s seemed to have been lost. The sort of problem which arose can be seen from the proposal by SCOW for a new hot mill at Port Talbot, but this was thought by the board to provide excess capacity. On the other hand the board did not 'wish to discourage the commercial enterprise of steel firms who were willing to risk large sums of capital', so it arranged for RTB to make the steel while SCOW turned it into sheet and tinplate. The reason for this was that RTB would have surplus capacity of steel as a result of the cabinet decision in 1958.

Ironstone is extracted by walking dragline near Corby (above). Scrap and ore are transported to steelworks, as at Ravenscraig (below), to be made into iron.

Coke ovens, as at Ravenscraig (above), are used to make coke which, mixed with ore and scrap, makes iron. Opposite Pig iron is seen at Workington.

Scrap is fed into an oxygen converter at Consett (above), *and the converters, as at the Abbey works* (below), *make steel, seen in molten form at Lackenby* (opposite).

The steel is 'teemed' into ingot moulds at Llanwern (above), *which are then cooled and reheated* (opposite).

Peech of United Steel took Rollason's place on the board in 1960, but otherwise it continued much as before. The 1961 development report was conceived in conditions of great optimism; it was the beginning of an era in national economic policy culminating in the creation of NEDC, of which Shone became director general in 1961, and the adoption of French-style 'purposive planning'. In the circumstances the demand for steel was thought likely to be extremely high. So in 1960 the board approved fifty-three schemes which would cost £223 million. Some of this new capacity was 'greenfield' (a new 'vogue' word), and some of it was to use new processes like the Kaldo process and L–D. Yet the recession of 1961 led to some doubts, which the board met by urging the scrapping of old plant, which it could not order firms to do. The situation of the 1920s might conceivably recur, where all firms had surplus capacity, and new capital (which had to be serviced) would be regarded as 'uneconomic'. In 1961 only twenty-one schemes, costing £78½ million, were approved, and they were essentially hang-overs from the 1960 plan. In 1962 only fifteen schemes, costing £8 million were approved. The whole programme rested, therefore, upon the decisions taken in 1960. By 1963 the board was referring to an excess of obsolescent capacity of 1 million tons still in operation to which it had referred in 1960 (and presumably the 1963 total was larger since three years had elapsed), and the massive programme of 1960 was tailing off. In addition, any schemes which had been approved had been delayed in starting. In 1963, only £16 million of new expenditure was authorized. It was the last report of the board – for 1966 – that gave voice to views that hitherto had been merely implicit. These views were that the second and third development plans had been a success, and that by the early 1960s capacity matched demand. But the demand expected in the 1960s had not materialized, so that the industry's technical momentum could only be kept up by withdrawing obsolete plant. 'The board has had no power to compel closures.' The board had sought in 1963 to amend the 1953 Act because of the need for positive planning of new capacity, to withdraw old capacity, and to reorganize the industry into large groups.

It is thus in the context of two major public agencies that the plans between 1952 and 1967 may be reviewed. ISHRA's main job was to sell the firms' shares on the market, which it almost succeeded in doing. The Iron and Steel Board increasingly felt frustrated by its terms of reference. Let us look at the plans in more detail.

Opposite The steel is continuously cast, saving on fuel costs, as seen at Panteg (above left). Strip is formed by pressure while it is hot and malleable as seen at Ravenscraig (above right), where the strip mill is fully automated and computer controlled (below).

K

The Plans

In order to clear the terminology, the various plans for the industry will be called the first plan, which refers to the period 1945 to 1952–3, was published in 1946, and was in large part a response to the Franks Report; the second plan, which covers the period 1953 to 1958, was published in 1955, and arose out of an examination ordered by the ISCGB and BISF in 1952; the third plan covering the period 1957 to 1962, which was published in 1957 by the Iron and Steel Board; and the fourth plan, published in 1961, which covered the period 1961 to 1965, and which was succeeded by a further formal plan – the fifth plan – just before the second nationalization in 1967. These last four plans provide a convenient framework within which to consider the development of the industry. It will be seen, if only from the unequal periods which they cover, and their diverse origins, that all save the 1957 plan were published in conditions of considerable political uncertainty, and that their publication was usually merely a formal act to celebrate, as it were, a long process of bargaining, conjecture and jigsaw puzzle making. The first plan was a major effort to rebuild the industry after the catastrophes of the slump and the deliberate neglect of capital equipment during the war. It took two years longer than envisaged because of shortages of capital goods and because of changes in the circumstances. The second plan arose out of somewhat more complex circumstances than the first plan. In a sense, the first plan had been thought of as a once-for-all effort, after which the industry would settle down. But the postwar problems of Europe, followed by the Korean War, and nationalization, completely unsettled the economic and political environment. By the time the original first plan was belatedly completed, circumstances had radically changed and it was thought that there would be a period of sustained economic growth. It was this that the second plan was about.

The second plan was published two years after it officially began and five years after the first plan was supposed to have been completed. The ISCGB in its second and final report showed that its staff, together with BISF, had drawn up and agreed the greater part of the plan well before the end of 1952. It looked forward to a £200 million programme of major programmes (together with £50 million for small schemes) to raise capacity to 21 million tons. In the Midlands and Lincolnshire, Appleby-Frodingham was to have two new blast furnaces, and there was to be a new blast furnace at Bilston. In Lancashire and Cheshire John Summers was to have a new blast furnace. In the North-East, Dorman Long was to have two large blast furnaces and a new universal mill, and there were to be further developments at South

Durham and Cargo Fleet, while Scotland was to have three new blast furnaces originally proposed for the first plan but not built. In South Wales the emphasis was also on blast furnaces. The implications of this programme are clear; a major bottleneck had to be broadened.

The main feature of the second plan was a chart showing a rate of growth of steel consumption changing from a rate of increase of 3·2 per cent a year to 4·5 per cent a year in 1953, and trailing off, over the edge, in a flurry of optimism. This led to the view that steel production should rise from $17\frac{1}{2}$ million tons a year in 1953 to $22\frac{1}{2}$ million tons in 1958 with a corresponding increase in capacity. This rested upon nine major projects – SCOW (1·0 million), John Summers (0·7 million), Dorman Long (0·5 million), South Durham (0·5 million), and others by Lancashire Steel, Consett, Colvilles, Stewarts & Lloyds, and Steel, Peech & Tozer, together with a further 1 million tons of smaller projects.

This was based upon a small proportionate rise in plate, a bigger growth in sheet, a doubling of tinplate, a fairly big growth of heavy sections, a 50 per cent rise in tubes, and smaller increases in other parts of the trade. In looking ahead the board felt that the tightness of supply of plates, sheet and tinplate was likely to continue. It was there that they concentrated their attention, and a veiled warning was given of the need for a fourth strip mill; so, too, was the need for a new continuous billet mill. The location of this mill depended upon the possibility of using home ore, which was 'crucial', though the use of Mauretanian ores was likely rapidly to increase, especially if bulk ore carriers and terminals could be developed.

The plan as a whole was to cost £257 million, and to lead to a marked rise in productivity. It was heavily weighted towards the section and plate works of the North-East coast and the Welsh sheet works. Since much of the work was underway it was not a forward-looking plan, in the sense that the first plan had been; and it was in essence conservative (especially on its technical side), despite its radical assumption of steadily increasing demand. Its emphasis was on the extension of capacity rather than on dramatic technical improvement.

By the time of the third plan which was drawn up in 1956 and published in 1957 the Iron and Steel Board was firmly in the saddle. It was more confident, too, that the optimists were right and that those who feared there would be no markets for the steel they were approving projects to produce were wrong. It was because of this that the board had asked in early 1956 for the 1958 targets to be raised to $23\frac{1}{2}$ million tons. Looking ahead to 1962 they saw a demand for 29 million tons, or 30 million tons, which imports would help to meet. This enabled them to approve massive plans for the expansion of blast furnace and pig iron capacity and it will have been seen that the second plan leant in that direction. They were also concerned about iron ore; both the first and second plans had emphasized the importance of home ore. In the event, foreign ore was available but in 1957 the board were still saying that they believed 'that still further exploitation of the English orefields is essential to the economic development of the industry in the years immediately after 1962'. (The Suez affair, of course, had raised freight rates so that the shipping position was unusually difficult.)

The third plan was optimistic about demand for steel – so optimistic that the board felt strong enough to draw attention to its residual powers to advise the Minister of Supply to build steel capacity himself should the firms not provide it – a point they re-emphasized in their final report. They wanted an integrated plant on a home-ore site 'north of the river Welland' – a sort of steel Shangri-La that haunted steel from the time that Brassert first conceived it – but neither United Steel nor Stewarts & Lloyds would agree to it. There was a need for more billet capacity than the firms proposed to build and, while sheet and tinplate capacity was growing rapidly, there was an acute dispute between the firms and the board about the need for a new hot strip mill. In other products, from wire to heavy plates, though the board thought the firms were too pessimistic, they were prepared to concede that by about 1962 there might be a rough balance; but there was a legacy of 'obsolete and ageing plant' that was likely to be still operative in 1962 that ought not to be operating, and should not be replaced on present sites. About £600 million was envisaged as a minimum programme – a doubling of the rate of investment that had taken place in the second plan.

In the event, the third plan was shattered by the strip mills decision of 1958, and by the onset of an era of surplus capacity. This is shown clearly in the fourth plan, published in 1961, which was a highly sophisticated document. Indeed, it must be noted that from the six-page Brassert Report, through the 222 paragraphs of the Franks Report to the fourth plan there is a major step forward in the quality of the technical and economic reasoning by which the industry was being governed, a step forward that may also be noted in the management of the constituent firms and plants. The fourth plan looked forward to a capacity of 32 million tons in 1965. By this time the Iron and Steel Board, which represented the 'best judgement' of the pundits of the industry, thought that the target would be achieved, indeed exceeded, but that it would be achieved only by using obsolete capacity. The plan was drawn up in the golden dawn of NEDO – the National Economic Development Office, which imitated the planning mechanism that was supposed to have led to sustained French economic growth – of which Sir Robert Shone was a senior official. It therefore posited a higher rate of economic growth than history showed to be probable and than the industry thought likely.

The board showed that 'for almost every product the potential production exceeds the capacity suggested as appropriate'. But the surplus was 'no more than equivalent to obsolete capacity'. The report was resolutely optimistic, talking indeed of a sixth strip mill by the end of the 1960s, the need for still more capacity for ferro-concrete rods and bars, and for replacing open-hearth crude steel capacity by new (predominantly oxygen) steel-making processes. The 1961 report marked the culmination of the home ore campaign, since it was shown that to use the ore 'north of the Welland' would require extensive underground mining which would raise costs above those of imported ore. The report concentrated, indeed, upon the need for adequate port and shipping facilities so that although the plans showed a greater use of home than imported ore it was already clear that the arguments were shifting towards a greater use of imported ore.

This was indeed confirmed by the fifth plan which was published in November 1964, just after the election in which Labour was returned by a narrow majority. Production had reached a peak of $24\frac{1}{4}$ million tons in 1960 and then fell back, to rise to $25\frac{1}{2}$ million tons by 1964. This was $6\frac{1}{2}$ million tons less than had been forecast for 1965 in the fourth plan. The level of capacity had reached 32 million tons and the major projects envisaged in 1961 had been completed. The obsolescent capacity had not been withdrawn, however. Since demand in 1970 was envisaged as lying between 27 and 30 million tons the emphasis of the fifth plan was on remodelling and renewal rather than on the dramatic expansion which the first four plans had emphasized, even though a margin of spare capacity was allowed for which envisaged a total capacity of some 33 million tons. The board said it would guard against excess capacity and specifically wanted to withdraw 5 million tons of obsolete capacity. There was need for more wire rod and bar in coil, but the emphasis was to be on renewing billet capacity and improving the quality of sheet. The statement was definitely made that there was no need for a new integrated works on a greenfield site.

Profitability in steel had fallen as demand had not kept up with capacity because of national economic conditions. Prices had been too low from the point of view of the industry. After the heroic heave in investment in the third plan, largely for the two strip mills, the level of investment had seriously declined. Labour productivity had not risen as had been hoped.

But behind this fifth (and last) plan were several serious questions that had to be put and answered. First of all, was technical progress as fast and as satisfactory as it could have been? Secondly, now that the era of great postwar growth was over, how was the industry to be kept on its toes, if productivity required old capacity to be closed down. And, thirdly, there was the question of location; this was conveniently dodged in the 1964 report but it was in fact a matter of central concern.

To answer these questions it will be necessary to examine closely management and research and technology. This is best approached, perhaps, by looking at the individual firms. In 1955 South Wales produced 23 per cent of the country's steel; the North-East coast produced 20 per cent; Scotland produced 12 per cent; Lancashire produced 9 per cent; Scunthorpe & Corby produced 15 per cent; Sheffield produced 13 per cent; and the rest came chiefly from Cheshire and Birmingham. The output of pig iron was differently located, and output of steel by value was of course different, because Sheffield, for example, produced high-quality and highly priced steels. The changes in steel had not been fundamental technical changes; they had been 'incremental' – that is the efficiency of existing ways of doing things had gradually improved. In the ten years from 1945, for instance, coke requirements per ton of steel had fallen by a tenth; the plants had become better balanced, by adding new units, and by using capacity more fully; and above all, the new capital equipment had saved labour. As a result, relatively speaking steel costs had fallen; and cheap scrap, ore and coal still gave Britain an advantage against its reviving Continental competitors.

In the preparation of the second development plan and in the subsequent approval of projects it is striking to see that the projects originated with the firms, and that the only way a firm could be effectively kept out of the programme, even if its proposals seemed unwise, was to use the threat that their proposals would be objected to by other firms who would regard them as encroachments on their territory. Thus Stewarts & Lloyds were used to dissuade Round Oak from a tube development. The Scottish firm of Colvilles was denationalized in 1955. Here was an instance, under the dynamic leadership of Sir Andrew McCance, of a firm that had big ambitions and considerable liquidity, as well as considerable political influence. The state still owned its debenture and preference shares but Colvilles was a major private concern, dominant in Scotland. In April 1951 Hardie gave a press lunch at which he pressed for a modern integrated steel works at Rosyth near the Fifeshire coalfield, relying on imported ore and scrap. Meanwhile the BISF was approving, on its own initiative, substantial developments on the Clyde and at Glengarnock: Colvilles were pressing for a large expansion of their own activities, and simultaneously suggesting that other Scottish firms were not likely to have much of a market for their products. In the event BISF found it prudent to accept Colvilles position which gave them about four-fifths of Scottish output. The BISF did not think the Scottish economy could absorb all the steel Colvilles proposed to produce, but they were also sure that the National Coal Board could not supply the coking coal to produce it. The excuse which was given to Sir Andrew McCance was that the Scottish Gas Board needed the coking coal that he wanted, which was an adventitious development in a situation where it was known that coal supplies were dwindling. It was sufficient, however, to divert Sir Andrew's wrath to the Gas Board and the Ministry of Supply for not sticking up for steel.

By contrast, the North-East coast was not a unified sector of the industry It was a matter for wide comment that no serious attempt was made to link Consett's works with other North-East coast firms. Dorman Long, for example, was denationalized in 1954, though half its capital remained in public ownership, in the form of loan stock and preference shares, yet its works at Cleveland, Lackenby and Redcar, on Tees-side, needed to be related to other North-East coast producers for full efficiency. Its profit record was excellent – a rise from £5 million in 1950 to nearly £10 million in 1955; on the basis of this it proposed to spend nearly £40 million in three years on a major renewal of its plant, and a big new universal beam mill. South Durham, denationalized in 1956, had major works on Tees-side, and was an important pipe producer. Its strength lay in its mixture of home and foreign ore; and when the relative prices of the ores shifted, as they did, to favour foreign ores, the possibility of a link with Stewarts & Lloyds was mooted. Yet it was still absorbing the consequences of its own amalgamation with Cargo Fleet. The North-East symbolized the difficulties of rationalizing the industry, as did Sheffield.

Thomas Firth & John Brown, at Sheffield, was denationalized in 1955; it produced special steels. Hadfields, a similar specialized producer, was also denationalized in 1955. The biggest steel-maker in Sheffield was United Steel, under Sir Walter Benton Jones. It had close links with other firms – its directors included Rollason and Richard Summers – and its two component Sheffield firms – Steel, Peech & Tozer and Samuel Fox – were both specialized steel-makers. It also had the Workington Iron and Steel Company that it sought to make profitable. Its chief interest, however, was now in Scunthorpe.

In the autumn of 1953 the ISRHA representatives – Sir John Morison, Charles Whishaw of Freshfields, and S. S. Wilson – attended a meeting of the United Steel Board. There were technical difficulties about raising money; but ultimately, in 1953, United Steel was denationalized. In 1957 £10 million of reserves were capitalized and £20 million of £1 shares were issued at par. The firm had a major plant at Scunthorpe — Appleby-Frodingham. This was to be the basis of the only major project to emerge in the late 1960s, Anchor. But United Steel had diversified interests – in

Sheffield, and at Workington – and it was not yet clear that its future most importantly lay at Scunthorpe. In Scunthorpe GKN, which had been partly nationalized, owned the important producer Lysaghts, linked to Baldwins and Briton Ferry in South Wales and Brymbo in North Wales. RTB owned Redbourn.

South Wales had been for years an area where attempts had been made to rationalize production, yet there was a serious break-up of concerns at the time of denationalization. The Steel Company of Wales (SCOW), whose chairman was Harald Peake, a banker, had Julian Pode, an accountant, as managing director. SCOW, set up by a group of other firms, RTB and GKB, had plans 'to rejuvenate the Welsh sheet and tinplate industry'. It was to be the basis for the major Welsh project and it already had a large Port Talbot works in operation, all of it of modern construction. RTB, under Sir Ernest Lever, and his assistant, G.H. Latham, was not de-nationalized, and its major works was at Ebbw Vale, with other smaller works at Redbourn (Scunthorpe) and in West Wales. Its separation from SCOW delayed the process of reorganizing production in South Wales.

The State of the Industry

Three major features stand out of this survey. The first is that the industry was based on a major development of existing sites. If all four plans were taken together, there was a shift of geographical emphasis. But there was no radical departure. The existing firms were the basis for growth, and this led to the decision in 1958 to have two strip mills, one in Scotland and one in Wales, despite all evidence to the contrary. Allied to this was the fact that many firms in the industry were still thought to be technically conservative. The L–D plants, for example, being developed in Europe were not the basis of the major new British works. This technical conservatism was allied to a somewhat diffident attitude to Europe. The European Coal and Steel Community had been set up earlier and Britain was not part of it. The reasons for this were fairly complex, but understandable in the light of events.

British relations with Continental Europe in the period immediately after the war in Europe were dominated by the need to relieve distress after the devastation, the obligation to disarm, de-Nazify and police the British zone of Germany, and the desire to resume normal trading relations. The crisis of payments and output of 1947 led to the Marshall Plan in which American and mutual aid formed the basis of a reconstruction of the Western Europe economy. The organization for the settlement of the intra-European policies was the Organization for European Economic Coopera-

Opposite A boiler drum is being forged at the River Don works, Sheffield.

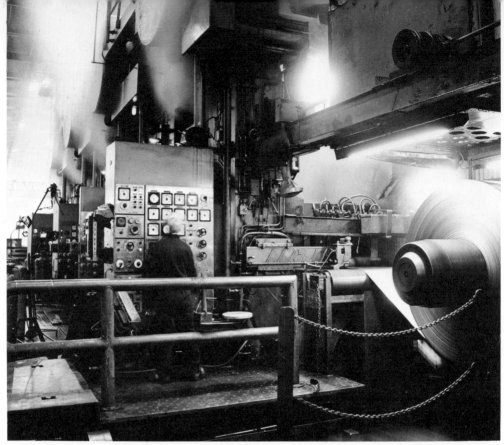

The cold mill at Llanwern produces special strip steel (above) *which is sometimes galvanized, as at Ebbw Vale* (below).

Corrosion resistant coatings may be applied to steel by electrolysis, as shown in the electrolytic tinning process (above) *or by coating with an organic compound* (below).

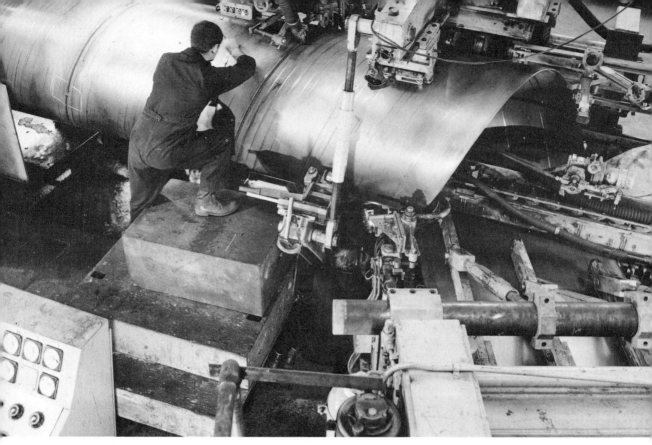

This strip (above) is being turned into spiral welded pipes. A pipe mill is shown below.

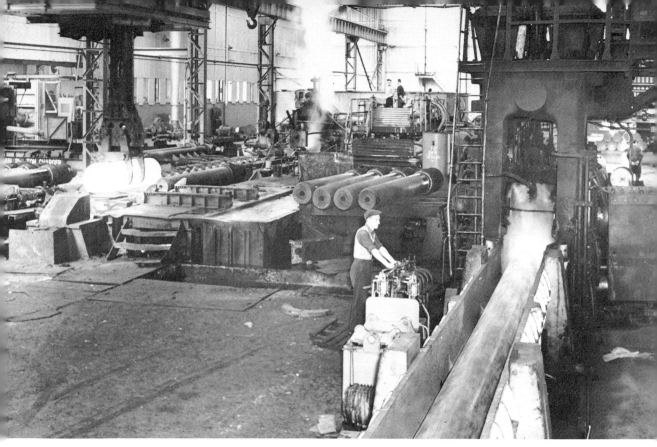

This seamless pipe is being made at Clydesdale (above), and (below) galvanized wire is drawn on to a frame.

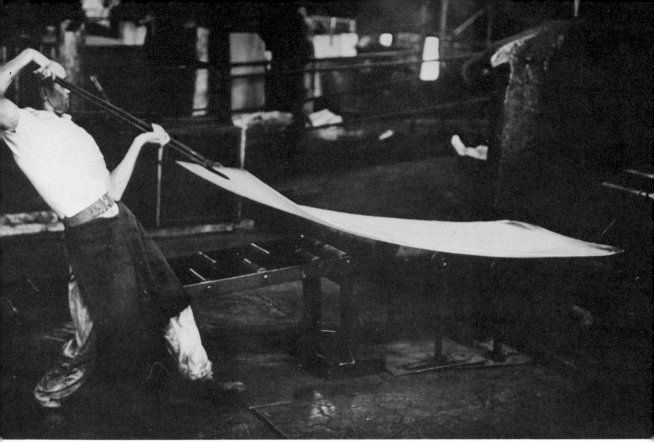

Hand-rolling of steel sheet, in South Wales (above), is an old and now obsolete process. The massive plate mill (below) is in striking contrast.

Making a modern product, like stainless steel (above), still involves hot and dirty work but the finishing mill (below) shows how much things are improving.

tion, seated in Paris, and under its aegis massive programmes of investment in Continental basic industries were undertaken. The European steel cartel had been used during the war to support the Nazi war effort. The British steel-masters looked forward to the end of the war with a certain amount of ambivalence. They expected to gain a larger share of a growing Continental steel market, though they also half-expected a recurrence of the interwar depression. Chiefly, they looked forward to the dismantling of the German steel industry and inheriting the major part of its market, as well as removing its international trade threat. It would almost be true to say that some steel-masters came close to implying that Britain should take Germany's place in the international structure, implying membership and leadership of the cartel.

Germany's recovery led to a pressure to export her steel, and by early 1949 a suggestion for a reconstruction of the coal and steel cartels. While the boom associated with the Korean War, which broke out in 1950, temporarily led to steel shortages, the major preoccupation of European steel-makers was to limit new capacity, to control prices and to supervise exports in what they were convinced would be conditions of chronic steel surplus, and every time demand fell off, as in 1953, the fall was taken to be the beginning of the period of surplus capacity.

The ECSC was founded partly – perhaps largely – on the initiative of Jean Monnet to whom credit was given, possibly with some justification, for the economic recovery of French industry in the late 1940s, because of his job as chief French economic planner. He and Maurice Schuman, the French Foreign Minister, sought to establish a community in Europe where coal and steel could be traded freely, within rules which would control pricing and investment within a broader concept of a guaranteed expanding market. The immediate political object was a reconciliation of France and Western Germany, whose relationships had been difficult, and where disputes over steel and coal, as in the question of the occupation of the Ruhr in 1923 and the ownership of the Saar, were perennial sources of trouble. The wider object, it was said later, was European unity, through the European Economic Community. The High Authority began in 1952, in Luxembourg after some considerable preliminary work, with a tight control over the coal and steel industries of the Six, of which those in Belgium, France, Germany and Luxembourg were the most important. It was in fact the old cartel raised to a new eminence and responsibility. The attitude of the United Kingdom to the association was compounded of several dissonant views, often held simultaneously by the same person or group.

The first and predominant attitude was one of distrust. The origins of the High Authority for coal, iron and steel in their view lay in the European

Opposite *In the end, as with these finished rings and tyres, there is steel . . .*

cartel, as a senior B I S F official wrote in a letter to Gerald Steel of United Steel, on 4 November 1949 about the first whispers of E C S C. 'Our [B I S F] policy . . . is rather to await events appreciating that some form of cartel [deleted] European industry cooperation may appear in the future, but in a somewhat different form to that of the prewar organization, and that it is not in our interests to hasten that appearance at this time.'

By 1954, however, after the European Coal and Steel Community had been set up, active discussions were under way and the Iron and Steel Board negotiated on the industry's behalf. The firms, through B I S F, retained the right, however, to 'speak direct to the minister' especially on dual pricing and tariffs. Their voice was uniformly hostile.

The E C S C model was to become a familiar one, though most British observers shared the Prime Minister, C. R. Attlee's, distrust of it, when he said that the British government 'do not feel able to accept in advance, nor do they wish to reject in advance, the principles underlying the French proposal'. The treaty set up a High Authority, with a Court and an Assembly, and with powers to regulate the production, pricing, trade and investment in coal and steel in the six countries of Benelux, France, Germany and Italy. Its chief features were the elimination of tariffs inside the Six, a common external tariff, a pricing system based on the agreed costs of production at a fixed point, near or at the production unit, with accepted costs of transport to the consumer. In principle, restrictive practices were illegal, a point on which the British industry were notably reserved in the light of the previous half-century's experience.

In 1957 the industry thought that 'Britain's early start in postwar development could still give her the advantage of lower capital charges', and 'labour productivity . . . is higher here than in most E C S C countries . . . due in part to superior management. The United Kingdom also has the advantage of cheaper home ore.' Indeed, even in 1958, the view was held that in productivity 'the British industry . . . may even have surpassed the American'.

These views turned out to be incorrect. To explain why this is so, it is necessary to examine the evidence carefully.

A leading factor in explaining the state of the industry at the time lies in its attitude to investment. It has already been shown that plans had to be approved by the Iron and Steel Board which theoretically had the right to initiate developments, though it never did. The firms were the same, their structure virtually unaltered, as those that had been nationalized. Each sought to get its fair share of development. It has been seen that no radical departure was envisaged, even in the Franks Report; certainly nothing so bold as the Bank of England scheme of 1930 was ever foreseen.

Partly this was because of finance. The firms were excessively cautious.

They ended the war with substantial reserves, partly due to high wartime levels of activity and hence high profits, which through the ingenious scheme of Andrew Macharg came back to finance development. The early postwar schemes were slow to start because of shortages of equipment, and cautions about prices. Once the first scheme was under way, nationalization was threatened and then occurred. Thereafter, the concern of the firms was to make denationalization work; and it was difficult to do so because G.R. Strauss, the Labour spokesman on steel, had said that 'in no circumstances will the total compensation [for nationalization] already paid out be increased'. This kept equity prices down, and the government, through the Iron and Steel Board, was a major supplier of new funds.

The Iron and Steel Board's view of future demand was at first cautious. But the firms were cautious too, and so was BISF. After Duncan's death, the 'independent chairman' was no longer much of a force and it is clear that Morison relied almost wholly upon views formulated by his staff, which made for playing safe.

A Major Development

A major problem arose in financing the expansion. The problem was a simple one. The firms had spent many of their reserves before nationalization. In the process of denationalization, much of the capital raised was debenture capital, bearing fixed interest charges. The companies found it hard to raise money on the market and relied for funds on the Iron and Steel Board, the Finance Corporation for Industry, and the banks. By 1960 the government stepped in with the Iron and Steel (Financial Provisions) Act, to supply money to Colvilles and RTB, promised in 1958 to finance the South Wales and Scottish Strip mills – £70 million to RTB and £50 million to Colvilles. At the time RTB was still nationalized, and was obliged to rely on public money; Colvilles was threatened in the 1959 election with nationalization; and the likely outcome of the schemes was a surplus of sheet steel capacity.

As Harold Lever, the Labour MP said in the Third Reading debate:

The reason why Colvilles did not raise the money was the circumstances in which this deal was done. The government came to the conclusion that it was very urgent in the interests of the country that there should be a vast increase in sheet steel production, planned, organized and financed in expectation of a greatly increased demand. The steel companies, among them Colvilles, did not take such a hopeful view of likely progress in demand. They were very unwilling to commit themselves to huge financial commitments and, not surprisingly, to meet a demand which they had no confidence would emerge.

This speech was made in a debate which raised several important matters. It will be seen that from about 1945 to about 1957 the industry had been successful in many respects. The disastrous interwar years had been followed by a substantial contribution to the war effort, and the peacetime expansion programme was marked by technical innovation, a re-jigging of management and a new self-confidence, despite shortages of raw materials and new plant, and the incessant commotion about nationalization. But in 1957 it was felt that the industry was reverting to its prewar sloth, the immediate issue being a fourth strip mill to supply the growing market for cars and domestic appliances. The big firms in the industry were not sure the demand was there. RTB, which was still nationalized, was the most willing to undertake the enterprise; naturally the other firms regarded this as an attempt to embark on a reckless project using public funds. Colvilles, the biggest firm, especially, wished to use whatever funds were available for its own purposes – a new steel plant. In the event, as will be seen, the government insisted not on one strip mill but two; they were located in Wales and Scotland for political-cum-regional reasons; and in the process the government lost the argument that steel could 'stand on its own [free enterprise] feet', while RTB was unable to be denationalized and Colvilles was brought into grave difficulty.

To start at the beginning, Colvilles planned a new plant at Ravenscraig. RTB planned a vast new plant at Newport. The issue was politically a difficult one. The Welsh background was itself especially complex, arising from differences between RTB and SCOW. In July 1953 RTB and SCOW became the property of the Iron and Steel Holding and Realization Agency. In the event, RTB remained such until it became the property of the British Steel Corporation in 1967. Sir Ernest Lever (as he became in the New Year's Honours List in 1954) remained in office there. The only major development on hand was the Midland works associated steel development scheme, to be built for £2·1 million. The board was reorganized in October 1955, as a result of the break of RTB with SCOW, which occurred chiefly because certain senior officials did not get on with Lever, and because SCOW was sold on the open market as part of the devesting procedure. Sir Hugh Beaver, managing director of Guinness's, the brewers, joined the RTB board, and at the prodding of the Iron and Steel Board, Lever proposed a large new hot strip mill at Newport. 'The chairman said that Sir Archibald Forbes was still obsessed with the idea that a new hot strip mill rather than a billet mill should be erected forthwith.' RTB was by now regarded as a thoroughly ill-run company with an elderly and ineffective management, 'apparently unable', according to Forbes, 'to proceed with what they themselves believe to be an essential scheme of development.' (Though publicly-owned, the company now gave £500 to the European Movement.)

It was agreed by the Iron and Steel Board and the government that Wales needed a new steel works. Fairly quickly, this became a notion that the steel works should be a new strip mill, to help supply the Midland car industry, now booming as the export drive for cars was succeeded by a wide domestic market. In June 1957, Lord Mills and Reginald Maudling, the two ministers concerned, and the Treasury, the Iron and Steel Board, the Holding and Realization Agency, and the BISF convened a meeting to confront Lever, Latham and Spencer; and as a result the matter was taken to cabinet level. What was at issue was, first, the efficiency of RTB, and second, the need to provide a new steel works in Wales. From the point of view of efficiency, as seen from the Iron and Steel Board, RTB was not a suitable unit for a big new works, except perhaps in the Midlands, where it would not be a serious candidate since the Midland group had first claim and Redbourn was too restricted a site. From the point of view of Wales, however, RTB was a powerful contender for new plant. RTB, putting the pressure on, closed its West Wales works in the autumn of 1957, on grounds of efficiency, paying up to £150,000 compensation to the employees concerned. The BISF strongly supported RTB's proposals for a new strip mill, probably because the other firms regarded a strip mill as uneconomic and therefore not competitive, and RTB set about expanding Ebbw Vale's steel-making capacity at a cost of nearly £11 million, with the reluctant agreement of Sir Archibald Forbes; the Iron and Steel Board had little confidence in RTB and preferred Colvilles in Scotland.

Eventually, in the autumn of 1958, Newport was agreed to, but only as a result of a cabinet decision to build a new works in Wales and another for Colvilles in Scotland, over-ruling Sir Archibald Forbes. But, as late as July 1958, it was thought that Colvilles would get a works in Scotland and RTB would not get the Newport works which it regarded as 'vital if the future of the company is to be assured'. When the announcement was made in Parliament, by the Minister of Power, Lever was about to retire and had been replaced by Geoffrey Eley. Newport was to cost £100 million. Lever's last board meeting, therefore, marked his biggest victory, as he had got a major new plant for RTB against strong opposition, just as Firth had got Ebbw Vale twenty years before.

In the event the Spencer works at Newport cost far more than expected. By 1961, the estimates were for £134 million, and as the company was still not devested, the money had to be raised for this and other activities to the tune of £190 million from the Holding and Realization Agency. By 1962 RTB was making a loss and the outlook, when Newport came on stream, would be far bigger losses. This was why RTB could not be devested. So when the Queen and the Duke of Edinburgh opened Spencer works, Newport, on 26 October 1962, it was to celebrate a technical and political achievement, but virtual financial bankruptcy. The technical achievement, too, was a little tarnished by the fact that despite L–D experiments elsewhere, they were not fully effective at Newport, and that there were no natural deep water berths for the iron ore carriers. By 1962, the full cost, excluding the deep water berths, was £150 million. Despite the sympathy of Sir Cyril Musgrave, chairman of the Iron and Steel Board, and Sir William Lawson, of ISHRA, RTB was in difficulties, and the prospective take-over of Whitehead's, a major RTB customer, by Stewarts & Lloyds meant that the publicly owned firm might collapse. Lawson therefore empowered RTB to take over Whiteheads, an irony when Stewarts & Lloyds was privately owned and RTB was still nationalized. Sir Henry Spencer (as he now was) became Whitehead's joint managing director. Yet the deep water harbour which was opposed in Parliament ran into difficulty; John Boyd-Carpenter, chief secretary, warned Eley that 'he could give . . . no support at all in the House . . . what he would have to say might harm our cause'. Sir William Lawson 'expressed doubts as to whether the City would feel that there was adequate security for financing the scheme until our results showed a great improvement'. The scheme was therefore deferred. The Iron and Steel Board and the British Transport Commission thereafter took on the provision of the docks on the Usk opposite the works, at a proposed cost of £15¼ million. By 1963, though results were thought to be improving, in fact they were not, and there was still no sign that the firm could pay its way. Eley was replaced by Michael Milne-Watson, as a full-time chairman; Sir Henry Spencer, who continued as managing director, fell ill and died. Sir Hugh Beaver, endlessly inventive, tried to get RTB to go into 'steel housing', in a big way, but the ministers concerned, Geoffrey Rippon and Sir Keith Joseph, poured cold water on the notion. The management of the company deteriorated, and it was not until December 1964 that Gwyn Lloyd Jones was made senior executive director, displacing Campbell Adamson and Gilbertson, and Hugh Weeks became deputy chairman in March 1965, that things looked up.

That, then, accounts for Newport. But in Scotland the story was equally dramatic. Ravenscraig was a logical development of a scheme linking the Dalzell works and the Lanarkshire steel works. It was linked to a new ore-unloading quay on the Clyde, already built as part of the second development plan, together with a huge blast furnace, and three open-hearth furnaces. It seemed both logical and economic to add to this a major new slabbing mill, especially as the shipbuilding firms in Scotland and Northern Ireland were adjacent, booming, and needed the steel. To this was to be added, reluctantly, the semi-continuous strip mill, wholly financed by the government, about which the House of Commons debated so fervently.

The name 'Ravenscraig' for the whole original £20·4 million project was suggested by Major W.R. Brown of Parkhead, and adopted by Colvilles. It inevitably became the name for the whole project, as will be seen. According to the firm the reason for choosing Ravenscraig as a site rather than the Clyde coast site at Inchinnan was that 'the coking fields lie towards Edinburgh', and it was a question of weighing the cost of taking ore to the coke, or coke to the ore; a coastal site would have required a writing-off and scrapping of all the existing Colvilles' plant. It was also held that it would have caused social problems in Motherwell and Lanarkshire, and that the Inchinnan site was too small and railways could not get to it. The memorandum giving these reasons was somewhat suspect, since its purpose was for public relations and the issues were more complex; nevertheless it carries some weight. The original scheme was for a new slabbing mill, alterations to the plate mills at Dalzell, with a major new blast furnace, designed to overcome the shortage of Scottish pig iron. Various alterations added to the cost, but by 1957 the scheme was developing as envisaged, and a new mill was proposed which would have yielded between 5·35 per cent and 6·6 per cent on an £18·2 million expenditure. All this was in the context of Colvilles as the major Scottish producer, behaving prudently, not expanding its markets, and deeply suspicious of the optimistic forecasts then being made of the demand for steel in the middle and late 1960s.

In 1958, however, as has been seen, the BISF and the Iron and Steel Board agreed that a fourth strip mill was necessary to meet the anticipated demand for steel for cars and other consumer durables in the middle and late 1960s. Colvilles were not convinced that this demand would materialize. RTB as has been seen eventually put in a claim for their Newport works, which made a great deal of sense – it was near deep water, it was fairly near the car firms in the Midlands, and it linked up with the rest of the South Wales iron and steel complex. The Iron and Steel Board examined several sites, but the problem was that under the Iron and Steel Act 1953 it had virtually no independent powers of initiative unless all steel firms had refused to provide necessary capacity. They looked at Grangemouth, Immingham, Kidwelly and Swansea.

By the spring of 1958 the Development Committee of BISF discussed the £135·5 million strip mill project for Newport. The pressure to build at Newport came from RTB, which was still not devested, and from Welsh political pressure. The plant would have to be built with public money, since sums of £100 million could not be met privately, especially as the market was being required to absorb steel stock as firms were denationalized. The counter-proposal from Colvilles was for Newport to make slabs and billets, now coming from Redbourn, while Redbourn should be developed so that its surplus iron could go into a new continuous billet mill. This would have upset the Midland group. But once a new strip mill was regarded as necessary, then RTB had a very strong case for having it. Lord Mills suggested Newport and his decision was accepted, probably reluctantly, by the Iron and Steel Board in the late spring of 1958. But the Minister of Labour, Iain Macleod, wanted a strip mill in Scotland to help support a car industry and other light industries. In this he was supported by Sir David Eccles, President of the Board of Trade, and John Maclay, the Secretary of State for Scotland, and their view was supported eventually by the Prime Minister and the Chancellor of the Exchequer. By the summer of 1958 Lord Mills, the Minister of Power, was asking Colvilles whether Scotland could sustain a strip mill, which would be Britain's fifth. Colvilles replied that Ravenscraig could be expanded to supply 100,000 extra tons of plates, and 250,000 extra tons of sheets, and it could possibly begin to justify a semi-continuous mill of 500,000 tons capacity. But it was doubtful whether there was a market for the steel.

Thereafter intensive discussions took place in the Ministry of Power and among ministers as to the possibility of building two strip mills – one in Wales and the other in Scotland. Colvilles told Mills in May 1958 that it would be years before the Scottish market could be big enough to absorb the output of a continuous strip mill and that the coke was not available for it. In June 1958, Colvilles told the Iron and Steel Board that 'this development was the outcome of political pressure. A full strip mill would be a financial disaster. . . .' In July, he suggested a smaller mill for Colvilles to meet the Scottish demand, and a smaller mill in Wales to meet future demand – demand which he did not think would materialize and would leave the losses on RTB's shoulders. Press leaks, thought to be of trade union origin, speeded the campaign for a Scottish strip mill so this proposal became politically unacceptable.

By September the pressure was really on, and Mills mentioned that one alternative was to let the Iron and Steel Board build a new works in Scotland with government money 'and do the job themselves'. At a crucial meeting in the Ministry of Power on 22 October 1958, the discussion with a senior official of the Ministry of Power and a senior official of the Treasury, together with a senior member of the Iron and Steel Board, was about the terms on which the government would advance the money, not about whether there should be a fifth strip mill. That was decided. Colvilles wanted a 'participating' loan at low interest rates – that is to say, the govern-

Opposite *Small steel rings are still hand-forged.*

ment shared the profits, if any, but effectively bore the risks. The civil servants sought to show that the mill would integrate well with Colvilles' existing development plan and raise its overall profitability. They also wanted interest at the going rate, and a high proportion (a ratio of 50:34) of the profits. Their view was tenable if the project was commercially viable which they all (except one) knew it was not. It was a political project.

But, as Colvilles pointed out, the shortage of cash (and the Scottish employment situation) was being used to 'bolster up its case for nationalization'. They got their terms – a low interest rate, postponed till the project was finished – though they gave the Ministry a debenture on the strip mill itself. Both strip mills were announced to the House of Commons in November 1958. Even so, the legal details took time to arrange – so long that Colvilles wrote in September 1959 that the agreement had to be signed 'before the election date as I would not have liked to face the risk of having the whole matter reopened should anything go wrong with the election'.

The scheme began, after Parliament had agreed to the money only provided that £45 million of the promised £50 million would be drawn. By December 1960 the cost had already risen to over £61 million, and the coking coal for which the site was chosen was not available, except from Durham, and the importation of American coal 'would be politically disastrous'. As the cost of building was now so high, and the running costs were going to be so great, Colvilles said they might not finish the project. By April 1962, after an extremely rackety 1961, Colvilles was almost bankrupt; it had to have £23 million to finish the project, and money had to be raised from FCI, and the banks, and by July the government had to give its original total of £50 million. By February 1963 so near to bankruptcy were they, that the Ministry of Power took up its security, lest in liquidation they would be merely among the unsecured creditors. So when Ravenscraig officially 'began hot strip mill production' on 1 May 1963, the firm's forebodings were correct; Colvilles was practically ruined because it had undertaken a project that it had thought unwise.

From this tale, then, which is the most dramatic in the postwar history of the industry, it will be seen that the steel industry was not freed from political pressures by the 1953 Act. In the process of the strip mill controversy the industry became subject once more to several criticisms – that it was over-cautious in its investment decisions, that it neglected Wales and Scotland, that it needed public money for new plant while continuing to pay good dividends, and that the division between an Iron and Steel Board and independent companies was not workable. The goodwill which came from the undoubted achievements of the industry was dissipated. The firms had expanded; technically they were well up to scratch; the managerial

Opposite *The Severn Bridge is an example of the modern use of steel.*

quality (especially of United Steel, Colvilles, SCOW and Stewarts & Lloyds) was high; and the prewar record of sloth and neglect had been expunged. From this time on, however, things began to seem to go wrong.

At the end of 1957 Sir Archibald Forbes, of the Iron and Steel Board, was dissatisfied with the progress of United Steel's investment programme and he wanted them to build a new plant to replace Consett's outdated plate-making capacity. There is some evidence of managerial slackness. Gerald Steel reported 'serious over-spending' amounting to £1¼ million on 'special expenditure schemes', at four places, due to faulty estimating and mistakes. This made major investment hazardous. But the slowness was partly due to the fear of nationalization – in early 1958 the *Daily Express* asked for advertising to support its anti-renationalization articles – and RTB was still not denationalized, making the arguments about 'free-enterprise' steel seem a little hollow. In 1958 the pressure for a new home ore site 'north of the Welland' became very strong; a possible scheme in North Oxfordshire was finally given up, and RTB offered to put down a billet plant at Redbourn to help supply United Steel. A decision was still not made – in October 1959 the United Steel Board agreed to allow all local branches to give £100 a year to their local Conservative associations. After the 1959 election, in December 1959, the steel-leaders saw the governor of the Bank of England to get his support for a scheme of floating the remaining ISHRA holdings of steel debentures, a scheme to which he assented. As part of this deal, United Steel sought to buy Redbourn from the still-nationalized RTB, and planned a £28 million works at Appleby-Froding-ham, to be built over the period 1960 to 1964. In early 1961, £10 million more ordinary shares were issued, and United Steel bought the Barrow steel works (which it had long managed on behalf of ISHRA) and began to contemplate the reorganization of Workington, which was once more 'uneconomic'. United Steel, with other firms, helped set up a body to buy up the small firms that ISHRA was unable to dispose of, namely Bairds and Scottish Steel, Skinningrove, and others, called Iron and Steel Investments, which soon became a competitor.

Apart from the strip mills, the major development underway was a new mill for United Steel at Appleby-Frodingham. But, what was interesting, the revolutionary developments of the 1960s, such as continuous casting, electric arc steel-making, and the L–D process, were but little thought about by most firms. The exceptions to this were United Steel, which was interested in the electric arc process and in continuous casting, and RTB, which was interested in the L–D process. So, too, were Colvilles, Consett and GKN. But in all these cases the new processes played but a small part in their view of the future. The sinter process, which increased blast furnace production, was used in the new Newport works, and it had spread to other firms. It was this which was chiefly responsible for the saving of fuel and of iron ore. Direct reduction was already in operation overseas; so, too, was oil injection instead of coke in iron-making.

Indeed, the industry was changing. Thomas Firth & John Brown's bought Beardmore in 1957, and part of Parkhead in 1958. Consett, which spent £28 million in 1958 to 1961 on a new plate mill and an oxygen steel-making plant, financed the development by £10 million internally, £9 million from FCI and £9 million from Lloyds and Barclays Bank – short-term loans to be repaid from future profits. For each major firm a roughly similar pattern of finance emerged.

But this decision to continue to allow the industry to develop piecemeal was accompanied by somewhat darker horizons. The first cloud was dissipated when Labour lost the 1959 general election. Nationalization then seemed a remoter threat.

The Early 1960s

But that election, like the earlier one, was followed by restrictive economic measures; it led to a fall in demand – the first such serious decline since the war. This altered British views of the European Economic Community, the Common Market, which the ECSC had become, since it seemed – incorrectly – that the European industries were expanding their capacities at a faster rate than that of the British, and that they were successfully overcoming certain difficulties that still faced the British industry. It was at this time that enthusiasm for European entry became a major political issue in Britain, and British industry, previously suspicious, became enthusiastic about the Common Market.

In 1962 the BISF was heavily concerned with the negotiations conducted by Edward Heath, then Lord Privy Seal, for entry to the EEC. Detailed position papers broadly rejecting the ECSC pricing system, transport policy and scrap system were sent to Heath's officials and used as his brief. There was a joint committee advising the Foreign Office at which there was deep disagreement with the National Coal Board, which wanted a protected domestic market, while the steel industry wanted cheap fuel imports from Europe. There was also concern that if the application for membership were successful, then the European Parliamentary Assembly might have in 1963–4 'a British Labour Party man' who might sympathize with the Coal Board. A keen effort was consequently made to get to know the politicians in Europe.

During the ten years leading up to nationalization the profitability of the steel industry tended to decline. The capital employed rose from £624 million in 1958 to £1,228 million in 1967, when steel was nationalized. There was a big leap in the amount of capital from 1961 to 1963, when Newport and Ravenscraig were installed and came on stream. Until then the level of profits rose from £108 million in 1958 to £141 million in 1960, and the rate of profits after depreciation rose from 17·3 to 18·8 per cent. After the new capacity was installed the profits fell from £141 million to £59 million and the rate of profit fell to 4·8 per cent. This was a period of economic recession and of severe price controls. Chetwynd Talbot of Cargo Fleet led a fearful outcry about the price-subsidy scheme, which he felt was penalizing efficiency, as it was. The steel pricing system was a complex one. Essentially it was designed to set prices at the level which would yield a normal rate of profit on a newly-built 'greenfield' site, for each major steel product. This would have had the effect of keeping the prices of steel produced from old plants at such a level that the rate of investment in new plant would be automatically settled by the difference between the costs of old plant and greenfield plant. When the old costs were higher than the new costs, investment would be profitable. The trouble was that in some circumstances there was no appropriate greenfield example to point to, that the costs of greenfield operations were usually underestimated and, above all, that steel is an industry whose profits are high when demand is high, but which makes losses when demand is low. If prices are fixed at too low a level, sufficient funds are not accumulated in the booms to keep up the investment in the slumps. Inevitably, therefore, the pricing system led to difficulties. There was a recovery of profits to 1964–5, and then a further fall. In the year in which the steel industry was nationalized, the profits were £23 million, that is 1·9 per cent on the capital employed. This last rate was due primarily to severe price control; but also to other factors.

It was difficult for the industry to finance its vast development programmes. Between 1954 and 1962 nearly £1000 million was spent, of which 10 per cent came from equity issues, 21 per cent from loans and debentures, and 69 per cent from internal cash flow. Obviously, if prices remained fixed at too low a level, as the industry continually argued, the profitability of the companies, or their development programme, would have to be sacrificed. The overall figures marked, too, a fall in internal financing, since the big strip mills were financed by government loans. In addition, as the 1964 general election approached, the prospect of nationalization was renewed.

In 1963 Morgan Grenfell, speaking for the City, spoke of the difficulties of raising money because of the possibility of nationalization, and they said the City would regard an 'outbreak of takeover bids in the steel industry as unfortunate and would defeat its own object'. So one way of restructuring steel and releasing cash was closed to the firms. Indeed this was a matter of considerable significance. The effect of the abortive nationalization was to freeze the firms as they were in 1949 and under the 1953 Act they had to be sold back if possible to their original owners. The merger movement which began in the 1950s restructured industry after industry and only steel remained immune from it. As a result the benefits of mergers (though there are many disadvantages too) were not gained; in particular the re-evaluation of assets, the concentration of output on least-cost plant, the alteration in cash flow and above all the restructuring of management, especially at board level, remained a matter for individual firms which were virtually free from outside pressure.

When the election took place Labour had a narrow majority. It was unable immediately to proceed to nationalization. Steel, too, had several good years of trade – 1963 to 1965 – but these same years were bad for profits, since the new capacity had to be utilized at the cost of writing off old capital and prices were kept down to a level possibly over 10 per cent lower than in Europe and the United States. In 1964, 26 million tons of steel were produced, and in 1965, 27 million tons. By 1966, a quarter of British steel was produced by oxygen processes, and a tenth by electric processes. Other new processes were being rapidly introduced. All this capital required rapid amortization of old equipment, and so led to a reduction in the profit rate. Indeed, at the time of the nationalization debate on steel, in 1965, the industry could be valued at anything between £500 million, based on capitalized profits, to £1000 million based on an optimistic notion of the appropriate return on sales if prices had been allowed to rise internally to world levels. In addition, many calculations suggested that there were serious areas of inefficiency in Britain. Nevertheless, in the twenty years since the end of the war, the industry had been transformed.

IO

A New World

Nationalization in 1967 differed significantly however from that attempted nearly twenty years before. The 1967 Iron and Steel Act covered fewer firms, but it led to the dissolution of organizations like the Federation which had remained independent in 1950. The legislation first proposed in the 1964 Parliament was confirmed by the 1966 election results and was then enacted. In 1971 the new Conservative government made clear that it would abide by what it had said in opposition, that the greater part of the industry would not be denationalized, though marginal changes might be made.

The British Steel Corporation, having been brought into existence in 1967, therefore had some prospect of permanence after 1971. A further element in making for this settlement was that the Act left to the Steel Corporation itself the task of recommending its own organization. Earlier nationalization statutes, those for gas, rail and electricity, for instance, had specified the structure which often had subsequently to be changed by statute.

The first chairman of the Corporation was Lord Melchett who was a young man, a merchant banker, whose appointment at an early stage to the preparatory body before the firms were nationalized was of cardinal importance. His drive and tact secured the co-operation both of the workers and managers in the industry and of successive ministers in creating a Corporation which would adequately serve the public interest whilst preserving that degree of managerial independence necessary for enterprise and initiative in a highly competitive world market. His death in the summer of 1973 at the age of forty-eight was a deep loss.

To centralize might mean to take all significant decisions about investment, production, pricing, wages, location, marketing in one place; or it might mean to take only 'crucial' decisions centrally. The Act transferred, on 28 July 1967, the fourteen largest crude steel companies to public ownership by the British Steel Corporation. The Act also dissolved the Iron and Steel Board. BISF was also later dissolved, by agreement. A substantial part of the industry, especially at the engineering and specialist product end, remained in non-public ownership, however, and the new trade association,

The British Independent Steel Producers Association which was created in 1967 to represent this part of the industry, had some one hundred and fifty members.

The first task of the new Corporation was to take charge of the nationalized part of the industry, organize its cash flow, and approve the ongoing investment programme. At the same time the decision was taken not to continue to operate through the existing firms, as had been done in the first nationalization, but to group the industry mainly on regional lines. This is broadly what had been proposed by Brasserts to Montagu Norman in 1930; what had been proposed by the trades unions in 1931; what had been proposed by the New Fabian Research Bureau in 1936; and what had, in fact, been 'official' policy until the mid-1950s. And it was also the logic of the Benson Report of 1966 on the Steel Industry, which was set up by the British Iron and Steel Federation to indicate how best the industry might be rationalized if it remained in private ownership.

The fourteen firms which were nationalized were not themselves giants, though among the bigger British companies. But combined they had a book value of £1,400 million, their turnover was £1000 million, and they employed over 250,000 people. There were thirty-nine crude steel producing works, including twenty-one that were fully integrated, together with a great miscellany of other assets. Some of the firms were mostly located in one area – Colvilles in Scotland for example, and SCOW in South Wales; some specialized in broadly one type of steel product, such as SCOW in sheet and tinplate, Consett and South Durham in heavy steel plate and sections, and Stewarts & Lloyds in tubes; but the remainder, for example, English Steel, John Summers, RTB, and above all United Steel, were geographically dispersed and produced a range of products. (Just before nationalization Dorman Long, South Durham and Stewarts & Lloyds had merged as British Steel and Tube Ltd, but it was too late to affect the argument.) If the Corporation decided not to continue the existing firms, should it seek to have specialist groups, or geographical groups?

Before the war it had been proposed by Brasserts and the Bank of England to have four regional groups – Scotland, North East, Midlands and South Wales. In the organization established by the Corporation in 1967, some of these areas were also specialized by product, though less so than in the nineteen-thirties scheme. In 1967, for sheer speed and managerial efficiency, it was decided first of all to organize the industry on the basis of individual companies, grouped mainly geographically. It was decided not to organize the industry by product group, since the works were geographically dispersed, and often works were multi-product. It was decided not to disperse existing management between works despite the earlier experience of the first amalgamation that management had remained loyal to the firms rather than to the Corporation. As a result, the organization was basically geographical; four groups were established, and these groups were big because they were basically company amalgamations. The structure that emerged resembled Montagu Norman's original scheme for the steel industry. The Midland Group was English Steel and United Steel in the Sheffield/ Rotherham area, including the former Tube Investments' steelworks at Park Gate; the Scunthorpe producers of Appleby-Frodingham, Redbourn and Lysaghts, and the Cumberland works of United Steel, i.e. Workington, Distington Engineering and Barrow Steel Works. The Northern & Tubes group was based on the Dorman Long, South Durham and Stewarts & Lloyds merger, together with Consett and Skinningrove. The Scottish and North West group was Colvilles, John Summers, Lancashire Steel and the Monks Hall subsidiary of RTB. South Wales was RTB and SCOW, together with Guest Keen's Cardiff works.

The Corporation said hopefully that 'the spur of competition other than in price between the groups and between units below them is in our view highly desirable'. The major reorganization was the severing of RTB from their Lincolnshire works. But apart from that it was a matter of amalgamation.

The essential task of those first four groupings was to bring together the managements of the companies, so that British Steel could begin to formulate a corporate identity and a corporate policy. It is often said that it takes at least ten years for a merger to be fulfilled; clearly, by the rate and degree of change the process of a merger can be accelerated or hindered.

By late 1968, when the Corporation had settled down, it decided that it would report to the Minister of Power on its working. The Corporation undertook a radical review of its structure. The four groups had been subdivided for operating purposes into sixteen divisions – six in the Midland group (Scunthorpe, Rotherham, Cumbrian, alloy and stainless steel, special steel, and general products), four in the Northern & Tubes group, (tubes, and pipes, iron and steel structural and engineering), three in the Scottish and North-West group (Colvilles, Lancashire, and Summers), and four in the South Wales group (RTB, SCOW, East Moors and Whitehead, and special steels and fabricated products).

The Corporation strongly urged the abolition of the old companies, all of which were vested in it, partly because while 'many companies have developed amongst their employees a valuable *esprit de corps* and loyalty. . . . It is of fundamental importance to build up a new loyalty with pride in the Corporation as a whole, and to make this compatible with local pride in the works and divisions.' The main reason was that the company structure was no longer relevant. The Corporation had left operations to groups and divisions, and operating plans, major investment, and sales were subject to central approval and initiative. But the system of multi-product groups 'impede rationalization and the optimum utilization of the Corporation's assets . . . and the disadvantages of a product grouping . . . would be out-weighed by the advantages in promoting rationalization. . . . Development of new capacity must . . . be planned on a product basis. . . . There is therefore a strong case for organizing the Corporation's activities on a product basis.' These arguments were accepted by the minister and were supported by the Iron and Steel Act 1969, which facilitated the dissolution of the company structure and also gave new financial support to the Corporation. The assets of the companies were transferred to the Corporation in 1970, and most of them dissolved so that the Corporation 'could operate as a single legal entity'.

The new arrangements, which began in early 1970, were for six product divisions. Two were for constructional engineering and chemicals; the remaining four were for steel proper. These were General Steels, based on Glasgow, Special Steels, based on Sheffield, Strip Mills, based on Cardiff, and Tubes, based on Corby. The geographical dispersal of the works in the divisions was substantial.

It would be impertinent to attempt to summarize the industry's record in order to pass a judgement on it. The questions that arise are self-evident. They relate to technical progress and the connection between technical progress and industrial organization. This in turn is connected with such topics as public control of prices and investment, and the relation of this public control to management and organized labour. It has to be recognized that quite apart from the merits or otherwise of nationalization as such, there are considerable differences between the British Steel Corporation and most other nationalized industries. The Corporation is a manufacturing business, international in its operations, its markets and its raw material supplies. It has vigorous competition both at home and abroad. In order to compete in its home and international markets the Corporation decided at an early stage in its life to maintain a highly commercial attitude to every aspect of its operations, to be market orientated, and, to this end, to obtain its raw materials and fuel and power at competitive market rates whether from within the UK or any other part of the world. The Corporation also attached considerable importance to ensuring that it remained competitive in its ability to attract and hold first class management and an efficient workforce.

Inevitably, this series of facts has had considerable implications for the relationship between the Corporation and the government: the Corporation has consistently taken the view that the minister, in assessing capital programmes for example, should rely on its judgment in technical, commercial and other matters. It will be recalled that the relations between the government and the industry had been a perennial topic of discussion for forty years or more.

The granting of £700 million of Public Dividend Capital in the Iron and Steel Act 1969 was a radical change made in response to proposals made by the Corporation with a view to bringing its financial structure more into line with that of ordinary commercial undertakings, including its main competitors at home and overseas. In the Iron and Steel Act 1972, the amount of PDC was reduced to £500 million and a reserve was created with the balance plus a provision for a further £150 million transferred to reserve from the Corporation's long term debt. The financing of investment has been a further perennial problem in steel.

Steady progress has been made with the rationalization of the Corporation's production facilities. Investment in new plant and equipment has risen very considerably from a rate of between £70 and £80 million a year between October 1967 and March 1970, to £143 million in the year ended March 1971, £237 million in the year ended March 1972, and an estimated £190 million for the year ended March 1973. Various major development schemes have already been carried through since 1967, especially at Scunthorpe, Lackenby, Ravenscraig and Llanwern and the Ten Year Development Strategy, agreed by the government in February 1973, marked the culmination of much planning work. It provided for the investment of £3,000 million over the decade, expanding the capacity of the industry considerably but concentrating steel production into fewer and larger units, with the object of achieving big gains in productivity and efficiency.

A considerable sector of the industry remained in private ownership, chiefly at the engineering and final product end. Rationalization arrangements with the private sector, designed to straighten out the 'ragged edge' left by the lines drawn by the nationalization act of 1967, have progressed, often on the Corporation's initiative. These have included the joint 50/50 ownership arrangement for Round Oak Steelworks, concluded by the Corporation with Tube Investments in 1967; the rationalization of the interests of the Corporation and Thos. Firth & John Brown in Sheffield; and the disposal of the Corporation's interests in building bricks, tool steels and tools, wire, stampings and engineering.

These rationalization procedures have not been uncontroversial. The actual and proposed closing of works has aroused controversy. So, too, has the decision to hive off.

British membership of the Common Market since 1 January 1973 is affecting the industry in a number of ways. At the end of a five-year transitional period it will lose its present tariff protection from producers in the Community. Conversely, its products will enter freely into the other countries in the Community. It has become subject to the decisions and recommendations of the ECSC for most of its products and to the rules of the EEC for the remainder. The ECSC requires all companies to publish price lists, which specify basing points at or near points of production, from which the prices apply and to which costs of carriage to the purchaser are added. It has superseded the statutory requirements of the Iron and Steel Act 1967 which established the Iron and Steel Consumers' Council with a duty of representing consumer interests and which empowered the minister to give directions to the corporation based on matters reported to him by the council. In April 1971, the Corporation was directed to reduce a price increase under the operation of these provisions. Since the Community has its own consultative machinery, the Iron and Steel Consumers' Council has ceased to be an official statutory body. In these and other ways the environment in which the industry operates has radically altered.

It will be seen, then, that the iron and steel industry is as subject to change and alteration as it has ever been. The rise of the industry, its achievements and its problems, have been indissolubly linked to a process of continuous change. Any search for finality would be an illusion.

General Steels Division

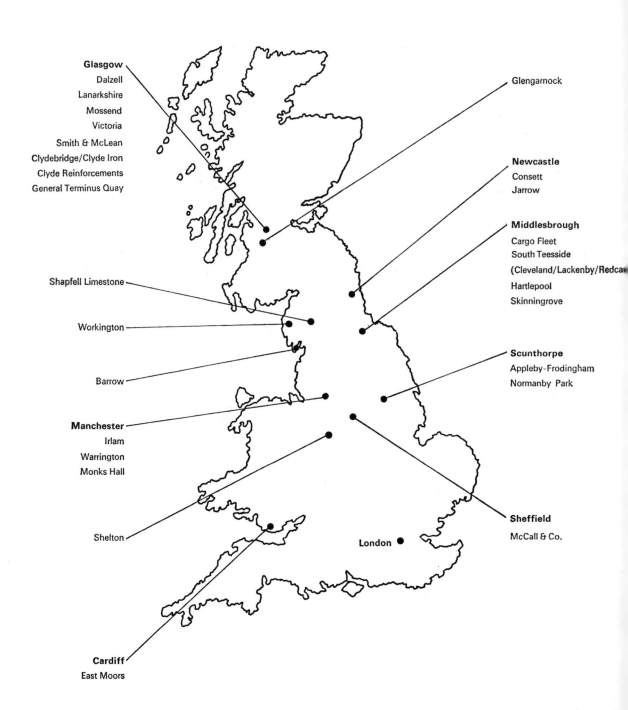

Glasgow
Dalzell
Lanarkshire
Mossend
Victoria
Smith & McLean
Clydebridge/Clyde Iron
Clyde Reinforcements
General Terminus Quay

Glengarnock

Newcastle
Consett
Jarrow

Middlesbrough
Cargo Fleet
South Teesside
(Cleveland/Lackenby/Redcar
Hartlepool
Skinningrove

Shapfell Limestone

Workington

Scunthorpe
Appleby-Frodingham
Normanby Park

Barrow

Manchester
Irlam
Warrington
Monks Hall

Sheffield
McCall & Co.

Shelton

London

Cardiff
East Moors

Special Steels Division

Glasgow
Fullwood
Hallside/Craigneuk/
Tollcross

Distington

Manchester
Trafford Park
Audenshaw

Sheffield
Stocksbridge
Tinsley Park
Shepcote Lane
Park Gate
Aldwarke
Roundwood
Templeborough
Brinsworth
River Don
Ickles
Grimesthorpe
Cyclops
Renishaw

Wolverhampton/
Birchley

Bilston

Birmingham

London

Swansea
Dowlais
Landore

Newport
Panteg

Strip Mills Division

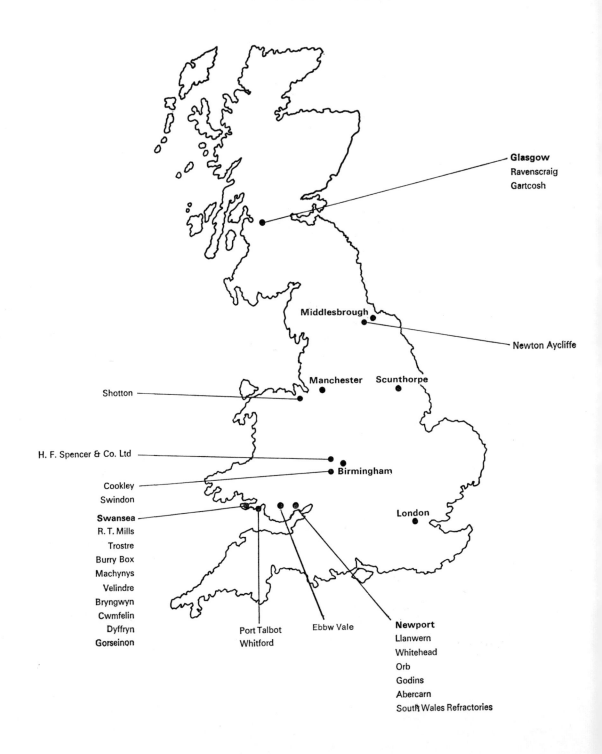

Glasgow
Ravenscraig
Gartcosh

Middlesbrough

Newton Aycliffe

Manchester   Scunthorpe

Shotton

H. F. Spencer & Co. Ltd

Birmingham

Cookley
Swindon

Swansea
R. T. Mills
Trostre
Burry Box
Machynys
Velindre
Bryngwyn
Cwmfelin
Dyffryn
Gorseinon

London

Port Talbot
Whitford

Ebbw Vale

Newport
Llanwern
Whitehead
Orb
Godins
Abercarn
South Wales Refractories

Tubes Division

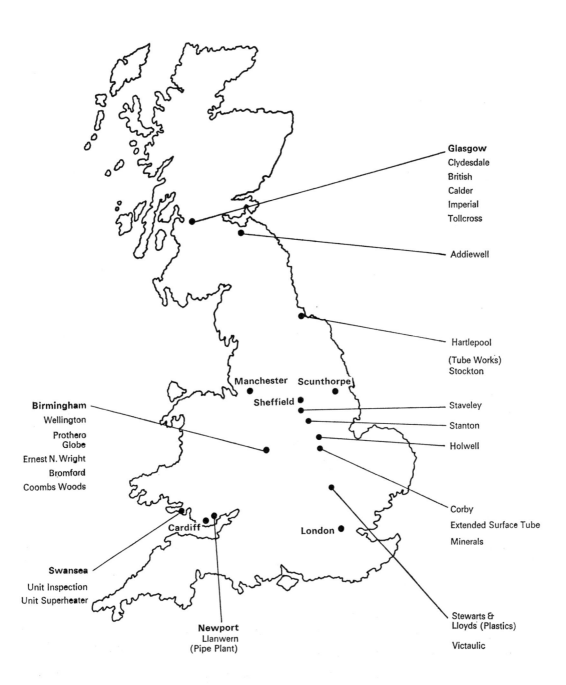

Glasgow
Clydesdale
British
Calder
Imperial
Tollcross

Addiewell

Hartlepool
(Tube Works)
Stockton

Manchester Scunthorpe
Sheffield

Birmingham
Wellington
Prothero
Globe
Ernest N. Wright
Bromford
Coombs Woods

Staveley

Stanton

Holwell

Corby
Extended Surface Tube
Minerals

Cardiff

London

Swansea
Unit Inspection
Unit Superheater

Stewarts &
Lloyds (Plastics)

Victaulic

Newport
Llanwern
(Pipe Plant)

Sources and Guide to Further Reading

In order to avoid overloading the book, the list of detailed references has been omitted from the printed text. It is available on application to the author, or to the Secretary to the British Steel Corporation. Most quotations and other factual material are drawn directly from manuscript sources, though in the first and last chapters printed sources have been extensively used.

Manuscript Sources

The manuscript sources used in the preparation of this book are mainly from inside the industry. Other collections which have been used are the Baldwin Papers, Cambridge University Library, the Dalton Papers, British Library of Political and Economic Science, and the Public Record Office. The Bank of England kindly allowed me to read the Brassert Report to Montagu Norman. They are not responsible for my interpretation of it.

Of the industry sources, many of the central papers of the British Iron and Steel Federation are now held by the British Steel Corporation. The Iron and Steel Board's main files are at the Public Record Office, together with those of the Iron and Steel Corporation of Great Britain, the nationalized body that was set up in 1950, and those of the Iron and Steel Holding and Realization Agency, established to denationalize the industry. These are catalogued.

The Corporation's records and archives inherited from the former steel companies are extensive and are in the process of being organized. When it is realized that the volume of records now belonging to the Corporation which have passed out of regular use runs to hundreds of thousands of cubic feet all of which will have to be appraised to determine their value, it will be understood that for the most part they are not yet systematically catalogued. Upwards of 5,000 cubic feet of records have already been identified as of archival value.

Most of these former company records are still held at the works, or at offices outside the works, owned by the firms before nationalization. They

Opposite Port Talbot, seen from the air, shows the size of a modern steelworks.

will in due course be systematically stored and catalogued under the Corporation's new arrangements, whereby archives will be stored in Records Centres in various regions of the country.

The records include board minutes, board committee minutes, share transfer certificates, letter books, reports by surveyors, architects, and other technical data, invoices and receipts.

To my surprise, and contrary to widespread opinion, the company minute books have been an invaluable source. In the first place they have not hitherto been much used in histories of steel; in the second place, when they have been used, they have been used for one firm, and without detailed references. To take a substantial number of companies is to see common problems from several perspectives. But, above all, the dictum that the minutes are designed to conceal and not to reveal is simply untrue. Nothing important was legal until it was minuted, and a careful eye can usually find the key minute and so know when and where to look for the other material. Further, over fifty years of monthly meetings, the hidden truth often slips out. What is most striking, too, is the way in which the personalities of individual directors and the atmosphere of particular firms shine out from their minutes.

In addition, I have had many conversations with people who have been concerned with the industry in many of its aspects. Notes of these conversations have been left in the Corporation's archives, together with successive drafts of this volume annotated with extra material.

This book has concentrated upon the industry as a whole. It has also sought to avoid easy judgements. One consequence of this, of course, is that the just commemoration of the work of hundreds of thousands of people in plants and firms up and down the country has not been directly made. But there are many histories of the major companies (all of which I have consulted and a number of which I have referred to) which go some way to fill this gap. For me to have covered the same ground might seem to the authors of the works concerned both otiose and possibly plagiaristic.

Printed Sources

The printed sources divide into three. First there are those that deal in general terms with the steel industry in the economy. Then there are those that deal specifically with the history of the steel industry. Lastly, there are specialized monographs. The first group is – broadly speaking – omitted here. The other two groups are listed together. The lists are not exhaustive – but they indicate the scope of further reading.

Opposite *Lord Melchett was the first chairman of the British Steel Corporation from 1967 to 1973. He was succeeded in September 1973 by Dr H. M. Finniston.*

Journals and Newspapers

British Steel, British Steelmaker, Daily Express, Economic Journal, The Economist, Iron and Coal Trades Review, Iron and Steel Institute Journal, South Wales Argus, Steel Review, Sunday Telegraph, Swansea Evening Post, The Times, Western Mail.

Books and Pamphlets

ANONYMOUS, *Allan Campbell Macdiarmid: A Memoir*, BISF, 1945.

ANONYMOUS, *The History of the English Steel Corporation*, (n.d.).

ANONYMOUS, *Tariff Commission*, Report on Iron and Steel, P. S. King, 1904.

ANONYMOUS, *Workington Iron & Steel Company Branch of the United Steel Companies Ltd*, Workington, 1956.

DEREK H. ALDCROFT (ed.), *The Development of British Industry and Foreign Competition, 1875–1945*, Allen & Unwin, 1968.

P. W. S. ANDREWS and E. BRUNNER, *Capital Development in Steel*, Blackwell, 1951.

ANGLO-AMERICAN COUNCIL ON PRODUCTIVITY, *Iron and Steel Productivity Team Report*, 1952.

T. S. ASHTON, *Iron and Steel in the Industrial Revolution* (2nd ed.), Manchester, 1951.

C. R. ATTLEE, *A Prime Minister Remembers*, Heinemann, 1961.

A. W. BALDWIN, *My Father: The True Story*, Allen & Unwin, 1956.

BALFOUR COMMITTEE FINAL REPORT, Committee on Industry and Trade, Cmd 3282, HMSO, 1929.

NORA BELOFF, *Transit of Britain*, Collins, 1973.

F. BENHAM, *The Iron and Steel Industry of Germany, France, Belgium, Luxembourg and the Saar*, London and Cambridge Economic Service, Special Memo. No. 39, 1934.

WILLIAM BEVERIDGE, *Full Employment in a Free Society*, Allen & Unwin, 1944.

ALAN BIRCH, *The Economic History of the British Iron and Steel Industry 1784–1879*, Frank Cass, 1967.

BRITISH IRON AND STEEL FEDERATION, (BISF) Annual Reports, *Battle for Steel*, 1945; *Steel – Fact and Fiction*, 1959; *Steel – The Facts*, 1964;

BRITISH IRON AND STEEL RESEARCH ASSOCIATION, Annual Reports.

BRITISH PRODUCTIVITY COUNCIL, Iron and Steel Report, 1956.

Steel and the Sixties, 1961; *The Iron and Steel Bill – Some Arguments for and against*, 1949; *Andrew Rae Duncan – A Memoir*, 1952; *The Iron and Steel Bill – Discussion in Committee*, 1949. Report to the Minister of Supply on the Iron and Steel Industry, Cmd 6811, HMSO, 1946.

BRITISH STEEL CORPORATION, Report on Organization, Cmnd 3362, 1967. Second Report on Organization, HC 163, 11 March 1969. Third Report on Organization, HC 60, 16 December 1969. Annual Report and Accounts 1967–8, and subsequently.

DUNCAN L. BURN, *The Economic History of Steelmaking 1867–1939*, Cambridge University Press, 1940. *The Steel Industry 1939–59*, Cambridge University Press, 1961. 'Steel', Chapter VII of *The Structure of British Industry*, Vols 1 and 2, a symposium, ed. Burn, Cambridge University Press, 1958.

J.C. CARR and W. TAPLIN, *History of the British Steel Industry*, Blackwell, 1962.

JOHN CLAPHAM, *An Economic History of Modern Britain*, Vols 1 to 3, Cambridge University Press, reprinted 1950–2.

SIR HENRY CLAY, *Lord Norman*, Macmillan, 1957.

HUGH DALTON, *High Tide and After*, Muller, 1962. *The Fateful Years*, Muller, 1957. *Practical Socialism for Britain*, Routledge, 1935.

A.F.L. DEESON, *The Great Swindlers*, Foulsham, 1971.

K.H.R. EDWARDS, *Chronology* (Private typescript in possession of BSC).

CHARLOTTE ERICKSON, *British Industrialists Steel & Hosiery 1850–1950*, Cambridge University Press, 1959.

W. FIENBURGH and R. EVELY, *Steel is Power*, Gollancz, 1948.

MICHAEL FOOT, *Aneurin Bevan, 1897–1945*, Vol 1, MacGibbon & Kee, 1962.

W.K.V. GALE, *The British Iron & Steel Industry*, David & Charles, 1967.

LORD GRANTLEY, *The Silver Spoon* (ed. Mary and Alan Wood), Hutchinson, 1954.

JAMES GRIFFITHS, *Pages from Memory*, Dent, 1969.

W. GUMBEL and K. POTTER, *The Iron and Steel Act, 1949*, Butterworth, 1951. *The Iron and Steel Act, 1953*, Butterworth, 1953.

W.K. HANCOCK and M.M. GOWING, *British War Economy*, HMSO, 1949.

E. HEXNER, *The International Steel Cartel*, The University of North Carolina Press, 1943.

J. HURSTFIELD, *The Control of Raw Materials*, HMSO and Longmans, 1953.

IMPORT DUTIES ADVISORY COMMITTEE, Recommendations and Import Duties Orders, Report on the Present Position and Future Development of the Iron and Steel Industry, Cmd 5507, HMSO, 1937.

'INGOT', *The Socialisation of Iron & Steel*, Gollancz, 1936.

IRON AND STEEL BOARD, (ISB) Annual Reports; Development Reports, 1955,

1957, 1961, 1964, 1966; Research in the Iron and Steel Industry, Special Report, 1963; The Iron and Steel Board – What It Is and What It Does, 1960.

IRON AND STEEL BOARD AND BRITISH IRON AND STEEL FEDERATION, Annual Statistics from 1955 to 1967.

IRON AND STEEL CORPORATION OF GREAT BRITAIN, (ISCGB) Annual Reports and Accounts.

IRON AND STEEL HOLDING AND REALIZATION AGENCY, (ISHRA) Annual Reports and Accounts.

IRON AND STEEL TRADES CONFEDERATION MAY 1931, What is wrong with the British Iron and Steel Industry?

SIR EDGAR R. JONES, *Toilers of the Hills*, The Griffin Press, Pontypool, 1959.

B.S. KEELING AND A.E.G. WRIGHT, *The Development of the Modern British Steel Industry*, Longmans, 1964.

J. M. KEYNES, *Essays in Persuasion*, Cambridge University Press, 1972.

KEITH MIDDLEMAS and JOHN BARNES, *Baldwin – A Biography*, Weidenfeld & Nicolson, 1969.

W. MINCHINTON, *The British Tinplate Industry: A History*, Oxford University Press, 1957.

HERBERT MORRISON, *An Autobiography*, Odhams Press, 1960.

DAVID MURRAY, *Sir John Craig, CBE, DL, LLD*, (Privately printed) n.d. (1955?).

NORRIS OAKLEY, *Iron & Steel Handbook*, (Privately printed), 1956 to 1966.

A.K. OSBORNE, *An Encyclopaedia of the Iron & Steel Industry*, The Technical Press, 1956.

ALBERT PAM, *Adventures and Recollections*, Oxford University Press, 1945.

R. PEDDIE, *The United Steel Companies Limited 1918–1968, A History*, C. Nicholls, Manchester, 1969.

M.M. POSTAN, *British War Production*, HMSO and Longmans, 1952.

SIR ARTHUR PUGH, *Men of Steel*, Iron and Steel Trades Confederation, 1951.

J.M. REID, *Sir James Lithgow*, Hutchinson, 1964.

L. ROSTAS, *Comparative Productivity in British and American Industry*, Cambridge University Press, 1948.

MICHAEL SANDERSON, *The Universities and British Industry 1850–1970*, Routledge and Kegan Paul, 1972.

H.R. SCHUBERT, *History of the Iron and Steel Industry* (from c. 450 BC to AD 1775), Routledge & Kegan Paul, 1957.

SCOBY-SMITH REPORT, Report of Departmental Committee on the Position of Iron and Steel Trades after the War, Cmd. 9071, HMSO, 1918.

SIR FREDERICK SCOPES, *The Development of Corby Works*, Stewarts & Lloyds, 1968.

J.D. SCOTT, *Siemens Brothers 1858–1958*, Weidenfeld & Nicolson, 1958.

ROBERT SHONE, *Problems of Investment*, Blackwell, 1971.

ROBERT SKIDELSKY, *Politicians and the Slump*, Macmillan, 1967.

A.J.P. TAYLOR, *English History 1914–45*, Oxford University Press, 1965. *Beaverbrook*, Hamish Hamilton, 1972.

G.R. WALSHAW and C.A.J. BEHRENDT, *The History of Appleby-Frodingham*, The Appleby-Frodingham Steel Co., 1950.

ELLEN WILKINSON, *The Town that was Murdered*, Gollancz, 1939.

W.G. WILLIS, *South Durham Steel & Iron Co. Ltd*, Eyre & Spottiswoode, 1969. *Skinningrove Iron Company Limited, A History 1880–1968*, Kidds Advertising, n.d. (1969 ?).

CHARLES WILSON, *A Man and His Times. A Memoir of Sir Ellis Hunter*, Newman Neame, 1962.

Some People Mentioned in the Text

DAME ELIZABETH ACKROYD (DBE 1970), b.? 1915; St Hugh's College, Oxford. Ministry of Supply and Board of Trade, Director Consumers' Council 1963–71.

LORD AIREDALE, b. 1863; Trinity College, Cambridge; iron and steel manufacturer and director Midland Bank; d. 1944. S. father 1911.

LIONEL BEAUMONT-THOMAS, b. 1893; director Richard Thomas; Conservative MP 1929–35; d. 1942.

SIR HUGH BELL, b. 1844; s. of Lowthian Bell; Edinburgh and Göttingen; director Dorman Long and Pearsons; d. 1931. S. father 1904.

SIR EDWARD BOYLE, b. 1878; barrister; Eton and Balliol; director Richard Thomas; d. 1945. S. father 1909.

SIR HERBERT BRITTAIN (Kt. 1955), b. 1894; Rochdale and Manchester University; Treasury 1919–57; chairman ISHRA; d. 1961.

SIR CHARLES BRUCE-GARDNER (Kt. 1938, Bart. 1945), b. 1887; St Dunstan's and Battersea Tech.; director John Summers; industrial adviser to governor of Bank of England; d. 1960.

SIR RICHARD CLARKE (Kt. 1964), b. 1910; Christ's Hospital, Clare College Cambridge; journalist, civil servant, Treasury 1945–66; Permanent Secretary Ministry of Technology, 1966–70.

SIR JOHN CRAIG (Kt. 1943), b. 1874; chairman and director Colvilles; d. 1957.

SIR CHARLES CRAVEN (Kt. 1934, Bart. 1942), b. 1884; Rossall, HMS Britannia; director Vickers; d. 1944.

LORD CRAWFORD AND BALCARRES, b. 1871; Eton and Magdalen; Conservative MP 1895–1913; mine-owner at Wigan; minister 1916–22; d. 1940. S. father 1913.

HUGH DALTON (Baron 1960), b. 1887; Eton and King's; university teacher; Labour MP 1924–31, 1935–59; minister 1940–7, 1947–50; President of the Board of Trade 1942–5; Chancellor of the Exchequer 1945–7; d. 1962.

SIR ARTHUR DORMAN (Kt. 1918, Bart. 1923), b. 1848; Christ's Hospital, and apprentice, chairman Dorman Long; d. 1931.

LORD DUDLEY, b. 1894; Eton and Christ Church; Conservative MP 1921–4, 1931–2; director of Earl of Dudley's Round Oak works, president BISF 1935–6; d. 1969. S. father 1932.

Some People Mentioned in the Text

SIR ANDREW DUNCAN (Kt. 1921), b. 1884; barrister; chairman BISF; MP 1940–50; President of Board of Trade 1940 and 1941; Minister of Supply 1940–1, 1942–5; d. 1952.

SIR LINCOLN EVANS (Kt. 1953), b. 1889; Swansea elementary school; general secretary ISTC 1946–53; member Iron and Steel Board 1946–9, deputy chairman 1953–67; d. 1970.

SIR WILLIAM FIRTH (Kt. 1932), b. 1881; chairman Richard Thomas; d. 1957.

SIR ARCHIBALD FORBES (Kt. 1943), b. 1903; Paisley, Glasgow University, accountant (Thomas McLintock); deputy secretary, Ministry of Air-craft Production; chairman of Iron and Steel Board 1946–9, 1953–9; chairman Midland Bank.

OLIVER FRANKS (Kt. 1946, Baron 1962), b. 1905; Bristol Grammar School, Queen's College, Oxford; Fellow and Provost of Queen's; Professor of Moral Philosophy, Glasgow; Permanent Secretary, Ministry of Supply; ambassador to Washington; chairman Lloyds Bank; Provost, Worcester College, Oxford.

LORD FURNESS (Viscount 1918), b. 1883; chairman Furness Group; d. 1940. S. father 1912.

SIR JOHN GREEN (Kt. 1949); b. 1892; member and then chairman ISCGB 1950–3; member ISHRA 1953–5.

LORD GREENWOOD (Hamar Greenwood) (Bart. 1915, Viscount 1937), b. 1870; Toronto University, Liberal MP 1906–22, Conservative MP 1924–9; minister 1919–22; president BISF 1938–9; d. 1948.

STEVEN HARDIE, b. 1885; Paisley Grammar School, Glasgow University; DSO First World War; chairman British Oxygen; chairman ISCGB 1950–2; d. 1969.

SIR ROBERT HILTON (Kt. 1942), b. 1870; Sedbergh; MetroVick 1919–28; managing director United Steel 1928–39; d. 1943.

SIR ELLIS HUNTER (Kt. 1948), b. 1892; accountant, partner in W.B. Peat (later Peat Marwick and Mitchell); Dorman Long 1938–61; d. 1961.

LORD INVERNAIRN (Baron 1921), b. 1856 as William Beardmore; Glasgow High School; Ayr Academy; School of Mines; d. 1936.

SIR JOHN E. JAMES (Kt. 1949), b. 1874; iron moulder at Cargo Fleet; chairman Lancashire Steel; d. 1963.

SIR WALTER BENTON JONES, b. 1880; Repton and Trinity Cambridge; director, chairman and president United Steel; d. 1967. S. father 1936.

SIR FREDERICK JONES (Bart. 1921), b. 1854; Repton and Trinity Cambridge; colliery owner and director United Steel; d. 1936.

LORD KYLSANT (Baron 1923), b. 1863 as Owen Philipps; Liberal MP 1906–10; Conservative 1916–22; controlled Harland and Wolff; imprisoned for city activities; d. 1937.

SIR WILLIAM LARKE (Kt. 1921), b. ? 1870; Colfe's Grammar School and engineering apprentice; engineer at BTH; director BISF, 1922–46; d. 1959.

SIR ERNEST LEVER (Kt. 1954), b. 1890; William Ellis School; joined Prudential Assurance Co. 1907; chairman Richard Thomas & Baldwins 1940–59; d. 1970.

SIR ALLAN MACDIARMID (Kt. 1945), b. 1880; Kelvinside Academy; Uppingham; accountant; chairman Stewarts & Lloyds; d. 1945.

SIR ANDREW MCCANCE, FRS (Kt. 1947), b. 1889; Morrison's Academy and Royal School of Mines; manager Beardmores; founder Clyde Alloy; managing director and chairman of Colvilles.

REGINALD MCKENNA, b. 1863; Trinity Hall, Cambridge; barrister; Liberal MP 1895–1918; cabinet minister 1907–16; Chancellor of Exchequer 1915–16; chairman Midland Bank 1919–43; d. 1943.

LORD MAY (Kt. 1918, Bart. 1931, Baron 1935); b. 1871; actuary; secretary to the Prudential Assurance Co.; chairman Economy Committee 1931; chairman Import Duties Advisory Committee 1932–46; d. 1946.

LORD MILLS (Kt. 1942, Bart. 1953, Baron, 1957, Viscount 1963); b. 1890; North-Eastern County School; businessman; Ministry of Production 1940–4; Minister of Power 1957–9; other government office 1959–62; d. 1968.

SIR FREDERICK MILLS (Bart. 1921), b. 1865; director Ebbw Vale; Conservative MP 1931–45; d. 1953.

SIR JOHN MORISON (Kt. 1945), b. 1893; Greenock Academy; accountant with Thomson McLintock; chairman ISHRA; d. 1958.

HERBERT MORRISON (Baron, 1959); b. 1888; elementary schools; Labour MP 1923–4, 1929–31, 1935–59; leader, London County Council 1934–40; Minister of Supply 1940; Home Secretary 1940–5; Lord President 1945–51; Foreign Secretary 1951; d. 1965.

LORD NORMAN (Baron 1944), b. 1871; Eton and King's; DSO in South African war; Governor of Bank of England 1920–44; d. 1950.

LORD PIRRIE (Kt. 1897, Baron 1906, Viscount 1921); b. 1847; Belfast Royal Academical Institution; apprentice Harland and Wolff and partner 1874, later chairman; d. 1924.

MAJOR ALBERT PAM, b. 1875; City of London, Germany and Lausanne; re-organized match industry in Venezuela; founded Marmite; joined J. Henry Schröder 1920; d. 1955.

SIR WILLIAM PLENDER (Bt. 1923), b. 1861; accountant and busybody; d. 1946.

SIR ARTHUR PUGH (Kt. 1935), b. 1870; elementary school Ross-on-Wye; smelter, general secretary ISTC 1917–36; d. 1955.

SIR PETER RYLANDS (Kt. 1921, Bart. 1939), b. 1868; Charterhouse; Trinity College, Cambridge; barrister; managing director Rylands Bros.; d. 1948.

LORD SANKEY (Kt. 1914, Baron 1929, Viscount 1932), b. 1866; Lancing and Jesus College, Oxford; lawyer and judge; d. 1948.

SIR ROBERT SHONE (Kt. 1955), b. 1906; Sedbergh, Liverpool University and Chicago; engineer and economist; BISF and Iron and Steel Board; director general NEDO 1962–6.

GEORGE STRAUSS, b. ? 1900; Rugby; Labour MP 1929–31, 1934–; Minister of Supply 1947–51.

BENJAMIN TALBOT, b. 1864; Fulneck School, and apprentice; managing director Cargo Fleet and South Durham; d. 1947.

LORD WEIR (Baron 1918, Viscount 1938), b. 1877; Director General of Aircraft Production 1918; Secretary of State for Air 1918; director G. and J. Weir; d. 1959.

JOHN WILMOT (Baron 1950), b. 1895; businessman, Labour MP 1933–5, 1939–50; junior minister in Churchill's coalition, Minister of Supply 1945–7; d. 1964.

Index

Aberdare, Lord, 84
Ackroyd, Dame Elizabeth, 133
Adamson, Campbell, 172
Adamson, John 89–90
Admiralty, demands steel, 11; demands more steel, 85, 88, 89
Aircraft Production, Ministry of, 157
Air-raids, 94
Alabama, 74
Alliance Assurance Co., 49
Allied Ironfounders, 58
Alsace-Lorraine, 74
Alsop, R., 93
American industry, develops, 6; competition 8–9; example 103, 113, 118, 132
Anchor project, 165
Andrews, P.W.S., 87
Anglo-American Finance Corporation, 55
Appleby-Frodingham, 41–2, 77–8; major development, 98, 103, 144–5, 154, 157, 160, 176
Armco, 81
Armstrong Whitworth, founded, 9; buys Rylands 32, 48
Atha, C.G., 73
Attlee, C.R., 135, 137, 168
Austin Friars Trust, 58
Ayton, H.R., 80

Bairds, 156
Baker, G., 124
Baldwin, Stanley, sees steel-masters, 32; pressure brought, 40; will not guarantee Vickers-Armstrong, 49; hears from Steel-Maitland and Weir, 50; possibly supports Ebbw Vale, 79; and cartel, 82, 92
Baldwins, founded, 9; grows, 11, 40, 61, 65; merges with Richard Thomas, 135–6, 166
Balfour Committee, 13
Bank of England, 48, 52–4, 60,

65, 81, 92, 93, 99, 118, 120, 121, 143, 168
Bankers Industrial Development Company, 52, 74, 91
Banks, involved in steel, 21, 42–4
Barclays Bank, 21; and Dorman Long, 49, 62, 84, 92; and South Durham, 61; and Consett, 177
Barlow, Sir Robert, 146
Beale, S.R., 80, 89, 138
Beardmore's, 54–5, 61, 177
Beaver, Sir Hugh, 170
Beaverbrook, Lord, 96
Belgian steel industry, 152
Bell Brothers, 29
Bell, Sir Hugh, chairman at advanced age, 23, 62
Bell, Lowthian, 7
Benton Jones, Walter, supports lock-out, 27; United Steel coal policy, 44; succeeds Peech, 57, 65; possible Midland Group, 75–6, 77–8; proposes merger with Summers, 81, 93, 95, 99, 123, 125, 144–5, 153, 165
Bessemer, 5
Bevan, Aneurin, 123, 125
Bevin, Ernest, on causes of slump, 49; supports nationalization 121, 122, 123
Bilston, 160
Bledisloe, Lord, 33
Bolckow Vaughan, founded, 9, 29; buys Redpath Brown, 31; taken over, 48
Bond, H.C., 33–6; supports merger of all steel firms, 55; retires, 61
Bowesfield Steel, 61
Boyd-Carpenter, John, 172
Boyle, Sir Edward, 22; supports Frank Thomas, 34; supports his resignation, 35; supports Firth, 61, 78; agrees to Ebbw Vale, 80; dies 136

Boynton, A.J., 64
Brasserts, important role, 23; advises Corby, 39; suggested by Bank of England, 49; agree with Sankey Committee, 51; surveys for Bank of England, 52–4; on Scotland, 59, 141; and North-East Coast, 61; and Lancashire, 63–4, 66; and Corby 73–5; and Consett, 84, 109; brevity, 162, 181
Bretton Woods, 114
British Foreign and Colonial Corporation, 40
British Indepenent Steel Producers' Association, 181
British Iron and Steel Control, see Supply, Ministry of
British Iron and Steel Control (Ore) Ltd, 95, 147
British Iron and Steel Control (Salvage) Ltd, 96
British Iron and Steel Control (Scrap) Ltd, 96
British Iron and Steel Corporation, 82, 92
British Iron and Steel Federation, 68, 69; origins, 70–3, 78; organization, 80–2, 84–7; influence, 93, 95, 100, 104–5; and Franks Report, 108–11, 115–16; and nationalization 118–20, 123–5, 127–8; and plan 129–31; and prices 133–4; and South Wales 138–9; and North-East coast, 140; and Scotland, 141; and Midlands, 143–4; reviews plan, 151; second plan 153, 155, 157–9; planning, 160; caution 169; dissolved, 180
British Mannesman, 73
British Oxygen, 128
British Steel and Tube, 181
British Steel Corporation, 56, 152, 180–5

Index

British Transport Commission, 172

Briton Ferry Steel, 78, 139, 166

Brittain, Sir Herbert, 156

Brown, John, 83

Brown, W.R., 89, 173

Bruce-Gardner, Charles, 52, 56, 62, 64, 140

Brymbo, 166

Cammell, 7

Cammell Laird, founded, 9, 48, 61, 85, 88, 156

Caretaker Government, 106, 109

Cargo Fleet, 30; difficulties, 31; refuses to amalgamate, 60; amalgamates, 61, 83, 89, 107; new plans, 139, 161

Carnegie, Andrew, 9

Cartel, 70–2, 81–2, 166–7 (see also European Coal and Steel Community)

Cazenove's, 56

Central Electricity Board, 71

Chamberlain, Arthur, 59

Chamberlain, Joseph, unofficial report, 9–10

Churchill, Winston, wartime promises, 40; seeks to support steel, 51, 62, 106, 118, 135, 152

Clarke, Sir Richard, 56, 72

Clore, Charles, 155

Clyde Alloy, 39

Clydebridge, 116, 142

Clydesdale works, 37, 74, 142, 145

Clydesmuir, Lord, 39

Coal industry, decline in productivity, 8; bad labour relations, 27; reorganization, 77–8; Sir William Firth on, 91; coal prices, 111

Cole, G.D.H., 121

Colville's, expands in First World War, 11; connection with Harland and Wolff, 39; takes over Dunlop's, 48; in chronic trouble, 54; in mergers, 59, 61, 65; virtual Scottish monopolist, 70, 82, 89, 92, 94, 104, 112, 134; scattered, 141; postwar plans, 141–2; sold, 155; new plant, 157–8, 161; influence, 164–5; new strip mill, 169–170; Ravenscraig, 172–5, 176, 181

Commercial Bank of London, 57

Conakry, 147

Conservative Party, 128; return to office, 152; again, 156

Consett, reopens, 22, 29; exceptionally well-managed, 31–2; and Lloyds Bank, 49; and South Durham, 61, 62; problems, 63, 83–5, 88, 89, 94, 103, 104, 107, 112; new development, 131, 139; sold, 156; new plant, 161, 176–7, 181

Cookson, Clive, 88

Corby, origins, 37; suggested by Brasserts, 39, 52, 72–5, 103; as an example, 107–8, 116, 126; new development, 131, 134, 147, 158

Craig, John, 39–40, 55, 56, 92, 141–2, 153

Craven, Sir Charles, 94

Crawford and Balcarres, Lord, 63, 64, 93

Crichton, Sir Robert, 93

Cripps, Sir Stafford, 121, 122, 123

Crowther, Geoffrey, 106

Cumberland, 6, 44–5, 77, 143, 166

Cwmfelin, 33

Cyclops works, 63, 88

Daily Express, 176

Daily Herald, 56

Dalton, Hugh, 121, 122, 125–6, 135, 136

Dalzell, 141, 173

Darby, Abraham, uses coke, 4

Davidson, Lord, 92

Davies, H. Leighton, 139

Davies, T.F., 61

Debenham, H.G.W., 125

Dividends, frequently passed, 20

Dorman Long, founded, 9; grows, 11; elderly chairmen, 22–23, 29; difficulties, 31; takes over Bolckow Vaughan, 48; and Barclays Bank, 49; and Cargo Fleet, 60; amalgamates with South Durham, 61; reorganization, 61–3, 65, 84, 104; arrangements with Consett, 140; sold, 155; new capacity, 160, 161, 165, 181

Dorman, Sir Arthur, dies, 22, 62

Dudley, Lord, 90, 92, 136, 153

Dunbar, Sir Alexander, 141

Duncan, Sir Andrew, 49, 52, 70–71, 74; and Midland Group, 75–6; and Richard Thomas, 79; and IDAC, 82, 84, 85–7, 93, 105; and nationalization, 118, 120, 122, 124, 125; and plan, 129, 132, 152, 156, 169

Duncanson, Sir John, 93, 96, 139

Dunlop's, 48, 56

Ebbw Vale, 65, 72; new plant, 80, 89, 107, 112, 116, 126, 134–6; enlarged, 171

Ebbw Vale Steel, Iron and Coal Company issues stock, 12, 20; seeks merger, 40

Eccles, Sir David, 174

Edgar-Thompson works, 7

English Steel Corporation, formed, 48–9, 52, 61, 63, 88–9, 103, 104; sold, 156, 181

Entente Internationale de l'Acier, 71

European Coal and Steel Community, 3, 107, 166, 167 (see also Cartel), 177, 185

European Economic Community, 167, 177, 184–5

Evans, Sir Lincoln, 157, 158

Evely, Richard, 126

Fabian Society, 56

Finance Corporation for Industry, 117, 139, 169, 177

Firth-Brown, 60, 61, 88; sold, 156, 165, 177, 184

Firth, Thomas, founded, 7; amalgamates, 61

Firth, W.J., joins Richard Thomas board, 35; manages Redbourn, 60; takes over, 61; possible link with United Steel, 75–6; negotiates possible mergers and builds Ebbw Vale, 78–81; hectic career and dismissal, 89–91; advocates coal nationalization, 111; opposes merger with Baldwin's, 136

Forbes, Sir Archibald, 123, 124, 129, 140, 142, 157–8, 170, 176

Foreign Office, 177

Franco, General, 94

Franks, Oliver, 96, 105, 108, 109, 118, 121, 122–3, 135, 136, 155

Franks Report, 52–3, 106, 108–17; iron ore, 110; coal and coke, 111–12; management, 113; size of industry,

114; investment, 114; inter-
national competition 115;
supports integrated works,
116; costs, 117; basis of
policy, 122; Elizabeth
Ackroyd and, 133; first plan
response to, 160; length, 162,
168
Frater Taylor, J., 32, 64
Freeman, Ralph, 80
Freshfields, 61, 155, 165
Frodingham Iron and Steel
Company, bought by Samuel
Fox, 11
Furness, Lord, 30
Furness Withy, founded, 9, 29

Gaitskell, Hugh, 123
Gartsherrie, 141–2
Gayley, 7
General Omnibus Company, 66
General Steels, 183
George E.J., 28, 32, 61, 76, 88
German industry develops, 6;
competition, 67–8
Gibb, Sir Alexander and
Partners, 80
Gilbertson and Co., 78, 139
Glengarnock, 141–2, 164
Goodenough, C.F., 61, 92
Gowers, Sir Ernest, 77
Grangemouth, 158, 173
Grantham, 144
Grantley, Lord, 58
Green, Sir John, 128, 155
Greenwood, Lord, 62, 90, 91–2
Griffiths, James, 27
Grimesthorpe works, 63
Grovesend, 139
Guest Keen, amalgamates with
Baldwins, 48, 61, 70, 112,
137–9
Guest, Keen and Nettlefold,
founded, 9, 80, 85, 137–9, 166
Guinness, 170

Hadfield's, 156, 165
Hardie, S.J.L., 128, 153, 164
Harland and Wolff, join David
Colville, 12; separated, 56
Hartlepool, 84, 140
Hatry, Clarence, 45, 54, 55;
career 57–8
Heath, Edward, 177
Henderson, James, 144
Hickman's, 38
Hicks, Sir John, 107
Hilton, Sir Robert, joins United

Steel, 44, 57; reorganizes,
58–60, 65, 76, 77–8, 144
Hodge, John, 26, 28
Holme Lane works, 63
Horne, Sir Robert, 40
Hunter, Ellis, 84, reorganizes
Dorman Long, 91–2, 104;
and nationalization, 124, 125,
128; and plan, 129, 140, 152,
153
Huntsman's crucible, 5

Ickles, 41
Immingham, 147, 158, 173
Imperial Chemical Industries,
56–7
Import Duties Advisory
Committee, 61, 67–8, 69–70,
82, 85–6, 97, 100, 114, 119,
133
Inchinann, 173
'Ingot', 56, 72, 121
International competition, 8,
21–2, 43–4, 85–6, 113–15,
129–30, 132, 164, 166–8
International Co-operative
Association, 126
Invernairn, Lord, proposes
amalgamations, 39
Iron and Coal Trades Review, 66
Iron and Steel Act, 1967, 180
Iron and Steel Act, 1969, 183
Iron and Steel Board, 120, 122–3,
127, 142, 152; becomes
statutory, 155–6, 157–9; and
plans, 160–3; caution, 169;
helps finance strip mills,
170–6; dissolved, 180
Iron and Steel Corporation of
Great Britain, founded,
127–8; wound up, 152–3,
155; and plans, 160
Iron and Steel Holding and
Realization Agency, 122,
155–8, 171,
Iron and Steel Institute,
founded, 6
Iron and Steel Investments, 156
Iron and Steel Trades
Confederation, advocates
nationalization, 2; paternalistic, 26; record in 1920s,
28–9
Iron-making described, 4
Iron ore, first developed, 6–7;
imported, 29; home ore, 30–1,
36, 37; in Lincolnshire, 41–2;
Cumberland, 44; Brasserts on,
53–4, 59; Corby and, 66, 74;

war and, 94–5; home ore
controversy, 106–7; 110–11,
130–1, 145, 147; imports,
147–8, 161
Iron output, grows from small
amounts to massive flows, 4,
29; worries in war, 95–6,
100–2, 114

James, John, at South Durham,
30; at Lancashire Steel, 61,
64–5, 76; at Ebbw Vale, 80,
90; in the war, 93; and fuel
supplies, 146
Jarrow, 84–5, 89, 126
Jeane, J.S., 5
John Baker and Bessemer, 156
John Brown, founded, 7; grows,
11; merges, 61
John Summers, 65, 76, 81, 89,
92, 99, 103, 143; sold, 155;
new capacity, 157, 160, 161,
181
Jones, Sir Frederick, 41, 57
Jones, T. Ivor, 36
Joseph, Sir Keith, 172

Kaldo process, 189
Keynes, J.M., on causes of
slump, 49; on office boys, 89;
at Treasury, 106
Kidwelly, 158, 173
Kieft, A.W., 61, 78; retires, 80
Killingbeck, W., 124
Kilnhurst Collieries, 37
Kitson, Roland, 62
Koppers, 64
Krupp, 83
Kylsant, Lord, 40, 56

Labour Party, 67–8; possible
victory, 87, 106; elected, 118;
manifesto, 121, 177, 179
Lanarkshire Steel, 56, 142
Lancashire, 32–3, 59, 61, 63–5,
93, 143–4
Lancashire Steel, wartime pay
arrangements, 26; organized,
33; financed, 49, 52; formed,
61; organized, 63–4, 65; and
Stewarts and Lloyds, 74–6, 83,
92, 93, 99, 134, 143; sold, 155;
new plant, 161
Larke, Sir William, 54, 70
Latham, G.H., 80, 82, 166, 171
Lawson, Sir William, 172
Layton, Sir Walter, 96
Lever, E.H., 63, 90, and South

Wales schemes 135, 138–9, 146, 153, 166, 170–1
Lever, Harold, 169
Lewis, Sir Alfred, 75, 77
Lewis, T.O., 61, 139
Lincolnshire, origins of industry, 12, 35–6, 60–1, 75; amalgamation, 79, 144–5
Lithgow, Sir James, 55, 65, 89, 90, 92, 135
Lithgow's, 56
Llanelli Associated, 139
Lloyd Jones, Gwyn, 172
Lloyd and Lloyd, 36
Lloyd, Samuel, 37
Lloyds Bank, and Colville's, 40; and Consett, 49; and Lancashire Steel, 54; and Dunlops, 56; and Richard Thomas, 60; and Consett, 63, 177; engrosses Richard Thomas debenture, 80
London County Council, 66
London Transport, 121
Lysaghts' 42, 61, 128, 137–9, 144, 156, 166

McAlpine, Sir Robert, 80
McCance, Sir Andrew, 39, 92, 124, 139, 141–2, 157, 165
McCosh, Andrew, 93
Macdiarmid, A.C., becomes chairman, 38, 65; and Corby, 73–5, 90, 93, 99; death, 125, 132, 144–5
Macdonald, Ramsey, 87
McGowan, Sir Harry, 55
Macharg, A.S., 33, 99, 169
McKenna, Reginald, seeks mergers 31, 48, 54, 56
Maclay, John, 174
Macleod, Iain, 174
McLintock's, 142
Macmillan, Harold, 96
McQuistan, A.N., 31, 61
Manchester, 63
Margam, 131, 138, 139, 146
Marmite, founded by Major Pam, 76
Marshall, Alfred, 87
Marshall Plan, 107
Martins Bank, 21; and South Durham, 49
Mather, L.E., 93
Mather, Richard, 153
Maudling, Reginald, 171
Maugham, Lord, 62
Mauretania, 147, 161
May, Sir George, 61, 67–8, 70;

proposes Midland Group, 76; concerned with Ebbw Vale, 79, 82
Melchett, Lord, 180
Metal Box, 146
Metropolitan Vickers, 58
Midland Bank, 21; loses United Steel account, 42, 57; seeks rationalization, 48; supports Colville's, 56
Midland Group, 75–6; proposal revived, 99, 107, 144–5; achieved, 182
Mills, Sir Frederick, 40
Mills, Lord, 171, 174
Milne-Watson, Michael, 172
Mitchell, Charles, 55, 61–2, 84
Monnet, Jean, 167
Morgan Grenfell, 178
Morgan semi-continuous mill, installed at Tredegar, 10
Morison, Sir John, 156, 165
Morrison, Herbert, 66, 121, 125, 128, 152
Morrison, W.S., 123, 169
Moss Hall collieries, 32
Munitions, Ministry of, takes control, 11; finances big extensions, 39, 67
Musgrave, Sir Cyril, 158, 172

National Bank of Scotland, 39, 55–6
National Coal Board, 124, 142, 165, 177
National Economic Development Council, 159, 162
National Provincial Bank, 21; and United Steel, 42–3, 49, 57; and Dorman Long, 62; stops merger, 77
Nationalization, 29, 56, 87, Chapter 7, Chapter 10
Neilson, Colonel, 136
New Fabian Research Bureau, 181
Newport scheme, 75, 156, 158, 170–2, 173–5
Norman, Montagu, finances steel, 49–51; gives evidence to Sankey, 52; approves Brassert Report, 53–4; opposes Hatry, 58; and Dorman Long, 61; and Lancashire Steel, 64–5, 69; and tariffs, 70; and Corby, 74–5; and Ebbw Vale, 79–80; stops United Steel and Summers merger, 81; and Jarrow, 85; and Sir William

Firth, 90; tributes to, 93; interferes, 95, 99, 109, 181
Normanby Park, 42
North Lincolnshire Iron Company, 37
Northamptonshire proposed plant, 103–4
North-East coast, 6, 12, 29–32, 61–3, 83–5, 89, 91–2, 139–40, 165
Northern and Tubes Group, 182
Norway, 94–5

Organization for European Economic Cooperation, 152–3, 166–7
Oxfordshire, possible site for steelworks, 147

Padbury, F.S., 90
Palmer's Ironworks, 84
Pam, Major, 59, 64–5; universal man, 76
Paris Universal Exposition, 6
Park Gate, 156
Partington Iron and Steel, 61
Peake, Harald, 166
Pearson Knowles, 64
Pease and Partners, 29
Peat, Sir Harry, 55
Peat Marwick, 84
Peech A.O., speaks out, 21; succeeds Steel, 43; removed, 57, 81, 159
Peel, Lord, 93
Penistone works, 63
Pirrie, Lord, 39; dies, 40, 54, 92
Plans, Franks 108–17; first plan, 134–45; its achievement, 146–51; second plan, 153–5; third plan, 157–9; terminology, 160; survey of, 160–3
Plender, Sir William, 39
Pode, Julian, 153, 166
Port Talbot, new plant 136–7, 158
Power, Ministry of, 156–7; and strip mills, 174–5
Price Waterhouse, 32
Prices, and fuel, 7–8; postwar, 13; dumping, 21–2, 43–4; rise after devaluation, 67–8; price-fixing, 70–71; under BISF, 85–6; accords with Marshall's principles, 87; wartime, 97–8; 99–100; and fuel and ore, 109–11; Franks on, 115–16; too high, 126; Shone scheme, 132–3;

Elizabeth Ackroyd on, 133–4;
and European cartel, 167–8;
complex, 178; British Steel
Corporation, 180, 185
Prudential Assurance Co., 49,
63, 77, 80, 90, 136
Pugh, Arthur, 26, 28, 83

Rationalization 48–68, 72, 75–6
Ravenscraig, 158, 172–5
Redbourn, 33–6, 42, 60, 77, 166,
171, 174, 176
Reith, Lord, useful dictum, 35
Richard Thomas, grows, 11;
frequent accidents, 26; early
history, 33; does well 60, 65,
70; links with Stewarts and
Lloyds, 75–6, 89, 103, 128, 132
Richard Thomas and Baldwins,
minutes sob, 26; controlled by
bank, 65; formed, 107, 134;
complex problems, 135–9,
146–7, 153; never denational-
ized, 155–6; plans for Newport
rejected and then approved,
158; new strip mill, 169–72,
173, 181
Rippon, Geoffrey, 172
River Don works, 63, 88, 103
Robert Addie collieries, 37
Robinson, Joan, 126
Rollason, 95, 157, 159, 165
Rostas, Laszlo, 106–7
Rosyth, 128, 164
Rother Vale collieries, join
United Steel, 12, 41, 77
Rothschilds, 80
Round Oak, 90, 92, 104, 144;
sold, 156; dissuaded, 164, 184
Royal Air Force, 88
Russell, Barnabas, a shareholder,
91
Rylands Brothers, 32, 63
Rylands, Sir Peter, 32, 63, 65,
92, 93

St Paul's School, 57
Samuel Fox, founded, 7; joins
Steel, Peech and Tozer, 11, 41,
143, 165
Sandys, Duncan, 152
Sankey Report, supports cartel,
29; criticizes industry, 51–2,
66,
Schroders, 59, 64–5, 76
Schuman, Maurice, 167
Scoby-Smith Committee, 13
Scotland's steel industry, 6, 12,

36–40, 54–6, 92, 140–2, 164–5,
172–5
Scott Smith, F.S., 41
Scottish Gas Board, incurs
wrath, 165
Scottish and North-West group,
182
Scottish Steel, 54, 59, 156
Securities Management Trust,
52, 62, 64, 80, 90
Shaw, G.B., 83
Sheffield's steel industry, 40–3,
165
Shelton Iron, Steel and Coal,
52, 81
Shone, Sir Robert, 131, 133, 157,
158–9, 162
Shotton, new strip mill, 79, 81,
89, 108, 134, 143, 157
Siemens, 5
Skinningrove, 125, 156
Slump, postwar, 14, and Chapter
2; interwar, 39, and Chapter 3
Smith, Clarence, 32
South Durham, 29; and Martins
Bank, 49; amalgamates, 61, 65;
refuses to merge with Dorman
Long, 83, 89; postwar plans
140; sold, 156; new plant, 157,
160, 161, 165; possible merger
with Stewarts and Lloyds, 165,
181
South Wales group, 182
South Yorkshire collieries, 78
Special Steels, 183
Spencer, H.F., 153, 171–2
Spens, J. Ivan, 58
Steel Company of Wales, 135,
153; sold, 156; new plant,
157–8, 161, 166; differences
with RTB, 170–1, 176, 181
Steel, Gerald, 77, 95, 144, 154,
168, 176
Steel, Harry, takes lead in
amalgamation, 11, 40
Steel Industries of Great
Britain, 58
Steel-Maitland, Arthur, 50
Steel-making described, 5
Steel, Peech and Tozer, 11, 41,
143, 161, 165
Stephen family, 54, 56
Stewart, A.G., 145, 153
Stewart's, founded, 6
Stewarts and Lloyds, founded, 9;
expand, 36–7; colliery
interests, 37; sells Froding-
ham, 37; buys Hickmans, 38;
difficulties, 38; calls in

Brasserts, 39; encouraged to
build Corby, 52; discuss
amalgamations, 55; arrangements with United Steel, 59,
65–6, 72; builds Corby, 73–5,
83, 99, 103, 104, 134;
negotiations with United
Steel, 139; arrangements with
Colvilles, 141–2; postwar
plans, 143, 145; Oxfordshire
site, 147; sold, 155; new plant,
157, 161; refuses new site,
162; dissuades Round Oak,
164; possible merger, 165,
172, 176, 181
Strauss, G.R., 125–6, 169
Strip mills decision, 169–74,
division 183
Summers, R.F., 153, 165
Supply, Ministry of, 92–3; Iron
and Steel Control, 94–6, 97–9,
Chapter 5 (on the Franks
Report), 118–21, 123, 127, 133,
135–6; Scottish pressure,
141–2, and United Steel, 144;
and productivity, 146; and
iron ore, 147; after
denationalization, 155, 157;
McCance angry with, 165
Swansea, 158, 173
Swindon, 58
Sydney Harbour Bridge,
ominous to Dorman Long, 23,
62,
Szavarzy, F.A., 40, 54, 55

Talbot, Benjamin, 30, 31, 55,
61, 84
Talbot, Chetwynd, 139, 155,
178
Tariffs, advocated, 9; recom-
mended by official commit-
tee, 13; introduced, 66–8;
formalized, 81–3
Taylor Brothers, 63
Templeborough, founded, 11,
41–3; in trouble, 57
Thomas, C.T., 80
Thomas, Frank, calls himself
dictator, 22; health collapses,
33; returns as dictator, 34;
resigns, 35; abroad, 36
Thomas and Gilchrist process, 7
Thomas, Ivor H., 91
Thomas, Jimmy, swallows
Treasury line, 51
Thomas, Lionel Beaumont, 33;
camps with territorials, 34,

78, 80; drowned, 136; son
killed, 136
Times, The, 56, 112
Trade, Board of, 135–7
Trades Union Congress, 56
Treasury, criticizes industry for
caution, 3; for excess profits,
98; Keynes at, 106; and South
Wales, 137; and strip mills,
174–5
Tredegar Iron and Steel Works,
10
Tube Investments, 36, 59, 145,
156
Tubes division, 183

United Steel, founded, 11;
issues stock, 12; run as
coalition, 23; General Strike,
27; shareholders fed up, 29;
buys Frodingham, 37;
difficulties in postwar slump,
40–5; and National Provincial
Bank, 49; taken over by Hatry,
57–8; arrangements with
Stewarts and Lloyds, 59; and
Lancashire Steel, 64; and
Corby, 74–5; recovery under
Hilton 76–8; relations with
BISF, 85, 95, 98–9, 103, 128,
134; negotiations with Stew-

arts and Lloyds, 139; postwar
plans 143–5, 152; sold, 155;
refuses new site, 162; future,
165–6; high managerial
capacity, 176, 181
United Strip and Bar Mills, 12,
57

Velindre, 157
Vicker's founded, 7, 9, 48, 83
Vickers-Armstrong, merger, 49;
hived off to English Steel, 61
85, 88, 156

Walmsley, Ben., 62, 84
Walsh, C.J., 95
War Office, 88–9
Ward, Ashley, 124
Watts, Cyril, 78
Weeks, Hugh, 172
Weir, Lord, does not lose heart,
50–1; commissions Brasserts,
52, 141
Welland, north of, 158, 162, 176
Welsh steel industry, 6, 33–6,
60–1, 78–81, 89–91, 135–9,
166, 170–2
Wendel, D.E., great steel-makers,
21
West Cumberland, 6
West, Sir Glyn, 32

Western Front, source of
management, 23
Westminster Bank, 21;
Armstrong Whitworths and,
32
While, G.A., 80, 90
Whishaw, C.P.L., 155, 165
Whitecross, 65
Whitehead, L.D., untypically
young, 10, 78
Whitehead's, 78–80, 172
Whitworths, founded, 7
Wigan Collieries, 63
Wilkinson, Ellen, 27, 85
Williams Deacons, 62
Williams, T.D., an historian, 149
Wilmot, John, 123, 124, 125
Wilson, Charles, 91
Wilson, Sir Horace, opposes
state aid, 51
Wilson, S.S., 165
Woodhall-Duckman, 64
Workington Iron and Steel,
founded, 9; joins United
Steel, 12; makes losses, 43;
recovers, 77; poor postwar
outlook, 143, 165
Wright, Sir Charles, 40, 65, 80,
90, 93, 125

Young, Allyn, 126